SHAKESPEARE'S MOULDY

LONGMAN MEDIEVAL AND RENAISSANCE LIBRARY

General Editors:
CHARLOTTE BREWER, Hertford College, Oxford
N. H. KEEBLE, University of Stirling

Leah Scragg

SHAKESPEARE'S MOULDY TALES
Recurrent Plot Motifs in Shakespearian Drama

LONGMAN
LONDON AND NEW YORK

Longman Group UK Limited,
Longman House, Burnt Mill,
Harlow, Essex, CM20 2JE, England
and associated companies around the world.

*Published in the United States of America
by Longman Publishing, New York*

© Longman Group UK Limited 1992

First published 1992

ISBN 0 582 07071 6 CSD
ISBN 0 582 07070 8 PPR

British Library Cataloguing in Publication Data

A catalogue record for this book is
available from the British Library

Library of Congress Cataloging-in-Publication Data
Scragg, Leah.
 Shakespeare's mouldy tales : recurrent plot motifs in
 Shakespearian drama / Leah Scragg.
  p.   cm. – (Longman medieval and Renaissance library)
 Includes bibliographical references and index.
 ISBN 0–582–07071–6 (csd). – ISBN 0–582–07070–8 (ppr)
  1. Shakespeare, William, 1564–1616 – Plots.   2. Plots (Drama,
 novel, etc.)   I. Title.   II. Series.
PR2997.P6S37   1992
822.3'3 – dc20   91–48356
                                                            CIP

Set in 10/12pt Bembo by 9
Produced by Longman Singapore Publishers (Pte) Ltd.
Printed in Singapore

Contents

Chapter 5   Exile   123
2 Henry VI
The Two Gentlemen of Verona
Romeo and Juliet
Richard II
As You Like It
King Lear
Coriolanus
Cymbeline
The Tempest

Chapter 6   ~~Putative~~ *Supposed* Death   156
Romeo and Juliet
Antony and Cleopatra
Much Ado About Nothing
All's Well That Ends Well
Measure for Measure
Pericles
Cymbeline
The Tempest
The Winter's Tale

Conclusion Shakespeare's Mouldy Tales   189

Further Reading   195

Index   198

Acknowledgements

The New Arden editions of Shakespeare's plays are quoted throughout, and I would like to thank the publishers (Methuen & Co. Ltd) for their kind permission to use them.

No doubt some mouldy tale
Like *Pericles*
(Ben Jonson)

Introduction

Mouldy Tales and Renaissance Attitudes to Originality

In his 'Ode to Himself', written after the failure of his penultimate play, *The New Inn* (1629), Ben Jonson, the most significant of Shakespeare's fellow dramatists, inveighed against the taste of contemporary audiences who preferred 'some mouldy tale / Like *Pericles*' to his own, more intellectually challenging compositions.[1] Jonson paid ample tribute to Shakespeare elsewhere in his work, and his comment derives from irritation at his own reception rather than animosity towards Shakespeare himself, but his complaint highlights a difficulty that troubles many readers and theatregoers when first encountering the plays. The tales enacted in Shakespearian drama are decidedly mouldy – and they are mouldy in two respects. In the first place, the stories which the plays unfold frequently have a long literary ancestry, while in the second, the plot motifs that they employ are repeated from play to play, making it difficult for the non-specialist to remember to which drama specific incidents belong. Numerous heroines disguise themselves as boys, for example (cf. *The Two Gentlemen of Verona*, *The Merchant of Venice*, *Twelfth Night*, etc.) feigned deaths occur with non-naturalistic frequency (cf. *Romeo and Juliet*, *Much Ado About Nothing*, *Antony and Cleopatra*, *The Winter's Tale*), while a sequence of gentlemen are deceived over the identity of a lady (cf. *Love's Labour's Lost*, *The Merry Wives of Windsor*, *All's Well That Ends Well*, *Measure for Measure*).

For the twentieth-century reader, dependency upon the work of others and the repetition of material from one work to the next suggest plagiarism on the one hand and a want of creativity on the

1. All quotations from Jonson's 'Ode' are from the text of the poem in M. Hattaway (ed.) (1984) *The New Inn*, Manchester University Press, pp. 204–8.

other. Following the advent of a technology that allows instant access to and reproduction of the literary stock, a strict code of practice has evolved in recent years to guard the written word against the predations which, to the modern mind, constitute varieties of theft. A writer's work cannot be quoted at any length without permission from the publisher, while the xeroxing of books is limited to single copies, intended for personal use, until fifty years after the author's death. At the same time, the process of composition is seen in post-Romantic terms as the product of 'inspiration'. The writer is popularly imagined to work at white heat, seeking to capture the 'overflow of powerful feelings'[2] before the tide of creative energy ebbs away. A species of composition which is patently rooted in another man's invention is consequently regarded today with suspicion, while the repetitious use of material is seen as signalling the lack of that spontaneous creativity which for many is a principal criterion of success.

Renaissance attitudes to the literary stock and the creation of an artistic work were at a considerable distance, however, from those that are in force today. Literary theory in the sixteenth century looks back, both directly and through Roman intermediaries, to the thought of Plato (c. 427–348 BC), and the work of his pupil, Aristotle (384–322 BC), and is founded upon the concept of imitation. Plato defined actuality as a flawed reflection of a world of ideal forms, and saw the artist as an imperfect imitator of that reflection, and thus at two removes from truth.[3] Aristotle, though he disagreed with Plato over the status of the artist, also regarded art as essentially mimetic, claiming that music, poetry and drama are all 'modes of imitation'[4] that give pleasure by expanding the understanding. This concept of art as *mimesis* evolved in the course of the classical period to embrace the creative process itself. Not only was art seen as imitating nature, but the artist himself was regarded as a species of copyist, learning his craft from, and finding his inspiration in, the compositions of those who had gone before him. Roman sculptors based their statuary on Greek originals, Roman playwrights drew on Hellenic plots, while the schools of rhetoric in which the Roman writers and

---

2. W. Wordsworth (1800) *Lyrical Ballads* (Preface). From W. M. Merchant (ed.) (1955) *Wordsworth: Poetry and Prose*, Rupert Hart-Davis, p. 230.
3. See *The Republic*, part X.
4. Quoted from J. Warrington (ed.) (1963) *Aristotle's Poetics*; *Demetrius on Style*; *Longinus on the Sublime* (Everyman's Library), Dent, p. 3.

orators were trained employed literary models as a means of inculcating the principles of composition. The concept of learning by imitation was taken up enthusiastically in the classically orientated schoolrooms of the Tudor period, and became the foundation of a programme of education, set forward most persuasively in Roger Ascham's *The Schoolmaster* (1570), designed to develop what might be known today as 'communication skills'. Having learnt the principles of grammar in his earliest years, the infant scholar would progress, via the translation of Latin texts, to the study of the rhetorical figures employed by his models, and thence to a composition of his own based on the passage of verse or prose with which he was currently engaged.

The assumption that the doctrine of imitation would, in Ascham's words, 'bring forth more learning and breed up truer judgment than any other exercise that can be used'[5] was not confined, furthermore, to pedagogues concerned to justify a teaching method. Literary critics and creative writers alike endorsed the methodology propounded by the period's educationalists. Sir Philip Sidney, for example, himself a distinguished poet, argues in his *Apology for Poetry* (written *c*. 1581–3), a work that encapsulates much of the critical thought of the age, that 'as the fertilest ground must be manured, so must the highest-flying wit have a Daedalus to guide him. That Daedalus. . . . hath three wings to bear itself up into the air of due commendation: that is, Art, Imitation, and Exercise.'[6] Similarly, Ben Jonson (for all his antagonism towards the purveyors of 'mouldy tales') declares in his *Discoveries* (published posthumously in 1641) that the successful poet requires three qualities, 'natural wit', 'Exercise', and 'Imitation', defining the last as the ability to 'convert the substance, or Riches of an other *Poet*, to his own use. To make choise of one excellent man above the rest, and so to follow him, till he grow very *Hee*: or, so like him, as the Copie may be mistaken for the Principall.'[7]

5. R. Ascham (1570) *The Schoolmaster*. Quoted from L. V. Ryan (ed.) (1967) *The Schoolmaster*. Cornell University Press (for the Folger Shakespeare Library), p. 118. All references to Ascham's work are to this edition.

6. Quoted from G. Shepherd (ed.) (1973) *An Apology for Poetry*, Manchester University Press, pp. 132–3. All references to *An Apology for Poetry* are to this edition.

7. Quoted from G. B. Harrison (ed.) (1966) *Discoveries 1641: Conversations with William Drummond of Hawthornden 1619* (Elizabethan and Jacobean Quartos), Edinburgh University Press, pp. 91–3. All subsequent references to Jonson's critical work are to this edition.

The theory of art as imitation led, inevitably, to a very considerable emphasis upon the mechanics of composition, and an appreciation of the writer's craft. The term 'artificial' during the Renaissance was regarded as an expression of praise, signifying the exhibition of a pleasing mastery of the principles governing a particular form. George Puttenham, for example, in his *Arte of English Poesie* (1589), maintained that 'it is a praise to be said an artificiall dauncer, singer, and player on instruments, because they be not exactly knowne or done, but by [i.e. except through] rules and precepts or teaching of schoolemasters', and that the poet 'may both vse, and also manifest his arte to his great praise, and need no more be ashamed thereof, than a shomaker to haue made a cleanly shoe, or a carpenter to haue buylt a faire house'.[8] Nevertheless, literary composition was not regarded merely as a craft which could be mastered through an apprenticeship in copying. Both teachers and literary theorists are adamant that the poet is born and not made, and is a being with exceptional gifts. Ascham was keenly aware of the different capabilities of the pupils in his charge,[9] while Sidney is very clear that 'no industry' can make a poet 'if his own genius be not carried unto it'.[10] Similarly, though Puttenham has no doubt that 'Poesie [is] an art not only of making, but also of imitation', he is quick to point out that 'this science in his perfection, can not grow, but by some diuine instinct . . . or by excellencie of nature and complexion: or by great subtiltie of the spirits and wit . . . or peraduenture by all or most part of them'.[11]

The goal to which the writer aspired, moreover, was not simply the slavish reproduction of an existing work. Ascham demonstrates considerable understanding of the processes of adaptation that are involved in the transmission of material from one generation to the next,[12] while Jonson is emphatic that imitation is an active, rather than a passive, response to a literary text. Having isolated one of the major characteristics of the poet as his ability to 'convert

8. Quoted from B. Hathaway (ed.) (1970) *The Arte of English Poesie* (Kent English Reprints), Kent State University Press, pp. 310 and 308. All subsequent references to *The Arte of English Poesie* are to this edition.
9. Cf. *The Schoolmaster*, pp. 21–5.
10. *An Apology for Poetry*, p. 132.
11. *The Arte of English Poesie*, p. 20.
12. Cf. *The Schoolmaster*, pp. 117–18.

the substance, or Riches of an other *Poet*, to his owne use', he continues:

> Not, as a Creature, that swallowes, what it takes in, crude, raw, or indigested; but, that feedes with an Appetite, and hath a Stomacke to concoct, devide, and turne all into nourishment. Not, to imitate servilely . . . but, to draw forth out of the best, and choisest flowers, with the Bee, and turne all into Honey.[13]

The recognition that both judgement and creativity are involved in the process of imitation is implicit in the programme of studies to which the more promising scholars of the period were introduced. Following Sir John Cheke, another eminent educationalist, Ascham advocates the parallel study of related Greek and Latin texts, with the student's attention directed towards the following points:

1. [The second writer] retaineth thus much of the matter, these sentences, these words.
2. This and that he leaveth out, which he doth wittily [i.e. consciously] to this end and purpose.
3. This he addeth here.
4. This he diminisheth there.
5. This he ordereth thus, with placing that here, not there.
6. This he altereth and changeth either in property of words, in form of sentence, in substance of the matter, or in one or other convenient circumstance of the author's present purpose.[14]

The procedures involved in this exercise are clearly those of literary criticism, but the end to which they are deployed is not solely the fuller understanding of specific works. In Ascham's view, his methodology furnishes 'all the necessary tools and instruments wherewith true imitation is rightly wrought',[15] and is designed to encourage the pupil to approach his own models with a clearer perception of the ways in which they might be adapted to produce new, and in Renaissance terms original, works.

The emphasis upon creative adaptation in the schoolroom and its endorsement by both practising artists and literary critics led, inevitably, to an immense outpouring of material during the sixteenth century that is rooted, to a greater or lesser degree, in

13. *Discoveries*, pp. 93–4.
14. *The Schoolmaster*, p. 118.
15. *Ibid.*

classical originals. While at one end of the spectrum writers were merely engaged in 'Englishing' their models, at the other end they were attempting to accommodate 'the excellentest artificiality of the most renowned worke-masters that antiquity affourdeth'[16] to compositions that spoke directly to their own generation. It was not only the classical authors who were studied in the classroom, moreover, who were imitated as the century evolved. The Renaissance had given birth to major writers in Italy long before it reached a comparable stage in England, and Italian *oeuvres* were embraced along with the Greek and Latin exempla to which they, in turn, were indebted. Spenser's *Faerie Queene* (1590–96), for example, a poem which celebrates England under Elizabeth and is concerned to define the ideal Renaissance gentleman, looks back not only to the epics of Homer and Virgil, but also to those of Ariosto and Tasso,[17] both of which were published in the sixteenth century. And Spenser was not alone in turning to more recent writers as a source of inspiration. Sidney's *Astrophel and Stella* (written *c.* 1581–82), which began the rage for sonneteering in England, is indebted to Petrarch (1304–74), while Spenser himself became a quarry for others, with Shakespeare, Jonson and Milton all drawing on his work.

The boundary between following the 'lines of example, drawn even in the ancients themselves'[18] and using the training supplied in the schoolroom in order to capitalize upon another author's success is clearly a narrow one, and by the last quarter of the sixteenth century that boundary had been effectively crossed. Lyly's *Euphues* (1578), for example, the most popular prose work of the period, was followed by a host of 'sequels', some of which, like Greene's *Euphues his Censure to Philautus* (1587), did not scruple to employ the name of Lyly's central figure. The practice of building upon the work of others was ratified, moreover, by the respect for 'authorities' that the Renaissance had inherited from the Middle Ages. In the early medieval period scholars felt some insecurity in relation to their own learning, and consequently

16. G. Harvey (1593) *Pierce's Supererogation*. Quoted from G. G. Smith (ed.) (1904) *Elizabethan Critical Essays*, Oxford University Press, vol. II, p. 277.
17. See J. C. Smith and E. De Selincourt (eds) (1912) *The Poetical Works of Edmund Spenser*, Oxford University Press, p. 407 ('A Letter of the Authors').
18. B. Jonson *Volpone* (dedication). Quoted from F. E. Schelling (ed.) (1910) *Ben Jonson's Plays* (Everyman's Library), Dent, vol. I, p. 402.

placed considerable reliance upon the validity of written records.[19] Convinced that anything that 'was old and was by a famous man and was widely admired was most likely to be true', they turned to 'authorities' and 'as often as not, copied them out verbatim'.[20] This attitude to the work of distinguished precursors lingered on long after scholars had cause to entertain a greater degree of respect for their own capabilities, and is summed up by Gower's assertion in *Pericles* (I. Chorus 10) that '*Et bonum quo antiquius eo melius*' ('And the older a good thing is, the better it is'). The respect in which 'authorities' were held during the Renaissance is illustrated most vividly perhaps by the popularity during this period of the 'commonplace book', a classified collection of noteworthy passages assembled in the course of private reading. Such collections not only furnished material for the improvement of conversation but acted as highly personal reference books that could be drawn on in the course of composition. The practice of imitation thus extended far beyond the adaptation of classical authors inculcated in the schoolroom. It embraced the remodelling of contemporary material, and the use of unacknowledged quotation as a means of lending weight or authority to an 'original' creative or scholarly work.

Renaissance dramatists were by no means aloof from the literary developments taking place around them. Following the suppression of religious drama (as tending to Papism) during the Reformation, the centre of histrionic activity had shifted during the sixteenth century from the Church to the academic institutions – both the grammar schools, in which acting was used as an educational instrument to foster the art of public speaking, and the universities, to which the budding scholar, reared on the doctrine of imitation and the study and performance of classical drama, eventually progressed. Not unnaturally, in the early years of the century the plays performed by academic troupes were principally in Latin, but in course of time the scholarly community learnt to adapt the classical material on which their studies were based to their own purposes. By the middle of the century, not only had a number of the major classical playwrights been translated into

19. See M. M. Gatch (1971) *Loyalties and Traditions: Man and His World in Old English Literature* (Pegasus Backgrounds in English Literature), Pegasus, New York, pp. 74ff.
20. M. M. Gatch (1971) p. 75.

English,[21] but dramatists such as Udall (in *Ralph Roister Doister:* 1545–52) and Stevenson (in *Gammer Gurton's Needle: c.* 1552–63) had begun to construct plays on English subjects using the ground-plan that Roman New Comedy supplied. With the opening of the first purpose-built playhouses in England during the 1570s, and the growing demand for new material that followed, university graduates gravitated towards London, applying the techniques acquired in the course of their training to supplying the needs of an expanding entertainment industry. Not only were classical plays translated and adapted for the contemporary playhouse but the work of Italian and French dramatists was rapidly assimilated into the new theatrical repertoire.[22] The Bible and traditional folk tales were also pressed into service,[23] while chronicle histories (like that of Holinshed), and the popular romances (often Italian in origin) that fed the Elizabethan appetite for amorous adventure, were recast in dramatic form.[24] At the same time, competition between troupes, and the attendant demand for fresh productions, thrust hard-pressed playwrights back on to the existing dramatic stock, and the remodelling of one another's work for different companies and occasions. Greene, for example, adapted Lyly's *Campaspe* (1580–84), originally a court comedy, into a play for the public stage; Bird and Rowley wrote some new scenes for a seventeenth-century revival of *Dr Faustus* (1588–92); while Ford transposed *Romeo and Juliet* (1594–96) into the grim world of late Jacobean drama. Since many of the sources of Renaissance plays (particularly the Bible and folk tales) were familiar to contemporary playgoers, audience expectation could be harnessed in a variety of ways to the projection of meaning, with writers engineering surprise or pro-voking thought by strategic departures from familiar motifs (cf. Marlowe's treatment of the morality play in *Dr Faustus*). The

---

21. Terence's *Andria* was first performed in English between 1516 and 1533, and was followed by plays by Euripides (1543), Sophocles (1543), Plautus (*c.* 1553–58) and Seneca (*c.* 1550–59).
22. Cf. Munday's (?) *Fedele and Fortunio (Two Italian Gentlemen)* 1579–84, a translation of Pasqualigo's *Il Fedele* and Kyd's *Cornelia* (pub. 1594), a translation of Garnier's *Cornélie*.
23. Cf. Peele's *David and Bethsabe* (*c.* 1581–94), and the collaborative *Patient Grissil* (1600).
24. Cf. the anonymous *Edward III* (1593–94?) which draws on both Holinshed's *Chronicles* and a romance adapted from the Italian by William Painter, and Greene's *James IV* (*c.* 1590) which is indebted to Cinthio's *Hecatommithi*.

Elizabethan–Jacobean theatrical community, in short, consisted of a highly self-conscious group of writers, feeding their imaginations on the work of others on both practical and aesthetic grounds.

Though there is little direct evidence relating to the education of the most influential member of this community, there is little reason to doubt that as the eldest son of one of Stratford's leading citizens Shakespeare would have attended the local grammar school in common with others of his class.[25] Like the pupils who studied under Ascham, he would have been introduced to the principles of Latin grammar at a very early age, and proceeded to the translation and imitation of classical authors, including (in all probability) the work of the Roman dramatist Terence, who was highly regarded by Renaissance schoolmasters for the purity of his style.[26] Emerging into a world in which the classics were regarded as an unfailing source of inspiration and creative adaptation was the accepted mode of composition, he turned naturally to the literary stock for the construction of his earliest comedies, modelling *The Comedy of Errors* (1590–93) on Plautus' *Menaechmi*, and drawing on the *Amphitruo* (also by Plautus) in *The Taming of the Shrew* (1589–92). Like his fellow writers, moreover, he was quick to extend the application of his training beyond the classical materials on which his education was based. Entering a theatrical environment in which plays were in constant process of revision, he drew freely on the work of his contemporaries, reworking the lost *Hamlet* (*c.* 1587–90), for example, and transforming the anonymous *King Leir* (*c.* 1588–94) from an undistinguished 'history' into a major tragedy. He also turned, like other writers of the period, to chronicle and romance[27] (sometimes transposing prose into verse with the

<hr>

25. Jonson's notorious comment that Shakespeare had 'small Latine and lesse Greeke' (commendatory verses published in the First Folio edition of Shakespeare's works, 1623) confirms, in fact, that the dramatist had some knowledge of both languages (merely implying that he had not proceeded to the advanced study of either), while the scene between Sir Hugh and his pupil William in *The Merry Wives of Windsor* (IV.i.11–70) bears witness to Shakespeare's familiarity with both Latin grammar and the teaching methods of contemporary schoolmasters.

26. See the remarks of Charles Hoole (a seventeenth-century schoolmaster) quoted in F. P. Wilson and G. K. Hunter (1969) *The English Drama 1485–1585* (Oxford History of English Literature, vol. IV, part I), Oxford University Press, p. 103.

27. The historical material in *Henry V* (1599), for example, derives from Edward Hall's *The Union of the Two Noble and Illustre Famelies of Lancastre and Yorke* (1548), both directly and through Holinshed's *Chronicles* (1587), while *As You Like It* looks back to *Rosalynde* (1590) a prose romance by Thomas Lodge.

minimum of verbal alteration)[28] while folk tales underlie a number of his plays.[29] At the same time, the rare passages of literary criticism that occur in his work bear witness to his knowledge (and implicit acceptance) of the literary theory of his age. Hamlet, for example, instructing the players on the dramatic performance through which he hopes to 'catch the conscience of the King' (II.ii. 601), invokes the concept that art is an imitation of life when he reminds them that the 'purpose of playing . . . was and is to hold as 'twere the mirror up to nature' (III.ii.20–2), while the amateur actors of *Love's Labour's Lost* (1593–94) and *A Midsummer Night's Dream* (c. 1595) turn automatically to classical subjects, like their real-life equivalents, when faced with the challenge of mounting a play.

Where Shakespeare differs from the majority of his contemporaries, however, is in the way in which he extended the practice of adaptation to his own compositions. Not only did he follow the accepted method of structuring his plays on literary sources, he also looked back, consciously or unconsciously, to his own plot material, utilizing old devices in new ways, and re-using situations for different effects. A number of items in the canon may thus look back to a single source, with plot motifs evolving into a variety of forms in their progress through the dramatist's imagination. While his contemporaries are caught up in a species of dialogue with their predecessors, Shakespeare is thus engaged in a much more complex debate, with the traditional connotations of inherited devices giving way to a succession of new meanings in the course of a continuing process of transposition.

Remote as such a self-referential and seemingly uninventive mode of composition may be from popular notions about the way in which 'great art' is produced, it nevertheless has the virtue of offering the twentieth-century critic a highly illuminating point of entry for an investigation of the plays. By following the methodology prescribed by Ascham, and exploring what the dramatist

---

28. See, for example, the Archbishop of Canterbury's speech on Salic law in *Henry V* (I.ii.35–95) which is borrowed with little alteration from Holinshed, and the celebrated description of Cleopatra in her barge (*Antony and Cleopatra*, II.ii.191–218) which is drawn from North's translation of Plutarch's *Lives of the Noble Grecians and Romanes* (1579).

29. Cf. *The Taming of the Shrew* (1589–92) among the early comedies and *Cymbeline* (1608–09) among the late plays (see Chapters 3 and 2 below).

'retaineth', 'leaveth out', 'addeth', 'ordereth . . . here, not there', 'altereth and changeth' in related compositions, the modern reader, like his or her Tudor forebears, may gain an insight, not only into the 'present purpose[s]' of a major writer, but the means by which those purposes were achieved. Following in the footsteps of Ascham's pupils, the twentieth-century student may thus reach a fuller understanding of the 'originality' of a given text, and acquire a deeper appreciation of the range of meanings that may be adduced from a single motif.

The purpose of the present study is to illustrate some of the critical insights that are afforded through Shakespeare's repetitious use of inherited material. Starting with *The Comedy of Errors*, which is directly structured upon a classical source and hence permits the most straightforward application of Ascham's methodology, the book examines a range of the traditional devices and situations that recur from play to play, and the changing implications which they generate. Since so many of Shakespeare's dramas look back simultaneously to a number of non-Shakespearian sources and one or more items in the canon, it would be impossible in the scope of a single volume to explore the entire spectrum of the playwright's 'tales', and it is consequently upon some of the more notoriously repetitive (e.g. gender exchange) and improbable (e.g. substitute coupling) that attention is focused. While seeking to define a fresh avenue from which to explore the plays, the study also attempts to demonstrate that far from bearing witness to his lack of inventiveness or culpable indifference to the laws of possession, Shakespeare's use of borrowed material supplies an index to an originality that is remarkable by the standards of any age. Though the tales that he draws on are unquestionably mouldy, the imagination that plays over them does indeed, as Jonson prescribed, 'turne all into Honey', triumphantly exhibiting the capacity of the supreme Renaissance artist to 'convert the substance, or Riches of an other *Poet*, to his owne use'.

Chapter 1

Sibling Confusion

The Comedy of Errors. Twelfth Night

The Comedy of Errors provides a natural starting point for the study of Shakespeare's use of inherited materials in that it is overtly structured upon a classical drama, and therefore lies closest to the type of creative adaptation inculcated in the Tudor schoolroom. At the same time, the plot of the Roman play lingered in Shakespeare's imagination, to be re-used at a later period in the construction of *Twelfth Night* (1601). A comparison between *The Comedy of Errors* and its Latin progenitor thus offers an insight into Shakespeare's purposes in shaping one of his earliest plays, while an analysis of the relationship between *The Comedy of Errors* and *Twelfth Night* affords an illustration of the contrasting 'meanings' that Shakespeare elicits from a single 'tale' at different stages of his career.

The similarity between *The Comedy of Errors* and *Twelfth Night* was apparent to the later play's earliest spectators. The lawyer, John Manningham, who was among the audience at the Middle Temple for the first recorded performance of *Twelfth Night* in 1602, noted in his diary

> At our feast we had a play called *Twelfth Night* or *What You Will*, much like *The Comedy of Errors* or *Menaechmi* in Plautus, but most like and near to that in Italian called *Inganni*.[1]

---

1. Spelling and punctuation have been modernized. For an exact transcript of the entry see J. M. Lothian and T. W. Craik (eds) (1975) *Twelfth Night*, Arden edition, p. xxvi.

The comment is a perceptive one, accurately locating the genealogy of both Shakespearian plays. As Manningham indicates, *Twelfth Night* looks back to *The Comedy of Errors* or Plautus' *Menaechmi* on the one hand, and an Italian comedy known as *Gl'Ingannati* (Manningham's *Inganni*) on the other, while *The Comedy of Errors* and the *Menaechmi* are themselves related. The Plautine comedy thus forms the common denominator of both Shakespearian plays, and it is consequently with this play that it is most useful to begin in tracing the history of Shakespeare's identical siblings.

The *Menaechmi* enacts the hilarious sequence of misunderstandings that spring from the arrival of one member of a pair of twins in a town in which, unknown to him, his brother is a leading citizen. The action opens with a speech by a parasite (a traditional character, hanging on the coat-tails of the rich), which serves to establish the wealth of the resident brother (Menaechmus), while the rest of Act I is devoted to the estrangement between this brother and his shrewish wife, whom he proposes to spite by giving one of her garments to a courtesan. Act II introduces the second twin (also known as Menaechmus) and sees the first error when he is accosted by the courtesan's servant, and then by the courtesan herself. Though he takes both to be mad, he nevertheless accepts their proffered hospitality, pretending to be the man they take him to be. Act III sees a further complication with the newly arrived twin being entrusted with the garment appropriated by his brother, and then with a gold chain, both of which he determines to keep. In Act IV the resident Menaechmus is challenged by his wife over the garment, and by the courtesan over both the garment and the chain, while by Act V the confusion has mounted to such a degree that all the characters regard one another as mad, before the source of the errors is revealed and the brothers are joyfully united.

The *Menaechmi* was well known during the sixteenth century (as Manningham's comment implies), and was performed at court on a number of occasions (e.g. in 1577 and 1583). It was available to readers in both Latin and English versions,[2] and though we cannot be sure with which text Shakespeare was familiar there can be little doubt in view of the similarities between its plot and that of *The*

---

2. See G. Bullough (1957–75) *Narrative and Dramatic Sources of Shakespeare*, Routledge and Kegan Paul, vol. I, pp. 3–5.

Comedy of Errors that one play is directly structured upon the other. The 'errors' of the Shakespearian comedy are also initiated by the arrival of one member of a pair of twins in a town in which his brother is a respected citizen. Like Plautus' Menaechmus, Shakespeare's Antipholus of Ephesus is torn between a shrewish wife and a courtesan, while his brother, Antipholus of Syracuse, is accosted by a servant who mistakes his identity, offered hospitality by strangers, and entrusted with a gold chain. Bemused by the conduct of the Ephesians, the newly arrived brother, like his Plautine predecessor, suspects that the citizens are mad, while the resident Antipholus, like his Roman counterpart, is threatened with incarceration as a lunatic before the source of the confusion is discovered and the family group happily reunited.

For all their similarities, however, *The Comedy of Errors* is not simply a translation of the Latin play. Though the story lines of the two comedies are broadly similar, Shakespeare appears to have felt (like the Italian adapters of the play before him)[3] that the plot was insufficiently complex to satisfy the expectations of a contemporary audience, in that he amplified it in a number of ways. In the first place, he supplied his identical masters with identical servants, thus more than doubling the scope for comic confusion, while endowing his married twin with an unmarried sister-in-law who could be paired with the newly arrived brother at the close. At the same time, he grafted on to the *Menaechmi* a scene from a second Plautine comedy, the *Amphitruo*, which supplies the out-facing situation of Act III scene i, while placing the entire action within an encircling frame plot (which has no place in Plautus' work) dealing with the fate of another member of the twins' family, their father, Egeon.

On the simplest level these additions are clearly designed to complicate the classical simplicity of the Plautine design in order to augment the potential for error, but they also form part of a much more fundamental process of adaptation that has taken place in the course of the Roman play's progress through Shakespeare's imagination. Though the plots of the two comedies follow a similar path, the motives and responses of those caught up in the

---

3. Though there is no direct evidence that Shakespeare was familiar with the work of these writers, he does appear 'to have been acquainted with the way in which the comedy of mistaken identity was exploited on the Italian stage' (K. M. Lea (1934) *Italian Popular Comedy*, Oxford, vol. II, p. 438).

action are markedly different, while the frame plot encircling the Shakespearian play widens the significance of the misunderstandings to which the central situation gives rise. The story line of the *Menaechmi* has thus become the vehicle for a 'present purpose' distinct from that for which it was initially deployed, with the divergencies between the two structures affording an insight into the later writer's intentions.

The exposition of the Shakespearian comedy offers a striking example of the very different meaning that is generated through the material that the dramatist 'addeth' to his source and that which he 'leaveth out'. Rather than opening, like the *Menaechmi*, with a parasite announcing his intention to fasten on an affluent patron, *The Comedy of Errors* begins with an old man under sentence of death. The audience is informed in the course of the opening scene that Egeon is the tragic survivor of a sundered family, who has fallen victim to the laws of Ephesus while in search of a lost son and his servant, who had set out together in their turn in quest of their identical siblings. Egeon lays his history before the Duke, rather than directly addressing the audience, heightening the self-contained nature of the play world, while his story excites the sympathies of the man he addresses, who allows him twenty-four hours in which to raise the ransom for his release. The comedy is thus set in a universe distinct from that of the spectator, while the conventional unity of time within which the source operates is transformed into a highly significant time-span within which the play's difficulties must be resolved.

The addition of Egeon to the inherited structure does not simply serve, however, to establish the self-contained nature of the later play, and to heighten the significance of its time scheme. It also contributes to the different kind of relationship that the dramatist engineers between the audience and the dramatis personae. Where Plautus' parasite ushers the spectator into a self-interested, economically orientated society, Egeon enlists the sympathies of the audience in the predicament of a caring individual. The old man has risked his life in order to recover his son, and now seems destined to die in a wholly isolated state. At the same time, his introduction in the opening scene serves to widen the play's focus from the individual to the family group. Where the *Menaechmi* turns upon the separation of one pair of brothers, *The Comedy of Errors* involves the division of an entire family – husband and wife, father and son, mother and son, brother and brother, master and servant. Moreover, the sequence of searchers established in the course of the exposition enhances the sense of personal deprivation that the dislocation of the family group entails in the Shakespearian play. Where Plautus' traveller is simply curious about the fate of his brother, the members of Egeon's family are searching, not merely for one another, but for a sense of personal identity that has been diminished by their separation. The 'errors' that occur in the main plot are thus not simply a product of the arrival of the second pair of twins. They are an extension of a process already at work – the disintegration of that sense of selfhood that derives, in part at least, from an acknowledged place within the family group.

It will be apparent from the above that the addition of Egeon to the inherited plot has served to move the Renaissance play away from its classical predecessor in two directions. While on the one hand the sense of gravity underlying the sequence of amusing events that the drama enacts is much greater in the Shakespearian play, on the other the process of fragmentation that is evoked in the opening scene elicits a measure of concern on the part of the audience for those whose security is at risk. The closing scene of the frame plot (which again has no counterpart in Plautus' work) emphasizes, moreover, both aspects of Shakespeare's departure from the tale on which he draws. Whereas the humorous potentialities of the situation are exploited in the central scenes of the play, when Egeon returns to the stage in the final act the potential seriousness of the situation is again recalled. Having failed to raise the ransom required for his release, the old man is on his way to execution when he encounters Antipholus of Ephesus, and believing him to be his lost son appeals to him for help – only to be repudiated by him (and his servant) in his hour of need:

> *Egeon.* Most mighty duke, vouchsafe me speak a word;
>   Haply I see a friend will save my life,
>   And pay the sum that may deliver me.
> *Duke.* Speak freely, Syracusian, what thou wilt.
> *Egeon.* Is not your name, sir, call'd Antipholus?
>   And is not that your bondman Dromio?
>   . . . .
>   Why look you strange on me? you know me well.
> *Eph. Ant.* I never saw you in my life till now.
> *Egeon.* O! grief hath chang'd me since you saw me last,

And careful hours with time's deformed hand
Have written strange defeatures in my face;
But tell me yet, dost thou not know my voice?
Eph. Ant. Neither.
Egeon. Dromio, nor thou?
Eph. Dro.   No, trust me sir, nor I.
Egeon. I am sure thou dost?
Eph. Dro. Ay sir, but I am sure I do not, and whatsoever
a man denies, you are bound to believe him.
Egeon. Not know my voice? O time's extremity,
Hast thou so crack'd and splitted my poor tongue
In seven short years, that here my only son
Knows not my feeble key of untun'd cares?
Though now this grained face of mine be hid
In sap-consuming winter's drizzled snow,
And all the conduits of my blood froze up,
Yet hath my night of life some memory;
My wasting lamps some fading glimmer left;
My dull deaf ears a little use to hear –
All these old witnesses, I cannot err,
Tell me thou art my son Antipholus.
Eph. Ant. I never saw my father in my life.

(V.i.283–319)

Here, the movement of the blank verse, with its run-on lines, and metrical irregularities, approximates to the rhythms of natural speech, enacting the emotion of the speaker, and enlisting the sympathies of the audience in his predicament. Though the mis-understandings through which his suffering is generated are rapidly resolved in the remainder of the scene, the danger implicit in his situation is vividly, if briefly, realized, giving the 'errors' of the main plot a resonance entirely lacking in the earlier play.

It is not merely the additions that Shakespeare makes to his source material, however, that serve to widen the implications of his action; that which he 'altereth and changeth' is equally signifi-cant. Whereas in the Plautine comedy the resident Menaechmus was parted from his father in childhood by being snatched away in a market place, the members of Egeon's family are separated during a storm at sea, which is powerfully evoked in the opening scene. The passage is too long to quote in full, but a brief extract affords some indication of the detail with which the incident is described:

Egeon. A league from Epidamnum had we sail'd
    Before the always-wind-obeying deep
    Gave any tragic instance of our harm,
    But longer did we not retain much hope;
    For what obscured light the heavens did grant,
    Did but convey unto our fearful minds
    A doubtful warrant of immediate death.
    ....
    The sailors sought for safety by our boat,
    And left the ship, then sinking-ripe, to us.
    My wife, more careful for the latter-born,
    Had fasten'd him unto a small spare mast,
    Such as sea-faring men provide for storms;
    To him one of the other twins was bound,
    Whilst I had been like heedful of the other.
    The children thus dispos'd, my wife and I,
    Fixing our eyes on whom our care was fix'd,
    Fasten'd ourselves at either end the mast.
                                    (I.i.62–85)

The sea journey is a traditional motif in European literature for the passage through life, while storm is emblematic of the cataclysmic events that beset man in his progress from the womb to the grave.[4] The tempest which severs the members of Egeon's family, unlike the random occurrence that separates the Plautine brothers, thus has symbolic overtones, suggesting the upheavals to which every human life is subject. In short, where the Roman play deals with a specialized instance, the Shakespearian drama has a universal application, and is consequently relevant to those outside the play world.

The central scenes of the play, which seem at first sight to constitute a straightforward amplification of the *Menaechmi*, also reveal on closer inspection a number of significant departures from the source. In the first place, Shakespeare's characters are far more attractive than their Roman New Comedy counterparts.

4. A large number of Shakespeare's plays make use of these motifs (e.g. *Othello, Pericles, The Tempest*), which occur frequently in Renaissance drama. Webster's *Vittoria Corombona* (*The White Devil*: 1612) describes her soul as 'like to a ship in a black storm . . . driven I know not whither' (V.vi.248–9), while Chapman's *Bussy D'Ambois* (1604?) expatiates on the danger of 'shipwrack' when wandering through 'the waves/of glassy glory' unguided by virtue (I.i.20–33). The concept is summed up in *Timon of Athens* (1604–05?) which describes life as an 'uncertain voyage' in 'nature's fragile vessel' (V.i.201 and 200).

Antipholus of Syracuse, for example, is a sensitive and imaginative man who feels the division of his family deeply (cf.I.ii.33–40). He responds with bewilderment, wonder and a degree of fear to the behaviour of the Ephesians (cf.II.ii.147–216), and accepts the gold chain that is given to him as further evidence of their extraordinary nature (cf.III.ii.178–84). The conduct of Plautus' Menaechmus, by contrast, is much more pragmatic and morally questionable. He quickly recognizes that he is the victim of some kind of error, accepting the items that are thrust on him with satisfaction, and resolving to keep them for himself. Similarly, though Shakespeare's Antipholus of Ephesus is at odds with his wife at the outset, the estrangement between them is clearly painful to both parties (cf.II.ii.110–80 and III.i.1–5), and they gain in understanding by the close, whereas Plautus' resident Menaechmus regards his wife as a shrew throughout, and is as anxious to be rid of her in the last scene as he was in the beginning. At the same time, the role of the courtesan is considerably reduced in the Shakespearian play, while a romantic element is introduced in the courtship between Antipholus of Syracuse and Luciana, allowing not merely for an additional dimension of comic interplay, but a further cementing of the family group through a future marriage. Where Plautus, in brief, projects an image of a mercenary, self-interested society, Shakespeare presents a much less predatory community, the members of which are motivated by emotional as well as economic needs, and are governed by moral as well as pragmatic considerations.

The combination of that which Shakespeare 'addeth' to his source and that which he 'altereth and changeth' has a significant effect upon the tonal range of the later play. Whereas Plautus' audience is amused throughout, from Menaechmus' determination to spite his wife at the outset to his regret at being unable to sell her at the close, Shakespeare's audience moves from a compassionate interest in Egeon's story, through the hilarity of the central acts, to momentary concern for the old father, and thence to a sense of joyous relief at the end. Though those outside the play world have been led to anticipate the reunion of both sets of siblings, and the restoration of the sons to their father, the revelation that Emilia, an old Abbess with whom Antipholus of Ephesus has taken refuge, is in fact the long lost wife of Egeon is wholly unlooked for, surprising the members of the audience in common with the dramatis personae, and hence generating a sense of wonder in the closing scene that has no counterpart in the source. The appearance of Emilia contributes, moreover, to a joyfulness of a very different order from that which attends the union of the brothers in the Roman play. Working in conjunction with the initial separation of the family group by storm, the arrival of the various members of the divided household in Ephesus (a city associated through the Bible[5] with magic and witchcraft), and the final assembly of the dramatis personae before the priory, the discovery of Emilia suggests the operation of a power external to the will of the protagonists, manipulating events towards a favourable outcome. The happiness of the closing scene (counterpointing the storm and stress of the opening) thus involves more than the recovery of a single person; it encompasses an entire family, and implies (for the audience at least) the intervention of benign forces in human affairs.

It is in the treatment of madness, however, that the distance between the 'present purposes' of the two dramatists is most clearly apparent. From first to last the characters of both plays define their situations in terms of a breakdown of rationality either among their compatriots or in the alien environments into which they have strayed. Menaechmus the traveller, for example, when first saluted by the courtesan's servant, immediately assumes he must be mad, and he reaches the same conclusion in relation to both the parasite and his brother's wife. Conversely, the inhabitants of Epidamnum, unable to account for the actions of the resident Menaechmus, decide he has lost his wits, and attempt to carry him to the house of a physician who has confirmed that he is mad. Similarly, in the Shakespearian play, Antipholus of Syracuse doubts the sanity of his own servant after an encounter with the Ephesian Dromio, while the Ephesians come to the conclusion that the resident Antipholus has taken leave of his senses, subjecting him to the ministrations of Dr Pinch. Nevertheless, though the madness motif has clearly been transposed from one play to the other, its significance differs considerably in the two works. In the Plautine comedy the characters' assumptions about one another are

---

5. Cf. Acts of the Apostles XIX. Shakespeare's audience, of course, would have been much more alive to the Biblical resonances of the location than spectators are today.

a register of the confusion that has been generated by the arrival of the second twin, while the binding of the resident Menaechmus functions as a mechanism for a fresh set of misunderstandings when he is freed by his brother's servant. In Shakespeare's play, by contrast, the term 'mad' acquires an expanding circle of significance as the drama unfolds. Whereas it is used initially as an expression of bewilderment in the face of the inexplicable behaviour of others, it comes to suggest an ultimate state of estrangement, and the operation of a diabolic force.

From the outset of the Shakespearian drama the protagonists are aware of themselves as moving towards a condition of isolation. Egeon grieves over the progressive disintegration of his family in the opening scene, Antipholus of Syracuse fears that he has lost himself in the course of searching for his missing relatives (I.ii.33–40), while his brother's wife in Act II scene i laments her distance from her husband (87–101). As the action progresses and the confusion mounts the characters become increasingly self-enclosed, unable to communicate effectively with one another in that every conversation that is initiated is based on a false premise. By the close of the play, though each of the dramatis personae is convinced of the rightness of his or her own position, none of them is able to rely on a shared perception of the situation on the part of those around them, and they thus lack any external support for the validity of their own stance. The amplification of the Plautine plot through the addition of the Dromios and Luciana, moreover, is highly significant in this respect. Whereas the misunderstandings in the *Menaechmi* are limited to a relatively small group of people, those of the Shakespearian play multiply throughout an entire society, involving not merely the brothers themselves, but their servants and their servants' acquaintance (cf. III.ii.71ff.), evoking an entire world of disorder, only one part of which is presented to the audience. At the same time, the elaboration of the plot heightens the pace as well as the complexity of the action, suggesting a world spinning into turmoil as individual after individual whirls from encounter to encounter in which his or her perception of the situation conflicts with another's or in which his or her sense of selfhood is challenged. Though the predicaments generated are highly amusing, their potential seriousness becomes increasingly marked, and the darker implications of the drama are particularly evident in its closing scenes. By Act V both Egeon and

Antipholus of Ephesus face a state of total estrangement from the social group. Egeon, confronting Antipholus of Ephesus, recognizes a man who does not recognize him, and the Duke promptly assumes that 'age and dangers make [him] dote' (V.i.329), dismissing his position, on which his life depends, as madness, while Antipholus of Ephesus, whose account of the day's activities does not accord with that of his fellow citizens, is threatened with imprisonment as a lunatic. At this point, it is not merely the humorous aspects of mistaken identity that are brought home to the spectator. Antipholus of Ephesus' frustration is strongly felt, while his father's plight reveals the vulnerability of human beings in a world in which a recognized place within the community is dependent not simply upon the individual's awareness of selfhood, but upon external endorsement of it. Deprived first of a wife and son, and then of a second son and his servant, Egeon is lost in an alien world in which his interpretation of actuality both isolates him and defines him as mad, in that it meets no answering response from his fellow men.

Madness in the Shakespearian play is not simply, however, an extension of that condition of alienation which is initiated by the severance of the family group. It is also an expression of the operation of external forces on the play world. Whereas Plautus' comedy is set in the morally suspect city of Epidamnum, Shakespeare's takes place in the spiritually dangerous environment of Ephesus, a city conventionally associated (as noted above) with sorcery. From the start of the play Antipholus of Syracuse and his servant are keenly aware of the reputation of the town in which they find themselves, and are quick to interpret the strange encounters that befall them as evidence of witchcraft. Antipholus of Syracuse, for example, after meeting the Ephesian Dromio, attributes his conduct to

> Dark-working sorcerers that change the mind,
> Soul-killing witches that deform the body,
>
> (I.ii.99–100)

while the Syracusan Dromio, faced with the seemingly bizarre conduct of Luciana, exclaims,

> O for my beads; I cross me for a sinner.
>
> (II.ii.188)

By the end of Act IV the Ephesians are convinced that the apparently insane resident Antipholus is possessed by the devil (cf.IV.iv.90–3 and 105), while Antipholus of Syracuse is in no doubt that the seemingly deranged citizens are witches and that he must leave the town as quickly as he can (IV.iv.145–55). Once again, the misapprehensions of the characters are amusing, but their conviction that they are in the grip of malign forces introduces a metaphysical dimension to the action that has no counterpart in the Roman play. It is only with the entrance of Emilia from the priory (a location that is clearly not without significance) that the madness associated by the protagonists with the diabolic is finally dispelled – the harmony that obtains in the closing scene thus having spiritual, as well as social and familial, dimensions.

It will be apparent from the above that though *The Comedy of Errors* is clearly structured on the Roman play the adaptations made by the later dramatist to his source are productive of a very different kind of dramatic experience from that offered by his classical model. Plautus' comedy is typical of the generality of his work, in that his characters display little human warmth, pursue their own interests with scant regard for those around them, and are largely motivated by material considerations. Drawn in broad outline rather than being conceived in depth, their interaction generates laughter rather than contributing to a pattern of meaning that emerges as the drama unfolds. *The Comedy of Errors*, by contrast, presents characters who are both more caring towards one another, and who elicit a greater degree of audience sympathy, while the 'mistaking' situations in which they are caught up contribute to a theme or statement about the nature of human life (the fragility of man's sense of identity, and the dependence of his selfhood upon factors external to his own consciousness) that is a product of the entire structure. Where the meeting between Plautus' brothers brings a series of misunderstandings to a close but leaves their society unchanged, the reunion between the members of Egeon's family restores order in the social, economic, intellectual and spiritual spheres, giving rise to both joy and wonder as each individual 'finds' himself in the fullest possible sense. By a process of reordering, adding and excising the later dramatist has thus transformed a drama designed to amuse its audience by presenting the improbable consequences of an improbable situation into one in which improbability is deployed to explore an aspect of reality.

Approximately ten years intervened between the composition of *The Comedy of Errors* and *Twelfth Night*, Shakespeare's second version of Plautus' errors plot. Unlike his first adaptation of the *Menaechmi*, however, the later play is not structured upon the Roman play alone, but is a product of a much more complex interaction in the dramatist's imagination between a variety of inherited materials. As Manningham noted in his diary in 1602, the ultimate source of the main plot of the play is neither the *Menaechmi* nor its Shakespearian offshoot, but *Gl'Ingannati*, an Italian comedy produced by the Academy of the Intronati in 1531.[6] This play concerns the amorous adventures of a young woman who, having been separated from her brother during the sack of Rome, and lodged in a convent by her father, has run away from the sisters to enter the service of the man she loves disguised as a page, only to be employed by him as emissary to the lady he wishes to marry. In executing her master's commission, the heroine becomes the object of her rival's affections, and is extricated from the triangular relationship she has unwittingly created only by the appearance of her brother, who is mistakenly afforded an opportunity to impose his own attentions on his sister's suitor. The play spawned a number of adaptations, some of which Shakespeare may have known, but it is generally agreed that it is to a non-dramatic version by Barnabe Riche recounting the adventures of Apolonius and Silla[7] that *Twelfth Night* is principally indebted. Once again, a brother and sister are divided, the former in this instance being involved in the African wars, while the latter is shipwrecked while in pursuit of a man who does not reciprocate her affections. Having survived the destruction of her vessel by clinging to a chest of clothes, the heroine disguises herself as her brother with the garments that are to hand, and enters the service of the man she is pursuing, only to be chosen by him as intermediary in his suit to another lady. Once again, the second lady falls

6. For a fuller account of the sources of *Twelfth Night* see G. Bullough (1957–75), vol. II, pp. 269–85, J. M. Lothian and T. W. Craik (eds) (1975), pp. xxxv–l and L. Scragg (1982) *The Metamorphosis of 'Gallathea': A Study in Creative Adaptation*, University Press of America, Washington DC, pp. 99–124.
7. The tale occurs in *Riche his Farewell to Militarie Profession* (1581).

in love with the first, the arrival of the heroine's brother again allowing, in course of time, for the situation to be resolved.

The similarity between the plots of *Gl'Ingannati* and Riche's romance on the one hand, and *Twelfth Night* on the other leaves no doubt of the tradition to which the Shakespearian play belongs. Like its dramatic and non-dramatic predecessors, *Twelfth Night* is also initiated by the separation of siblings, with the heroine's decision to disguise herself as a youth in order to enter the house of a nobleman with whom she subsequently falls in love leading to her master's choice of her as emissary in his suit to another lady, the second lady's infatuation with the first, and a knot of cross-affections that can be loosened only by the arrival of the heroine's brother. Nevertheless, for all their similarities, the story derived from *Gl'Ingannati* is not the sole source of the Shakespearian play. The Plautine elements of the tale (notably the separation of siblings) appear to have reminded the dramatist of his own earlier work, in that some aspects of plot clearly look back to *The Comedy of Errors*. Whereas the sundered siblings of the Italian play and its derivatives are merely brother and sister, their counterparts in *Twelfth Night*, like the brothers of *The Comedy of Errors*, are identical twins, with all the divisible indivisibility which that traditionally mysterious relationship implies. At the same time, the cause of the division between the central figures is also reminiscent of the earlier play. Whereas in *Gl'Ingannati* it is the sack of Rome which parts the siblings, while the storm that befalls the heroine of Riche's romance occurs after her separation from her brother, in *Twelfth Night*, as in *The Comedy of Errors*, it is a storm that functions as the agent of severance, with the expositions of both plays evoking the painful consequences of a sea journey.

It is in the career of Sebastian, however, that the Plautine antecedents of the later comedy are most plainly visible. Though Viola's history patently derives from *Gl'Ingannati*, whatever the precise route of its transmission, her brother's looks back to the *Menaechmi*, and (more immediately) to the adventures of Antipholus of Syracuse. Like his *Comedy of Errors* counterpart, Sebastian finds himself in an unfamiliar country as a consequence of a shipwreck in which he has been separated from his identical twin. Having been advised to lodge at the Elephant (Antipholus of Syracuse 'hosts' at the Centaur), he sets out to 'see the relics' (III.iii.19) of the town, while his companion 'bespeak[s his] diet'

(III.iii.40) at the inn (cf. Antipholus of Syracuse: 'Within this hour it will be dinner time; / Till that I'll view the manners of the town, / Peruse the traders, gaze upon the buildings' (I.ii.11–13). Like Antipholus of Syracuse he is greeted familiarly, to his amazement, by the citizens, and has a series of encounters with strangers who claim some knowledge of his affairs. In the course of the ensuing action, he is accosted, like his *Comedy of Errors* predecessor, by a servant (cf. *Comedy of Errors*, I.ii.43ff. and *Twelfth Night*, IV.i.1ff.), invited to the house of a lady he has not met (cf. *Comedy of Errors*, I.ii.43ff. and *Twelfth Night*, IV.i.1ff.), and addressed fondly by a woman he does not know (cf. *Comedy of Errors*, II.ii.110ff. and *Twelfth Night*, IV.i.50ff.), before being reunited with his *alter ego* and 'finding' not only himself but a marriage partner. Like his counterpart in the earlier play his experiences cause him to question his own sanity (cf. *Comedy of Errors*, II.ii.213 and *Twelfth Night*, IV.i.60), while in the recognition scene at the close he is saluted as a spirit or ghost (cf. *Comedy of Errors*, V.i.332–7 and *Twelfth Night*, V.i.233–6).

Sebastian is not the only character in the later play whose origins may be found in *The Comedy of Errors*. Antonio, the sea-captain who 'took [him] from the breach of the sea' (II.i.21–2) has affinities with Egeon, in that both are regarded as enemies by the society into which they have intruded, and are consequently arrested and threatened with death. Having lent his purse to Sebastian, Antonio is obliged by his changed circumstances to ask for its return, only to be met with blank incomprehension on the part of the youth whom he addresses, who is not Sebastian but the disguised Viola. Both the misunderstanding over the purse of gold and the repudiation of an older man by a younger are clearly recalled from *The Comedy of Errors*, and so too is the scene in which the captive Antonio is brought before the Duke. Required, like Egeon before him, to explain why he has jeopardized his life by trespassing into a hostile country, he responds with a speech laden with resonances of the earlier play:

> . . . A witchcraft drew me hither:
> That most ingrateful boy there by your side,
> From the rude sea's enrag'd and foamy mouth
> Did I redeem. A wrack past hope he was.
> His life I gave him, and did thereto add
> My love, without retention or restraint

All his in dedication. For his sake
Did I expose myself (pure for his love)
Into the danger of this adverse town;
Drew to defend him, when he was beset;
Where being apprehended, his false cunning
(Not meaning to partake with me in danger)
Taught him to face me out of his acquaintance,
And grew a twenty years' removed thing
While one would wink; denied me mine own purse,
Which I had recommended to his use
Not half an hour before.
Viola.   How can this be?
Duke. When came he to this town?
Ant. Today, my lord: and for three months before
No int'rim, not a minute's vacancy,
Both day and night did we keep company.
. . . .
Duke.   Fellow, thy words are madness.
Three months this youth hath tended upon me;
But more of that anon. Take him aside.

(V.i.74–98)

Numerous aspects of this exchange serve to confirm Shakespeare's
dependence here on his previous composition. Not only is Antonio's story initiated, like Egeon's, by a shipwreck, but the prisoner
has been drawn to an alien town by his love for a younger man,
only to be repudiated by him in his hour of need. Like his
predecessor in *The Comedy of Errors*, he is informed by his accusers
that the youth whose acquaintance he claims is a resident of the
city, while the time-span that he evokes to express their changed
relationship echoes the earlier play (cf. *Comedy of Errors*, V.i.326–8
and *Twelfth Night*, V.i.87–8). Like the Syracusans before him
Antonio ascribes his experience to witchcraft, while the Illyrians
follow the Ephesians in assuming their captive to be mad (cf.
Comedy of Errors, V.i.329 and *Twelfth Night*, V.i.96).

Though the Antonio/Sebastian plot supplies the most obvious
link between Shakespeare's two versions of the *Menaechmi*, other
characters and incidents are also transposed from the earlier into
the later play. Just as Antipholus of Ephesus, for example, having
been driven to seemingly insane behaviour by the errors to which
he is subjected, is diagnosed as mad and incarcerated as a lunatic,
so Malvolio is the victim of an error (in this instance a practical

joke) which induces a species of 'mad' behaviour leading to his imprisonment in a dark room. Both characters escape from their confinement vowing vengeance, with Malvolio, unlike his predecessor, still unreconciled at the close. In this instance, the experiences of the more irascible of Shakespeare's first set of twins have been adapted to form the central interest of a sub-plot independent of the sibling confusion from which they initially derive.

There can be no doubt, then, that in constructing *Twelfth Night* Shakespeare has turned back to his earlier work, but the later play is far from being *The Comedy of Errors* revamped. The addition of the strand of action deriving, via Riche's romance, from *Gl'Ingannati*, has effected a major change in the function of the errors plot and in the meaning that it generates. In the first place, the environment in which the events of the drama take place has undergone a significant change. *The Comedy of Errors*, like its classical predecessor, is firmly set in the Roman world. The action is located in Ephesus, a city associated with St Paul on the one hand,[8] and a celebrated statue of the goddess Diana on the other, while the central figures have 'Roman' names. The relationship between master and man is that of *dominus* and *servus*, rather than gentleman and servant, and admits physical correction, while the ready resort of a respectable citizen to a courtesan suggests a Roman milieu rather than a Renaissance one. The observation of the unities of time, place and action reinforces the play's link with a culture other than that of its original audience, as do the insistent references to the 'mart' (evocative of the Roman forum), and to such towns as Epidamnum and Corinth. *Twelfth Night*, by contrast, is set in a very different milieu. 'Illyria' is far less precise in its associations than Ephesus, suggesting the world of romance rather than any specific culture. the names of the characters – Orsino, Olivia, Viola / Sir Toby Belch, Sir Andrew Aguecheek, Maria – evoke the elegance and refinement of the Italian city state on the one hand, and contemporary English society on the other, while their pursuits – hunting (cf.I.i.16), participating in masques and revels (cf.I.iii.111–12), and listening to music (cf.II.iv.1–67) – contribute to the image of a courtly, sophisticated society. At the same time, a movement has taken place up the social scale. With the exception of the Duke, who passes judgement at the opening

8. See Acts of the Apostles XIX and St Paul's epistle to the Ephesians.

and the close, the dramatis personae of *The Comedy of Errors* are monied citizens and their servants, with the interests and preoccupations of their class, while the characters of *Twelfth Night* are aristocratic, with the leisure for introspection and the pursuit of pleasure rather than the need to secure their daily bread. The sex of the principal figures has also undergone a notable change. Whereas it is upon the brothers and their attendants that attention is focused in the earlier play, it is a woman (Viola) in *Twelfth Night* who stands at the centre of the action, while her relationship with a member of her own sex forms one of the principal concerns of the plot. The female mind is thus much more fully delineated than it was in *The Comedy of Errors*, with the ambiguous nature of Viola's role (in her disguise as Cesario) allowing for a far richer complex of relationships and responses than is afforded by the Plautine confusion between identical brothers. At the same time, the focus on female experience heightens the vulnerability of the central figures, while a shift in the marital status of the protagonists gives rise to a new set of concerns. Whereas in *The Comedy of Errors* (as in the *Menaechmi*) the action focuses on the married (or presumed to be married), in *Twelfth Night* (as in *Gl'Ingannati* and its offshoots) it centres on those in the process of forming relationships, and hence is evocative of the insecurity and heightened emotion associated with that particular phase of human life. In brief, where *The Comedy of Errors* evokes the rumbustiousness of its Roman New Comedy source, *Twelfth Night* transposes the 'errors' plot into the world of Italianate romance, infusing it with all the sophistication of feeling implied during the Renaissance by that context.[9]

It is not merely the general ambience of the action arising from his additions that serves, however, to distinguish Shakespeare's two versions of the *Menaechmi*. That which he 'altereth and changeth', and in particular the relationship that he engineers between the dramatis personae and the audience, also contributes to the very different kinds of dramatic experience afforded by the two plays. In *The Comedy of Errors*, although those outside the play world are encouraged to relate to Egeon in the frame plot, they are distanced from the figures caught up in the central action by the

9. Cf. G. K. Hunter (1978) *Dramatic Identities and Cultural Tradition*, Liverpool University Press, pp. 21ff. Hunter notes the potency of this image of a 'land of wit, of pleasure and of refinement' (p. 21) in English Renaissance comedy and tragedy.

speed with which the plot develops, their superior awareness (in that they understand the causes of the characters' confusion), and the kind of language that the speakers are assigned. The use of rhyming couplets, for example, helps to frustrate dramatic involvement by their distance from natural speech, and the same effect is produced by accentuating the regular pulse of the iambic pentameter, by elaborate punning, and by the use of artfully managed images in the course of 'impassioned' speech. The employment of these devices works against the illusion of naturalism, heightening the spectator's awareness of the play as play, and encouraging the members of the audience to laugh at the individual's predicament, rather than inviting a sympathetic involvement in his or her experience. Adriana's rebuke to her seeming husband for appearing to side with his servant against her is a typical example:

> How ill agrees it with your gravity
> To counterfeit thus grossly with your slave,
> Abetting him to thwart me in my mood;
> Be it my wrong, you are from me exempt,
> But wrong not that wrong with a more contempt.
> Come, I will fasten on this sleeve of thine;
> Thou art an elm, my husband, I a vine,
> Whose weakness married to thy stronger state,
> Makes me with thy strength to communicate:
> If ought possess thee from me, it is dross,
> Usurping ivy, briar, or idle moss,
> Who all for want of pruning, with intrusion,
> Infect thy sap, and live on thy confusion.
>
> (II.ii.168–80)

In *Twelfth Night*, by contrast, a far more intimate relationship is established between the dramatis personae and those outside the play world. The members of the audience are privy to Viola's disguise from the outset, and thus have a double perspective on the scenes in which she is involved, appreciating the complexities of her position, even while laughing at the errors to which her masculine exterior gives rise. At the same time, the use of the aside (cf.I.iv.41–2 and III.iv.307–9) and of innuendo (cf.II.iv.20–8 and 104–16) serve to place the members of the audience in a conspiratorial relationship with the central figure, and a similar effect is achieved in the sub-plot, with the audience aligned (initially at least) with Maria and Sir Toby through their shared knowledge in the plot against Malvolio. The slow pace of the action, moreover, allows the spectator to linger upon personality and motive, rather than being borne along on a current of events, while the language that the characters are assigned is appropriate to each individual, serving to initiate those outside the play world into the workings of a specific mind. While Orsino, for example, plays with pleasing ideas (cf.I.i.1ff.), Sir Toby is involved with the physical, the world of 'cakes and ale' (cf.II.iii.*passim*), and this contrast between their psychologies is expressed through the medium each employs (blank verse against prose), and the field of reference upon which they draw. And distinctions of this kind do not simply serve to distinguish main from sub-plot characters – they also operate within social groups. Though Sir Toby and Sir Andrew, for example, are almost invariably seen together, their personalities are sharply distinguished, as is their intellectual stature. Sir Andrew's weakness of wit and will are signalled by his eagerness to respond to the leads the other man supplies, by his linguistic blunders and lack of self-awareness, while Sir Toby's superior vigour, and fundamental contempt for his companion are implied by the ease with which he manipulates him into exposing his folly, and the enjoyment that he derives from doing so. The scene in which he introduces Sir Andrew to Maria (and thus to the audience) illustrates the point:

> *Sir And.* Bless you, fair shrew.
> *Maria.* And you too, sir.
> *Sir To.* Accost, Sir Andrew, accost.
> *Sir And.* What's that?
> *Sir To.* My niece's chambermaid.
> *Sir And.* Good Mistress Accost, I desire better acquaintance.
> *Maria.* My name is Mary, sir.
> *Sir And.* Good Mistress Mary Accost –
> *Sir To.* You mistake, knight. 'Accost' is front her, board her, woo her, assail her.
> *Sir And.* By my troth, I would not undertake her in this company. Is that the meaning of 'accost'?
> *Maria.* Fare you well, gentlemen.
> *Sir To.* And thou let part so, Sir Andrew, would thou might'st never draw sword again!
> *Sir And.* And you part so, mistress, I would I might never draw sword again. Fair lady, do you think you have fools in hand?

Maria. Sir, I have not you by th'hand.
Sir And. Marry, but you shall have, and here's my hand.

(I.iii.46–67)

Not only are the characters of *Twelfth Night* more fully differentiated, moreover, than those of the earlier play, they also create
the illusion of being complex human beings, rather than stereotypical (or two-dimensional) figures. Whereas Antipholus of Ephesus
merely becomes angrier and angrier as the action of *The Comedy of
Errors* progresses, while his twin grows more alarmed and confused, the inhabitants of Illyria gradually reveal more about themselves as the drama unfolds, displaying the destructive tendencies,
in some instances, concealed beneath their courtly veneer. For
example, whereas at the outset of the drama the members of the
audience might be disposed to regard Orsino as a typical embodiment of Petrarchan love, they are rapidly obliged to modify this
assessment as his rapprochement with 'Cesario' becomes increasingly marked. Here the spectator is simultaneously aware of the
character's own view of his emotional predicament, and of the
actual state of his affections, and is thus able to formulate both a
truer and a more complex judgement of his position than is
available to Orsino himself. At the same time, the seemingly effete
nature of the Duke's character is qualified in the final scene in
which his abrupt determination to

. . . sacrifice the lamb that I do love,
To spite a raven's heart within a dove,

(V.i.128–9)

tears aside the fanciful mask of courtly lover that he has worn
throughout the play. And Orsino is not alone in being a more fully
developed figure than the characters of *The Comedy of Errors*. From
Olivia at one end of the social spectrum to the members of her
household at the other, the dramatis personae are constantly
engaged in revealing aspects of their personalities to the audience
which complicate any attempt to categorize them. Olivia, as
Sebastian remarks in Act IV scene iii (16–20), displays considerable
strength of mind and judiciousness in her conduct of her household, yet she has no capacity to govern her passion for 'Cesario',
and demeans herself in her pursuit of him. The seamy underside of
Sir Toby's affability becomes increasingly evident as the action
evolves (cf. his attitude to Sir Andrew in III.ii. and V.i.), while

Feste in the final scene betrays a vindictiveness towards Malvolio of which the audience has had no previous suspicion.

Twelfth Night, then, constitutes a different kind of dramatic experience from its dramatic progenitor in that it involves those outside the play world in a sophisticated universe peopled by complex human beings, rather than inviting the spectator to sit back and laugh at (as against with) whose caught up in the sequence of events. This shift in the nature of the play world and the stance of the audience towards it is crucial, moreover, to the 'present purposes' of the dramatist, and the meaning of his play. In the earlier comedy, the 'errors' to which the characters are subject are the product of external agencies. They are initiated by the chance arrival of Antipholus of Syracuse (and his Dromio) in Ephesus, and compounded by the fortuitous encounters between the Ephesians and the Syracusans. Man in this play is not, therefore, seen as master of his own fate, in that his attempts to control his situation – by seeking a lost brother, for example, rebuking a slave for his negligence, or courting a seemingly eligible lady – are constantly frustrated by factors he is unable to anticipate or comprehend. Though the resolution of the action is productive of a sense of wonder and wholeness, the achievement of this state is arrived at by a process as arbitrary as that by which the preceding chaos was generated, with man's security in his universe, and even his grasp of his own identity, being seen as dependent upon forces beyond his control. In *Twelfth Night*, by contrast, the errors in which the characters are caught up are largely self-generated. Where Antipholus of Syracuse duplicates his brother by an accident of birth, Viola consciously models herself on Sebastian, for whom she could not normally be mistaken, in assuming the role she elects to play, cf.:

> I my brother know
> Yet living in my glass; even such and so
> In favour was my brother, and he went
> Still in this fashion, colour, ornament,
> For him I imitate.
>
> (III.iv.389–93)

At the same time, Viola's disguise, while serving to generate the mistaken courtship of Olivia, and the 'errors' to which Sebastian falls victim, also functions as a literal representation of a metaphorical role-playing that is characteristic of all the inhabitants of the play world. Orsino has cast himself as Olivia's suitor, a role that leads only to frustration since Olivia fails to reciprocate his passion; Olivia has assumed the part of a devoted sister, grief-stricken by the death of a brother, a pose she finds inimical to the satisfaction of her emotional needs when she meets, and falls in love with, Cesario; while Malvolio, having cast himself as Olivia's suitor with even less justification than Orsino, finds himself contorting his face in an effort to be agreeable, and restricting his circulation in an attempt to be seductive, only to be incarcerated in a dark room for his pains. And the fate of Malvolio (which may be seen as a literalization of the 'madness' infecting the dramatis personae as a whole) is again significant in terms of the contrast that it affords with the earlier comedy. Though in both plays the madness motif suggests the isolation of the individual and his inability to communicate with those around him, in *Twelfth Night* the causes of this isolation spring from the characters themselves, rather than fate or external circumstance. The seeming madness of Antonio is a consequence of Viola's decision to conceal her identity, the absurd behaviour of Malvolio a product of the interaction between Maria's plot and his own delusions, the confusion of Feste with Sir Topas the outcome of a role deliberately assumed. Thus, whereas *The Comedy of Errors* might be said to be a play that exhibits man's puppet-like role in the universe he inhabits, *Twelfth Night* is concerned with individuals, and the way in which human beings jeopardize their own happiness. In the course of its progress through Shakespeare's imagination the sibling plot has thus been turned inside out, with the well-being of the dramatis personae of the later play at risk, not because an alien identity has been imposed on them from without, but because one has been generated from within. The movement from the world of Roman New Comedy to that of romance, the introspective nature of the characters, the greater degree of differentiation between individuals, and the shift in actor/audience relationships all contribute to a transfer of attention from events to emotional states, and from chance or fate as the initiator of action to an interplay between external circumstance and human impulses.

The forces militating against human happiness are clearly much more complex in the later play than they were in the earlier, and its resolution is correspondingly more tenuous. Whereas in *The Comedy of Errors* all the difficulties are resolved when the twins come face to face, in *Twelfth Night* the problems confronted by the characters are not immediately dissipated by the reunion of Sebastian and Viola. Though a number of misunderstandings are cleared up, and some more substantial difficulties overcome (for example, Olivia's infatuation with 'Cesario'), the tendency for human beings to adopt attitudes prejudicial to their own well-being is not eradicated from the play world, with Malvolio, for example, vowing revenge on those who deluded him. Though a sense of wonder, as in the earlier play, pervades the final scene, it is tinged with a wistfulness born of the characters' experience of loss, and of the spectators' awareness of the precariousness of the happiness that has been achieved. Man's capacity for self-delusion remains evident to the close, and it is significant that whereas in *The Comedy of Errors* the identity of all the dramatis personae is fully established in the last scene, in *Twelfth Night* Viola leaves the stage still dressed in her masculine clothes.

It will be clear from the above that though *The Comedy of Errors* and *Twelfth Night* both look back to the *Menaechmi*, the versions of reality that the three plays project are radically different. Plautus' play presents a financially orientated, competitive society, and is designed to amuse the spectator by a fast-moving series of misunderstandings. *The Comedy of Errors*, by contrast, presents relationships that are based on emotional, rather than economic, considerations, while the interaction between main and frame plots exposes the fragility of man's sense of selfhood, and the pain that social dislocation entails. By *Twelfth Night*, not only has the location of the action been transferred from the world of Roman New Comedy to that of romance, but the focus of attention has shifted from the plot, and the ludicrous situations to which it gives rise, to the characters, and the frustrations and disappointments which their multiple errors occasion. For all their superficial similarities the three plays consequently differ in terms of tone. The Plautine comedy is essentially boisterous, and much of its gusto is carried over into *The Comedy of Errors*. The laughter is momentarily stilled, however, in the final act of the Shakespearian play, allowing for a more profound sense of relief when the misunderstandings are resolved. In *Twelfth Night*, by contrast, the boisterousness of the Roman play is found only among the sub-plot characters. Since the forward motion of the plot serves only to increase the discrepancy between disguise and self (moving

Viola, for example, further and further from her hoped-for union with Orsino, and plunging Olivia deeper into her passion for Cesario), it is pathos and frustration that are communicated to the audience rather than comic perplexity, giving rise to a much more sympathetic, less unqualified laughter than that generated by comparable situations in the two earlier plays. The mouldy tale that forms the starting point for the two comedies has been restructured, in short, for very different purposes, and is productive of markedly different effects.

The Comedy of Errors and *Twelfth Night* afford a natural starting point for the study of Shakespeare's repetitious use of inherited materials not simply because the former may have been the dramatist's first experiment in the comic mode, but because the relationship between the two plays, and with their Roman antecedent, is relatively clear cut. A careful examination of Shakespeare's alterations and additions to the Plautine source offers a clear line of approach to the playwright's immediate purposes in the two comedies, and his changing preoccupations at different points in his career. At the same time, a comparison between the three versions of the sibling plot readily reveals that Shakespeare did not simply carve his success from another man's materials, or shamelessly repackage his own compositions under different names. As his imagination plays over the tale on which he draws, he elicits new meanings from its incidents, and fresh dramatic potentialities from its design. Rather than testifying to the limited range of his inventiveness, the close relationship between the three plays thus bears witness to his creativity, to his capacity to transmute the 'substance' of another writer into 'honey' of more than one kind. Shakespeare's use of the literary stock is rarely as uncomplicated, however, as in his handling of sibling confusion. The motifs to which he returns in his plays frequently derive from a variety of traditions, and undergo a much more intricate process of transformation in the course of their progress through his work. It is with these more complex versions of literary 'conversion' that subsequent chapters will be concerned.

Chapter 2

Gender Exchange

The Two Gentlemen of Verona. The Merchant of Venice. As
You Like It. Twelfth Night. Cymbeline

There can be few students of Shakespearian drama or regular
visitors to the theatre who have failed to remark the readiness with
which Shakespeare's female characters discard their petticoats and
farthingales and disguise themselves as youths. From Julia in *The
Two Gentlemen of Verona* (1593), via Jessica, Portia and Nerissa in
The Merchant of Venice (1596–98), to Rosalind in *As You Like It*
(1598–1600), Viola in *Twelfth Night* (1601), and Imogen in *Cymbeline* (1608–09), the mere mention of adverse circumstance is
seemingly sufficient to prompt a swift recourse to the dressing
room and a re-entry in masculine form. The paucity of invention
implied by this constant resort to a single plot mechanism was
apparently shared, furthermore, by Shakespeare's major contemporaries. Lyly's *Gallathea* (composed 1584), arguably the most
important pre-Shakespearian comedy, also involves the disguise of
two central figures as youths, while in Greene's *James IV* (*c.* 1590)
the Queen of Scotland becomes a squire as a means of saving her
life. Marston's *Antonio and Mellida* (1599), roughly contemporary
with *The Merchant of Venice* and *As You Like It*, not only has the
heroine in the garb of a man, but the hero dressed as an Amazon,
while Ben Jonson in *The New Inn* (1629) presents a girl brought up
as a boy in the guise of a fashionable lady.

An explanation for the frequency with which gender exchange
occurs on the Renaissance stage is often sought in the practical
difficulties surrounding the production of plays in the Eliza-

bethan–Jacobean period. The acting companies who performed in both the public and private playhouses were exclusively male,[1] with youths taking the female roles. The transfer of the heroine into doublet and hose is thus seen as a means of sustaining the spectator's 'willing suspension of disbelief' in the dramatic fiction, in that a young man playing a youth is assumed to be more convincing than a boy impersonating a woman. The explanation is a convincing one at first sight, but it fails to take into account a number of important considerations. In the first place, having never experienced the execution of female roles by actresses, the members of an Elizabethan audience would be unlikely to criticize the performance of those parts by youths on naturalistic grounds. The casting of boys as girls was a theatrical convention, and no more intrinsically absurd than the representation of a house by a painted flat, or the impersonation of a devil by a human being. In fact, the members of an audience do not equate what takes place in the theatre with 'real life'.[2] They recognize a set of conventions, which they interpret in the light of their previous experience, and an Elizabethan spectator would have found no greater difficulty in accepting a boy in woman's clothes as Imogen than a modern playgoer finds in crediting that the 'Antony' of yesterday's performance is the 'Hamlet' of today's. The responses of a contemporary audience to a puppet show are indicative of the degree to which the spectator is capable of surrendering to the dramatic illusion. While on one level the onlookers clustered around a Punch and Judy booth are fully aware that the figures that they are watching are lifeless dolls, endowed with voice and motion by a human manipulator, on another they respond to their actions as if they were flesh and blood, shouting at them, for example, to beware of danger or hissing them for their evil designs.

An equally potent objection to the theory that it is the want of female performers that is responsible for the prevalence of sexual disguise on the Renaissance stage is supplied by the dramatists of the period themselves. Though the late twentieth-century spectator

1. The performance of female roles by women dates from the reopening of the theatres in 1660.
2. Shakespeare himself explores the distinction between artifice and actuality (and laughs at those who confuse the two) in *A Midsummer Night's Dream* (cf. the scenes involving the Mechanicals' problems with the representation of a wall, moonlight, and a lion).

may have reservations about the ability of youths to play women's parts, the playwrights of the late sixteenth and early seventeenth centuries had clearly no doubts about the capacity of their boy performers to create (and be convincing in) the most demanding of female roles. The part of Cleopatra was written not for a woman but a youth, and the same is true of Webster's Vittoria (*The White Devil*, 1612) and Middleton's Beatrice-Joanna (*The Changeling*, 1622). Powerful female figures dominate the stage in a surprising number of dramas, testifying to their creators' faith in their actor's talents, and suggesting that the sexual exchanges of the comedies may derive not from the need to mask the deficiencies of the boy performers, but from a desire to exhibit their histrionic skills.

The most telling argument, however, against sexual disguise as an index to the limitations of the Elizabethan–Jacobean dramatic companies is the popularity of the motif in non-dramatic literature. Shakespeare, Lyly and Greene did not invent the device as a means of overcoming a practical difficulty, they inherited it with the stories on which their comedies were based. *Twelfth Night*, as noted in Chapter 1, draws not only on the *Menaechmi* by Plautus, but on a romance by Barnabe Riche, involving the principal character's disguise as a youth, and her employment by the man she loves. Similarly, Lyly's *Gallathea* looks back to the sex change in Ovid's tale of Iphis and Ianthe (*Metamorphoses*, ix), while Greene's *James IV* has its origins in Cinthio's *Hecatommithi*,[3] which includes the story of the unhappy Arenopia who is obliged to exchange her woman's clothes for those of a man in order to evade an attempt upon her life. These playwrights did not simply structure their comedies on popular non-dramatic works, however. Reared on a system of composition rooted in the theory of imitation, and writing under considerable commercial pressure, they drew freely on one another's successes, creating a complex interaction between a variety of influences. Both *Twelfth Night* and *As You Like It*, for example, draw on romance material, but they also look back to *Gallathea*,[4] while Greene was keenly aware of his

3. A collection of prose romances published in Italy in 1565. The stories found their way into England via a number of routes including William Painter's *The Palace of Pleasure* (first published in 1566 and augmented in 1567 and 1575). They furnished the plots for a number of Renaissance plays including Shakespeare's *Othello* (c. 1603–04).

4. See L. Scragg (1982) *The Metamorphosis of 'Gallathea'*, pp. 79ff.

fellow writers throughout his theatrical career.[5] The epicene figures who stand at the centre of so many Renaissance plays spring, in short, not from the shortcomings of the Elizabethan playhouse, but from an interaction between literary sources and an evolving theatrical tradition, with Shakespeare's own plays contributing to the increasing complexity of the sexual disguise motif.

Two principal motives govern a change of gender both on the Renaissance stage and in the non-dramatic literature upon which the plays of the period were based. On the one hand, a masculine exterior supplies a defence from aggression, while on the other it affords access to a member of the opposite sex who is otherwise incapable of approach. The defence motif is probably the older of the two traditions, and occurs in a variety of contexts. In Ovid's story of Iphis and Ianthe, for example, Iphis is brought up as a boy because her father has decreed that she should be killed at birth should she prove to be a girl, while in Lyly's *Gallathea* Tyterus and Melebeus disguise their daughters as youths in order to evade a sacrifice to Neptune. Cinthio's Arenopia becomes a man to frustrate her husband's malign intentions towards her, while Greene's Dorothea has a similar motive in transforming herself into a squire. A number of Shakespeare's heroines clearly belong to this tradition in that they embrace their masculine roles for defensive purposes. Rosalind, in *As You Like It*, for example, is very conscious of the dangers to which her sex exposes her when she is banished from her uncle's court, and is quick to propose the conventional solution:

> *Ros.* Alas, what danger will it be to us,
>   Maids as we are, to travel forth so far?
>   Beauty provoketh thieves sooner than gold.
> *Celia.* I'll put myself in poor and mean attire,
>   And with a kind of umber smirch my face;
>   The like do you. So shall we pass along
>   And never stir assailants.
> *Ros.*   Were it not better,
>   Because that I am more than common tall,
>   That I did suit me all points like a man?
>   A gallant curtle-axe upon my thigh,
>   A boar-spear in my hand, and in my heart,

5. His *Friar Bacon and Friar Bungay* (c. 1589–92), for example, looks back to Lyly's *Campaspe* (1580–84), while *Alphonsus, King of Aragon* (c. 1588) is modelled on Marlowe's *Tamburlaine* (1587–88).

Lie there what hidden woman's fear there will,
We'll have a swashing and a martial outside,
As many other mannish cowards have
That do outface it with their semblances.

                                        (I.iii.104–18)

Similarly, Imogen, in *Cymbeline*, is quickly persuaded that a masculine disguise is the most effective means of securing her safety when she learns that her husband is planning her death:

Pis[anio]. I'll give but notice you are dead, and send him
        Some bloody sign of it. For 'tis commanded
        I should do so: you shall be miss'd at court,
        And that will well confirm it.
Imo.   Why, good fellow,
        What shall I do the while? where bide? How live?
        Or in my life what comfort, when I am
        Dead to my husband?
. . . .
Pis. You must forget to be a woman: change
        Command into obedience: fear, and niceness
        (The handmaids of all women, or, more truly,
        Woman it pretty self) into a waggish courage,
        Ready in gibes, quick-answer'd, saucy, and
        As quarrelous as the weasel: nay, you must
        Forget that rarest treasure of your cheek,
        Exposing it (but, O, the harder heart!)
        Alack, no remedy) to the greedy touch
        Of common-kissing Titan.

                                        (III.iv.126–65)

Disguise as a means of pursuit is clearly more limited in its range of applications and is principally found in amatory contexts. As noted in the previous chapter, Lelia in *Gl'Ingannati* assumes the role of a page in order to serve the man she loves, while the heroine of Riche's romance of Apolonius and Silla follows her beloved to Constantinople, adopting her brother's identity on being ship-wrecked.[6] Similarly, Julia, in *The Two Gentlemen of Verona*, determined not to be parted from her lover, enlists the aid of her maid, Lucetta, in devising a stratagem to follow him to Milan:

Jul. Counsel, Lucetta; gentle girl, assist me,
        And ev'n in kind love I do conjure thee,

─────────────────────
6. See above pp. 24–6.

> Who art the table wherein all my thoughts
> Are visibly character'd and engrav'd,
> To lesson me, and tell me some good mean
> How with my honour I may undertake
> A journey to my loving Proteus.
> *Luc.* Alas, the way is wearisome and long.
> *Jul.* A true-devoted pilgrim is not weary
> To measure kingdoms with his feeble steps.
> . . . .
> *Luc.* But in what habit will you go along?
> *Jul.* Not like a woman, for I would prevent
> The loose encounters of lascivious men:
> Gentle Lucetta, fit me with such weeds
> As may beseem some well-reputed page.
>
> (II. vii. 1–43)

Imogen, in *Cymbeline*, also belongs to this tradition in that she consents to disguise herself as Fidele not simply in order to save her life, but in the hope of seeing her husband:

> *Pis[anio].*   Th'ambassador,
> Lucius the Roman, comes to Milford-Haven
> To-morrow. Now, if you could wear a mind
> Dark, as your fortune is, and but disguise
> That which, t'appear itself, must not yet be
> But by self-danger, you should tread a course
> Pretty, and full of view; yea, haply, near
> The residence of Posthumus; so nigh (at least)
> That though his actions were not visible, yet
> Report should render him hourly to your ear
> As truly as he moves.
> *Imo.*   O, for such means,
> Though peril to my modesty, not death on't,
> I would adventure.
>
> (III. iv. 143–55)

The assumption of a male exterior gives rise, in both dramatic and non-dramatic literature, to a number of stock situations. On the one hand, disguise allows the heroine access to the masculine world, subjecting her to physical danger, and frequently involving her in the courtship of another lady on behalf of the man she loves. On the other hand, the heroine herself becomes the agent of another's suffering, in that she engages the affections of a member of her own sex. The numerous offshoots of *Gl'Ingannati* illustrate the first point. In the tale of Apolonius and Silla, for example, Silla enters the house of her beloved disguised as a servant, only to be employed by him as emissary to the woman with whom he has fallen in love, and the same plot motif is used by Shakespeare in both *The Two Gentlemen of Verona* and *Twelfth Night*. The second stock situation also occurs in a range of literary contexts. In Ovid's story of Iphis and Ianthe, for example, Iphis is reared as a boy as a means of preserving her life, and her betrothal to Ianthe is a logical consequence of her ambiguous existence. In Greene's *James IV*, by contrast, the intimacy that springs up between Lady Anderson and the wounded 'youth' she helps to save gives rise to an emotionally charged sexual triangle, in that Lady Anderson herself is a married woman. It is this kind of development which links the second class of plot to the first, in which a supposed page woos on behalf of his master only to be loved by the lady he courts, in that both generate an emotional interplay between figures actually and superficially of the same sex.

The repetitious nature of these plot motifs might well lead a modern reader to suppose that the exit of yet another imperilled lady to don doublet and hose was greeted by the Elizabethan spectator with a yawn, or had him demanding the prompt return of his penny from the inner reaches of the 'gatherer's' box. In fact, however, the meanings elicited from the use of the device are by no means as uniform as might appear at first sight. Nearly one-third of Shakespeare's comedies and romances involve a girl disguised as a youth, and in one of them (*The Merchant of Venice*) all three female characters exchange their petticoats for masculine clothes. Nevertheless, the experiences afforded by these dramas are widely divergent, and it is in the novel application of the device, and the different kinds of universe that it helps to define, that the interest of the spectator lies. Whereas the return in *Twelfth Night* to a plot mechanism previously employed in *The Comedy of Errors* simply permits the student of Shakespearian drama an insight into the distinct nature of the dramatist's purposes at different stages of his career, the repeated use of a change of gender affords a demonstration of Shakespeare's capacity to re-work seemingly hackneyed material into a dazzling variety of forms.

The motif appears first in *The Two Gentlemen of Verona* and is derived, either directly or through a dramatic intermediary, from *Diana* (1559), a romance by the Portuguese writer, Jorge de

Montemayor, translated into French in 1578 and published in English in 1598. The principal interest of Montemayor's tale concerns the adventures of the lovers Diana and Syrenus, but this thread is interwoven with another strand concerning a second pair of lovers, Felix and Felismena. These two are forced to part by the former's father, and Felix travels to the Emperor's court, where he falls in love with another lady. Felismena follows her lover, and having entered his service disguised as a page is employed by him in his suit to Celia, who falls in love with her wooer's emissary. On the death of Celia further tribulations follow, but the lovers are finally united when Felismena saves Felix's life. The similarities between this plot and that of *The Two Gentlemen of Verona* will be immediately apparent. Shakespeare's play also involves two pairs of lovers, a parting enforced by a peremptory parent, the unfaithfulness of one of the two gentlemen, and the disguise of the lady as a page. Nevertheless, Shakespeare has not simply recast Montemayor's romance in dramatic form. In the first place he has omitted the second lady's infatuation with the seeming youth sent to win her affections (a situation he exploits in *Twelfth Night*), while in the second he has married the disguised lady motif to another traditional story (cf. the fusion of disparate sources in *Twelfth Night*) to produce a more complex range of relationships than is offered by the original 'tale'.

Whereas the origins of Shakespeare's disguised lady may be found in the history of Felismena, the experiences of her partner look back to the love and friendship literature popular throughout Europe in the Renaissance and Middle Ages. This type of story occurs in a variety of forms, but at its core lies the tension set up between a pair of friends when they fall in love with the same lady. In Chaucer's *The Knight's Tale*, for example, the brothers-in-arms Palamon and Arcite are divided by their love for Emily, and a resolution is achieved only with Arcite's death, while in Sir Thomas Elyot's *The Boke Named the Governour* (1531) the noble Gysippus surrenders his bride to his comrade on being informed of his passion for her. Similarly, in *The Two Gentlemen of Verona* Valentine and Proteus both fall in love with Silvia, and the former offers to withdraw in favour of the latter (cf. V.iv.82-3) though assured of the lady's love. The interweaving of the love and friendship and sexual disguise motifs in the Shakespearian play gives rise, however, to a much more complicated situation than that which proceeds from the traditional desire-versus-comrade-ship device. The lover who is pursued by the disguised lady not only comes into conflict with his friend in seeking to court his mistress, he also betrays his own lady in transferring his affections to another woman. Rather than setting up an emotional triangle as the two sources separately invite, the play thus presents a four-cornered mesh of relationships, exhibiting a range of amatory experience.

Valentine and Proteus, the two gentlemen of the play's title, are presented at the outset as devoted friends, the latter in love with Julia, the former determined to expand his knowledge through travel, rather than being chained by the bonds of love. Having taken leave of his friend, Valentine departs for the Emperor's court, but is quickly joined by Proteus, who is obliged by his father to follow a similar course. Julia, unable to bear her lover's absence, follows him disguised as a page, only to discover on reaching Milan that he is now a suitor to the Duke's daughter, with whom Valentine has fallen deeply in love. Having entered Proteus's service, Julia is employed by her lover as a messenger to her rival who, though ignorant of her identity, proves sympathetic to her plight. Valentine seeks to elope with Silvia, but is betrayed by his former friend, who then attempts to force his own attentions on the lady he professes to love. Though Valentine intervenes to prevent Silvia's rape, he magnanimously offers to renounce her to the other man when Proteus repents of his misdeeds. Julia faints, however, from emotional strain, and with the revelation of her identity the two couples are happily reunited.

It will already be evident to anyone familiar with the comedies of Shakespeare's middle period that the use of sexual disguise here gives rise to a number of situations that have no counterpart in later plays. In *As You Like It*, for example, though Rosalind's disguise as Ganymede allows her access to Orlando, and the opportunity to assess the nature of his love for her, Orlando himself remains faithful throughout, and proves worthy of her affection, while in *Twelfth Night* though Viola is sent by Orsino to woo Olivia on his behalf, the courtship in which she is implicated does not constitute a conscious betrayal of either a friend or a mistress. In *The Two Gentlemen of Verona*, by contrast, a pattern of pursuit and rejection, commitment and disloyalty is enacted between the four central characters, inviting a much less favourable response on the part of the audience to some at least of the dramatis personae.

The term 'pattern' is an important one in relation to Shakespeare's early comedies, in that the element of design constitutes a major part of the species of enjoyment which they offer. *The Two Gentlemen of Verona* is no exception in this respect, with both the organization of scenes and the delineation of character contributing to the complex sequence of analogies and contrasts that emerges as the drama unfolds. The play opens, as noted above, with an elaborate parting between friends, and this scene is first echoed in an exchange of farewells between lovers (II.ii), and then parodied through a servant's account of his dog's hard-hearted conduct during a succession of familial leave-takings (II.iii). Similarly, Julia is first seen in Act I scene ii tearing up a letter from Proteus in order to prove her assumed indifference to him, while Silvia destroys a letter from him in Act IV scene iv to show her genuine distaste for his suit. These correspondences encourage the audience to view situations from different perspectives, and to reflect upon their significance, and Julia's role as Sebastian plays an important part in this projection of meaning through pattern. In the first place, her disguise constitutes a visual expression of a process of reversal that takes place as the drama evolves. The names of the play's two gentlemen – Valentine and Proteus – invite the spectator to view the former as the epitome of constant love, and the latter as subject to change, but when these characters are introduced their roles appear to be reversed. In Act I scene i it is Proteus who plays the part of the faithful lover, and Valentine that of the heretic, indifferent to amatory affairs. It is not until the young men reach the Emperor's court that the expectations generated by their names are fulfilled. Valentine, on encountering Silvia, becomes the embodiment of constant love, while Proteus betrays his fickleness through his desertion of Julia. Julia's progress through the play provides an implicit commentary on these events. She changes her outward form (in adopting the role of a page) in order to demonstrate her constancy, while Proteus erects a façade of fidelity in order to mask his inner disloyalty to both his friend and his mistress. Julia's translation from maiden to youth and mistress to servant is thus emblematic of the metamorphoses that the principal characters undergo, while presenting a mirror image of her lover's experience through a species of elaborate conceit.

While forming an integral part of the pattern of changes that the drama enacts, Julia's decision to adopt her masculine disguise also testifies to her strength of character, and this too is significant in terms of the network of contrast and analogy that the drama sets up. At the outset of the action, three of the four principal characters leave Verona for Milan. Valentine elects to go there in order to broaden his experience. Proteus, by contrast, opts to stay in Verona, but is obliged to follow his friend by his father, against his own inclinations. Proteus' failure to play the man here by asserting his commitment to his mistress is in striking contrast to the conduct of Julia, who resolves to follow her lover to Milan in spite of the dangers that the journey represents. Once again, a process of reversal is at work in terms of audience expectation in these scenes. It is the man here who is submissive in the face of an arbitrary exercise of authority, and the woman who exhibits a masculine resolve. The persona Julia adopts thus conceals her sex but reveals something about her nature, while Proteus' male exterior is belied by his lack of inner resolve.

While contributing to the definition of character and the sequence of changes that the drama enacts, Julia's metamorphosis into Sebastian also furthers the educative process that takes place in the course of the play. At the outset of the action, Valentine, as noted above, regards travel as the pathway to knowledge, rejecting Proteus' enslavement to love as folly:

> *Pro.* So, by your circumstance, you call me fool.
> *Val.* So, by your circumstance, I fear you'll prove.
> *Pro.* 'Tis Love you cavil at, I am not Love.
> *Val.* Love is your master, for he masters you;
> And he that is so yoked by a fool
> Methinks should not be chronicled for wise.
>
> (I.i.36–41)

Paradoxically, however, the educative process in which he becomes involved on reaching Milan is the product not of study, but of love, in that his involvement with Silvia leads him to a fuller understanding both of his own impulses and the nature of his friend. Similarly, Proteus' experiences at the Emperor's court involve the discovery of aspects of his personality of which he was unaware, enforcing a recognition, again through sexual experience, of his capacity for treachery and violence. Julia's role as Sebastian allows her to participate in this learning process, while contributing to the education of others. It gives her access to both Proteus and Silvia, enabling her to recognize the full extent of her lover's treachery, and thus to accept him with a mature awareness of his limitations at the close, while affording Proteus objective evidence of the worth of the woman he has despised. Antithetical patterning, once again, is evident in this aspect of the play's structure, in that Julia's deceptive appearance provides her with the means of discovering the truth about Proteus, while Proteus' pose of friendship blinds Valentine to the true nature of his friend.

It will be apparent from the above that the addition of the love-and-friendship story to the disguised lady motif has enabled the dramatist to devise a kind of structure that encourages the spectator to view the dramatis personae in a sequence of contrastive relationships. Julia stands in opposition to Proteus in her constancy, while being Protean in terms of appearance; she is the female counterpart to Valentine in being betrayed by the man she trusts; and is juxtaposed against Silvia in pursuing rather than being pursued. It is not merely his additions to his source, however, that distinguish Shakespeare's treatment of sexual disguise in this comedy from his use of the motif in later plays. That which he leaves out is equally significant. Though Montemayor's *Diana* includes the rival lady's infatuation with the seeming youth sent to woo on another's behalf, the scenes between the metamorphosed Julia and her lover, and between 'Sebastian' and Silvia do not seek to exploit the tension between the masculine and feminine aspects of the 'boy's' personality, or to involve him/her in the masculine world, and thus in a different order of experience. The initial exchange between Proteus and Sebastian (IV.iv.40–89) is designed to exhibit the former's infidelity and the latter's faithfulness, while the subsequent encounter between Sebastian and Silvia (IV.iv.108–75) evokes sympathy for the former's plight, while stressing the propriety of the latter's conduct. Though a rapprochement springs up in both instances between the speakers (cf.IV.iv.62–8 and 171–5), these scenes carry none of the complex sexual undercurrents that are a feature of later comedies, while the audience remains firmly aware of the 'youth' as Julia throughout. The interview between Proteus and his page is a short one (forty-nine lines including a substantial interruption), allowing insufficient time to establish the kind of relationship between the youth and his master that evolves in the course of *Twelfth Night*, while Proteus' decision to send him to Silvia arises as much from the deficiencies of his other servant as from the good opinion that he has of him (cf.IV.iv.62–8). At the same time, the true identity of the page is constantly enforced by references to Julia (cf.IV.iv.72–84), while the positioning of a soliloquy between the disguised lady's encounter with her lover, and her meeting with the woman she has been directed to woo sustains the audience's awareness of her identity, and hence dissolves the reality of her fictive personality:

> How many women would do such a message?
> ....
> This ring I gave him, when he parted from me,
> To bind him to remember my good will;
> And now am I (unhappy messenger)
> To plead for that which I would not obtain;
> To carry that which I would have refus'd;
> To praise his faith which I would have disprais'd.
> I am my master's true confirmed love,
> But cannot be true servant to my master,
> Unless I prove false traitor to myself.
> (IV.iv.90–105)

Though rather longer than the scene with Proteus, the interview between Silvia and Sebastian also undermines rather than authenticates the role that Julia has assumed. Already in love with Valentine, Silvia is attracted to neither Proteus nor his messenger, and it is on the plight of the neglected Julia that the scene focuses throughout. As in the previous exchange with Proteus, very little sense of 'Sebastian' as an independent personality is established in the course of this passage. Julia speaks of and for herself, evoking sympathy for her own plight, rather than participating, on one level, in the experience of the opposite sex.

It is the degree of distance between the disguised heroine and the role that she assumes that differentiates Shakespeare's treatment of sexual disguise in *The Two Gentlemen of Verona* from his second foray into the field of gender reversal in *The Merchant of Venice*. The two plays have much in common (a proposed elopement, recognition through rings, a servant named Launce/Launcelot, etc.) and at first sight the multiplicity of seeming youths in the later comedy appears to offer a particularly striking example of the dramatist's lack of inventiveness and readiness to plunder his own work. In fact, however, the disguised heroine motif is derived, once again, from the play's source, rather than being transplanted directly from the earlier composition. The story of the bloody bargain, and the evasion of its terms through the intervention of an unrecognized lady, is an old one, occurring in a variety of forms throughout the Middle Ages, but it was probably *Il Pecorone*, an Italian version by Ser Giovanni Fiorentino (*c.* 1378, pub. 1558), that was the immediate source of the Shakespearian play.[7] The action in Fiorentino's narrative is set in Venice, and involves a confrontation between a Jew and the newly married wife of the central figure, whose friend has mortgaged his own person in order to furnish him with the money to woo his bride. The lady disguises herself as a lawyer, and defeats her opponent by a quibble, insisting that he must cut an exact pound of flesh in exacting the forfeit, and that no blood must be split. The similarities with the plot of the Shakespearian play are too extensive to be merely coincidental. Antonio also mortgages a pound of his own flesh in order to supply Bassanio with sufficient money to woo Portia, while Portia poses as a lawyer and defeats Shylock by the same legalistic means. Moreover, a second strand of the action that might appear at first sight to have its origins in *The Two Gentlemen of Verona*, the recognition of the lady by means of a ring (cf. *The Two Gentlemen of Verona*, V.iv.87–98 and *The Merchant of Venice*, V.i.142–285), also has its origins in Fiorentino's work. Having won the lawsuit, the disguised lady begs a ring from her husband's finger, having previously engaged him not to part with it. The husband is reluctantly persuaded to give up the token, and the lady subsequently accuses him of infidelity before revealing all that has passed. Portia too, as the lawyer Balthazar, asks for the ring that she herself gave Bassanio as a reward for saving Antonio's life, and then accuses her husband of adultery on his return to Belmont before producing the ring and revealing her own part in the affair.

Shakespeare's first two epicene figures thus have their origins in different sources, and their roles within the structures in which they function are strikingly different. In the first place, whereas Julia follows Proteus to Milan because she cannot bear to be parted

---

7. The doubt in relation to the attribution springs from the fact that Giovanni Fiorentino's work was not translated (as far as is known) into English.

from him, and is reduced by her decision to a position of subservience, Portia sets out for Venice in order to go to her husband's aid, assuming a position of dominance during the trial scene, and winning the gratitude and admiration of the principal characters. At the same time, while the translation of Julia into Sebastian forms one element of the analogical patterning that *The Two Gentlemen of Verona* enacts, Portia's role as Balthazar plays a part in the clash between personalities and values that lies at the heart of the later play.

It is clear from the very outset that *The Merchant of Venice*, like *The Two Gentlemen of Verona*, deals in oppositions. The generosity of Antonio is contrasted with the niggardliness of Shylock (cf.I.i.130–60 and I.iii.37–40), the life-affirming nature of the Christians, with their love of revels, with the life-denying attitudes of the Jew (cf.II.v.28–36), the commercialism of Venice, with the liberality of Belmont (cf.I.iii.98–132 and III.ii.296–306). Whereas, at the start of the play, the Christian position is sustained by Antonio (who is prepared to jeopardize his own safety in order to secure the happiness of his friend), once his fortunes fail and he falls victim to Shylock the negative and destructive tendencies embodied in the Jew are in the ascendancy until Portia irradiates the Venetian world with the values of Belmont through her intervention in the trial. Nevertheless, though an age-old opposition underlies the conflict, it is not upon a pattern of attitudes that the attention of the audience is principally focused, but upon the characters of those by whom that pattern is enacted. Both parties are personally motivated and strongly defined – Shylock aggrieved by his treatment at the hands of the Christians (cf.I.iii.101–24), and incensed by the elopement of his daughter (cf.III.i.22–120), Antonio deeply committed to Bassanio (cf.I.i.130–85), Portia concerned for the safety of her husband's friend (cf.III.ii.290–301). Portia's intervention in the trial scene is thus designed, not simply to enact a process of reversal, but to define a world view in opposition to Shylock's and to register the triumph of one group of individuals over another.

It is not merely the more dominant role of the disguised lady, and her function as spokesperson for, and guarantor of, the values that the drama upholds, however, that distinguish Shakespeare's second epicene creation from his first. Whereas in *The Two Gentlemen of Verona* he largely neglects the opportunities supplied by his source for developing 'Sebastian's' autonomous existence, in *The Merchant of Venice* he follows Fiorentino in distinguishing the lawyer who intervenes in the trial from the wealthy lady whose courtship allows the Jew his opportunity for revenge.

The audience is first introduced to Portia in the context of the casket plot. Here she is the rich and beautiful lady who is to be won by means of a lottery, and Bassanio proves his worthiness as a suitor by choosing in accordance with her father's will. *Il Pecorone* also involves the borrowing of money for the purposes of courtship, but the means by which the lady is achieved in the Shakespearian play do not derive from Fiorentino's work. The casket story has its origins in a different tradition,[8] and its fusion with the bond plot in *The Merchant of Venice* is typical of the way in which the dramatist brings together disparate sources (or 'addeth' one to another) in the process of creation. In Fiorentino's tale the hero is invited to go to bed with the lady, and twice falls into a drugged sleep before finally remaining awake and making love to her, and thus winning her for his bride. The substitution of the casket plot for this strand of the Italian narrative allows Shakespeare to heighten the moral status of his heroine, by removing her from sexual intrigue, while simultaneously stressing her lack of control over her own destiny. The will of a dead father governs her conduct towards her suitors, and she has no freedom of choice in relation to her own marriage. When the news of Antonio's arrest reaches Belmont, and Bassanio hastens back to Venice, Portia announces her decision to follow him in terms that locate the device within the never–never-land of romance:

> *Por.* Come on Nerissa, I have work in hand
>   That you yet know not of; we'll see our husbands
>   Before they think of us!
> *Ner.*   Shall they see us?
> *Por.* They shall Nerissa: but in such a habit,
>   That they shall think we are accomplished
>   With that we lack; I'll hold thee any wager
>   When we are both accoutered like young men,
>   I'll prove the prettier fellow of the two,
>   And wear my dagger with the braver grace,
>   And speak between the change of man and boy,

---

8. This tale, like that of the bond plot, exists in a variety of redactions and there is some doubt about the immediate source of the Shakespearian version.

With a reed voice, and turn two mincing steps
Into a manly stride; and speak of frays
Like a fine bragging youth: and tell quaint lies
How honourable ladies sought my love,
Which I denying, they fell sick and died:
I could not do withal:- then I'll repent,
And wish for all that, that I had not kill'd them;
And twenty of these puny lies I'll tell,
That men shall swear I have discontinued school
Above a twelvemonth: I have within my mind
A thousand raw tricks of these bragging Jacks,
Which I will practise.

(III.iv.57–78)

Once in Venice, however, Portia is effectively translated not only into a different role, but a different world. The bloody bargain, struck between Antonio and Shylock in the much darker, emphatically masculine, environment of Venice, though instigated by the need to finance Bassanio's journey to Belmont, has constituted a separable strand of interest from the outset, and this division between the two areas of the play's action is largely maintained until the closing scenes. Though the members of the audience have been acquainted with Portia's decision to pose as a youth, neither Portia nor Nerissa appears in masculine form before the trial, and there is no aside or ambivalent comment when Nerissa appears as the lawyer's clerk to link this figure with the lady's maid of the casket scenes. Similarly, when Portia enters as the lawyer Balthazar, she functions in that role for the duration of the trial, saving Antonio from Shylock not through means relating to her feminine identity, but by ways directly compatible with her assumed role. The authoritative figure who commands the respect of Christian and Jew alike in the trial scene, and who has power over life and death, is thus at a considerable remove from the passive heroine of the casket plot, bound to conform to her father's will, and from the waggish youth that in Belmont this figure proposed to play. Only one ironic exchange in the course of the trial scene links these disparate personalities (IV.i.278–90), allowing a momentary relaxation of tension, while reminding the audience of concerns common to the two areas of interest.

The distance that the dramatist engineers between Portia and the young lawyer who bows Shylock's will to his own is significant in a number of respects. In the first place, the audience's perception of the disguised lady is very different from their stance towards Julia in her role as Sebastian in the earlier play. In *The Two Gentlemen of Verona* the use of aside and innuendo ensures that those outside the play world remain on intimate terms with the heroine throughout, and she thus retains her feminine personality regardless of the clothes she wears. In *The Merchant of Venice*, by contrast, the figure of Balthazar is much more remote from the spectator, and a much greater degree of uncertainty consequently surrounds his/her ultimate identity. Jessica's assumption of a masculine form in order to elope with Lorenzo points up the contrast between these two kinds of role playing. Jessica's disguise, like Portia's, serves to translate her into a different world, the one moving from Venice to Belmont, the other from Belmont to Venice, but her personality undergoes no comparable metamorphosis. Where Portia embraces her part with enthusiasm, intending to 'become' a youth in outlook, not merely in appearance, (cf.III.iv.57–78), Jessica is acutely conscious of the distance between self and role, and hence of the impropriety of her garments:

> *Jes.* I am glad 'tis night – you do not look on me, –
>   For I am much asham'd of my exchange:
>   But love is blind, and lovers cannot see
>   The pretty follies that themselves commit,
>   For if they could, Cupid himself would blush
>   To see me thus transformed to a boy.
> *Lor.* Descend, for you must be my torch-bearer.
> *Jes.* What, must I hold a candle to my shames? –
>   They in themselves (goodsooth) are too too light.
>   (II.vi.34–42)

Moreover, whereas Portia adopts a masculine persona in Venice and reverts to a feminine one in Belmont, never functioning as her alternative self in either environment, Jessica discards her disguise on her arrival in her new location thus equating, in the minds of the audience, the young woman who elopes from Shylock's house with the lady who (with her lover) governs Belmont in Portia's absence.

The greater degree of autonomy enjoyed by the lawyer and his clerk is also signalled by the responses of those within the play world to the three 'youths'. Whereas, in the final act, Lorenzo recalls the night on which 'Did *Jessica* [my italics] steal from the wealthy Jew' (V.i.15), Bassanio and Gratiano experience considerable uncertainty over the identity of the doctor and his clerk, and this uncertainty is heightened when Portia and Nerissa claim to have slept with the two 'men'. Though by the close of the play the husbands are convinced, on one level, that the ladies were the lawyers, on another they continue to resist a total identification between the two, the 'doctor' and 'clerk' still being referred to (albeit jokingly) at the close.

The function of this interplay between real and fictive personalities is a complex one, and intimately related to the themes of the play. The uncertainty surrounding the figure of Balthazar, and Bassanio's failure to recognize his wife, are symptomatic of a play world in which man's nature is not easily determined, or his motives readily understood. Antonio, at the start of the play, is in the grip of a sadness he is unable to comprehend, while Gratiano asserts in the same scene that human nature is beyond rational explanation:

> then let us say you are sad
> Because you are not merry; and 'twere as easy
> For you to laugh and leap, and say you are merry
> Because you are not sad. Now by two-headed Janus,
> Nature hath fram'd strange fellows in her time:
> Some that will evermore peep through their eyes,
> And laugh like parrots at a bagpiper:
> And other of such vinegar aspect,
> That they'll not show their teeth in way of smile
> Though Nestor swear the jest be laughable
>
> (I.i.47–56)

At the same time, Portia's assumption of a masculine persona signals her entry into uncharted areas of experience. In becoming Balthazar she sheds the passivity and acquiescence that attend her female role, functioning in a male universe on more than equal terms. Her part in the trial scene enhances her understanding of her husband and his relationship with his friend (cf.IV.i.278–83), while allowing her to exhibit the strength of character and moral awareness (cf.IV.i.180ff.) that are part of the 'wealth' that Bassanio achieves in winning her, but which cannot be displayed within the confines of her role in the casket plot. Above all, the distance between Portia and the lawyer contributes to the muted sense of wonder that pervades the final scenes. Antonio comes close to death in the course of his trial, and his salvation, both physical and later financial, is achieved by means that are neither anticipated by those within the play world, nor fully understood (cf.V.i.273–9). The terms in which this process is defined, moreover, are redolent with theological implications. The young lawyer is seen by both sides as a 'Daniel come to judgment' (IV.i.219), he appeals to mercy (IV.i.180ff.) as against the law (IV.i.196–201), reflects on man's unworthiness for salvation (IV.i.194–8), and warns Shylock of the danger of shedding Christian blood (IV.i.305–8). He thus embodies, on one level, the religious values that oppose the attitudes upheld by the Jew, encouraging the audience to reflect on the wider implications of the conflict. A closer identification between Portia and this figure would reduce the instrument of Shylock's downfall from an agent in a spiritual process to the 'witty wench' of folk tale, or the 'clever wife' of romance.

If Jessica in *The Merchant of Venice* looks back to Julia in *The Two Gentlemen of Verona*, Portia looks forward to Rosalind in *As You Like It* and Viola in *Twelfth Night*. Of all Shakespeare's comic heroines, Rosalind and Viola have probably enjoyed the greatest popularity in the theatre, and are most frequently seen as variations on the same theme. In fact, however, for all their obvious similarities, the two characters are not a direct product of the dramatist's tendency to re-work his own material, but have separate origins in the sources from which their adventures derive. *As You Like It* is structured upon a romance by Thomas Lodge[9] in which the heroine, Rosalynde, disguises herself as a youth, Ganimede, in order to escape the animosity of the tyrant who has usurped her father's throne, and becomes a shepherd in the forest of Arden accompanied by her friend Alinda (disguised as Aliena). Once in Arden she is courted by her lover, Rosader, in place of the 'real' Rosalynde, while the shepherdess, Phoebe, falls in love with her in her masculine form. *Twelfth Night*, by contrast, though it too involves sexual disguise and cross-affections, has its origins (as noted in Chapter 1) in Riche's tale of Apolonius and Silla in which the heroine, having entered her lover's service, is obliged to woo another lady on his behalf. Nevertheless, though the situations in *The Merchant of Venice*, *As You Like It* and *Twelfth Night* are clearly

9. *Rosalynde: Euphues Golden Legacie* (1590).

derived from different sources, there are striking similarities in the treatment of the epicene figures who stand at the centre of the three plays. In the first place, as in *The Merchant of Venice*, the autonomous existence of the seeming youths of the two later comedies is strongly felt. Whereas in Lodge's romance Rosalynde's role as the beloved of Rosader and friend of Alinda is never fully distinguished from her existence as Ganimede, Shakespeare's central figure is a much more complex creation. Though Rosalind's feminine identity is firmly established in the opening scenes, and resumed with her marriage at the close, she appears in masculine garments for a large part of the play, functioning as a woman in relation to Celia, and as a youth with Orlando, Phebe, and Silvius. Her assumption of a masculine persona is not merely confined, moreover, to a change of dress. She consciously adopts the manners and attitudes of a youth (cf.I.iii.110–18 and II.iv.3–7) and maintains them in her dialogues with Orlando. Similarly, whereas Riche's heroine is still referred to as 'Silla' after her transformation into Silvio, Viola appears as a woman in only one scene (I.ii) in which the causes of her disguise are established. She enters Orsino's court already translated into a youth, and is received as a young man by the entire society in which she functions. Unlike Rosalind, who moves between the persons of Rosalind and Ganymede as she turns from Celia to Phebe, Viola remains within the parameters of her role throughout, thus entering more fully than any of her predecessors into the world of masculine experience.

The greater degree of assimilation into the fictive role in these plays is accompanied in *As You Like It*, as in *The Merchant of Venice*, by an enlargement of freedom. Whereas in her own person Portia is constrained by the will of her father, entertains unwelcome suitors, and is the passive object of Bassanio's affections, as Balthazar she dominates her lover, and controls the destinies of Antonio and Shylock. Moreover, the authority she exhibits in the trial scene is carried back with her to Belmont, enhancing her stature in the play world as a whole. Similarly, though as the daughter of an exiled father Rosalind is obliged to flee from her uncle's tyranny, as the youth Ganymede she enjoys considerable physical and intellectual freedom. She is able to explore her feelings for Orlando (and his for her) in a way not normally available to a member of her sex, while her superior knowledge of the situation allows her to manipulate the misplaced affections of Phebe towards a more fruitful relationship. In *Twelfth Night*, by contrast, Shakespeare exploits the opposite potentiality of gender exchange. Whereas disguise for Portia and Rosalind constitutes a species of liberty, freeing them from the conventional restraints governing the conduct of women, and enabling them to function in a larger arena than their sex would normally permit, for Viola it emerges as a trap, progressively diminishing her area of manoeuvre. Though, like her predecessors, she assumes her masculine garments to secure an immediate goal (cf.I.ii.41–61), her role rapidly emerges as disadvantageous when she meets, and falls in love with, Orsino. At the same time, her success as Cesario militates against her own happiness, in that it leads Orsino to choose her as emissary to Olivia, and Olivia's infatuation with her proxy wooer. Where Portia and Rosalind are in control of their situations once they have adopted their assumed roles, Viola becomes increasingly aware of the intractability of her position and of her own incapacity to change it, cf.:

> O time, thou must untangle this, not I,
> It is too hard a knot for me t'untie.
>
> (II.ii.39–40)

Her attitude to the part that she plays is consequently very different from that of earlier heroines. Whereas Portia and Rosalind relish the opportunity of posing as youths and regard their roles as beneficial, Viola sees her disguise as an error, referring to it as a 'wickedness' (II.ii.26). The term is in striking contrast to the field of reference surrounding Portia's operation as Balthazar in *The Merchant of Venice*, and this negative attitude to role playing is integral to the meaning of the play. As noted in Chapter 1, the dramatic universe in which Viola functions is one in which men and women are held captive by their affectations, and her disguise is a literal representation of the mental prisons in which the dramatis personae have cast themselves. Orsino's affection for Cesario cannot lead to a fuller relationship, not simply because they appear to be of the same sex, but because the Duke is locked into the pursuit of another woman, while Olivia's emotional predicament is complicated by the mourning ritual she has adopted for her brother. The assumption of an alien persona is consequently associated here not with the discovery of truth but with confusion and misapprehension, and it leads not to freedom of action and self-fulfilment but to passivity and emotional attrition.

For all the frequency with which an exchange of gender takes place, then, in his major comedies, Shakespeare's handling of the device is far from repetitive. Not only does he draw on different sources, but he adapts those sources towards different ends, developing his own earlier departures from others' tales. And it is not simply in their degree of autonomy and capacity for self-determination that distinctions may be drawn between his central figures. Just as Portia, Rosalind and Viola are differentiated from Julia and Jessica by their fuller assimilation into their masculine roles, so Rosalind and Viola are distinguished from Portia by the sexual situations to which their disguises give rise. Portia is married to Bassanio before her departure for Venice, and the arena in which she functions as Balthazar is an economic and legalistic, rather than an amatory, one. Rosalind, by contrast, is still on the threshold of courtship when she embarks on the part of Ganymede, and she uses her disguise as a youth as a means of educating and testing her lover. The encounters between the two consequently have strong sexual undercurrents, and these are heightened when 'Ganymede' encourages Orlando to court him in place of his mistress, and to participate in a mock betrothal. The presence of other lovers in the forest also contributes to the sexual confusion. Whereas it is arguable that Orlando is attracted to Ganymede because of his unconscious recognition of him/her as Rosalind, Phebe undoubtedly bestows her affections on 'him' as a member of the opposite sex, regarding him as a more acceptable partner than her rustic lover, Silvius. The sexual identity of Ganymede/Rosalind is thus much more complex than that of earlier disguised heroines. While on one level the members of the audience are aware of him/her as a woman throughout (an awareness that aside and innuendo, as in the case of Julia, helps to sustain, cf.IV.iii.164ff.), on another the attitudes of Phebe and Silvius serve to authenticate his/her role as Ganymede, with the scenes between Orlando and Ganymede-as-Rosalind straddling these two positions. Viola's stance in *Twelfth Night* seems, at first glance, to duplicate this situation. She too functions as a boy in relation to both the man she loves and a member of her own sex, while aside and innuendo communicate her feminine responses to those outside the play world (cf.I.iv.41–2). In fact, however, Viola's predicament is not as similar to that of the earlier heroine as initially appears. In the first place, her entry upon amatory experience takes place after her assumption of a masculine form. Where Rosalind falls in love with, and is loved by, Orlando prior to her metamorphosis into Ganymede, Viola does not meet Orsino until after her translation into Cesario, the rapprochement between them thus having both homo- and heterosexual overtones. At the same time, although at first sight the emotional triangle involving Orsino, Olivia and Viola seems to constitute a particularly glaring example of Shakespeare pillaging his own work, in fact the emotions that the situation generates are far more complex, and ultimately more violent, than those explored in the earlier play. Whereas Phebe's affections are transferred to Silvius once Ganymede's true identity is revealed (cf. V.iv.148–9), Olivia's passion for Cesario is such that it cannot be accommodated by an alternative lover, and it is only the appearance of Viola's *alter ego*, the twin brother whom she both emulates and resembles, that allows for the situation to be resolved. Similarly, Orsino's sense of betrayal when Olivia finally repudiates him draws the action into a much darker arena than that in which the cross-affections of *As You Like It* are played out:

> Why should I not, had I the heart to do it,
> Like to th'Egyptian thief at point of death,
> Kill what I love? – a savage jealousy
> That sometime savours nobly. But hear me this:
> Since you to non-regardance cast my faith,
> And that I partly know the instrument
> That screws me from my true place in your favour,
> Live you the marble-breasted tyrant still.
> But this your minion, whom I know you love,
> And whom, by heaven, I swear I tender dearly,
> Him will I tear out of that cruel eye
> Where he sits crowned in his master's spite.
> Come, boy, with me; my thoughts are ripe in mischief:
> I'll sacrifice the lamb that I do love,
> To spite a raven's heart within a dove.
>   (V.i.115–29)

Consequently, when at the close of the action the masculine and feminine aspects of Cesario divide (into Viola and Sebastian), the relationships that are formed among the dramatis personae allow for the fulfilment of a far wider range of affections than those satisfied by the heterosexual couplings of the earlier play, while the wonder and relief that the resolution occasions is correspondingly more profound (cf. V. i. 214ff.).

The pathos and constraint that surrounds the playing of roles in *Twelfth Night* foreshadows Shakespeare's handling of his last epicene creation, Imogen/Fidele in *Cymbeline*. Once again, however, though this figure has obvious affinities with previous heroines, his/her immediate origins are to be found not in Shakespeare's own compositions but in the non-dramatic literature of the period, in this instance the ninth novel of the second day of Boccaccio's *Decameron* (assembled 1349–51).[10] As in the Shakespearian play, the heroine of Boccaccio's story is the victim of a wager made on her chastity, and she assumes the disguise of a youth as a means of escape when her husband is persuaded of her infidelity. Nevertheless, though Imogen's situation is clearly derived from the tradition to which Boccaccio's story belongs, the *Decameron* is not the sole source of the Shakespearian drama. Just as in previous comedies he 'addeth' to his exemplum by combining incidents from different literary traditions (love and friendship with sexual disguise in *The Two Gentlemen of Verona*, gender exchange with sibling confusion in *Twelfth Night*), so in *Cymbeline* he fuses the defamed wife motif with elements drawn from other kinds of inherited material. The title figure, Cymbeline, for example, is not a deluded ruler from romance, but a character drawn from British history, and the events that surround his relationship with Rome are adapted from Holinshed's *Chronicles* (1587). The treatment of these episodes is far from historical, though, in the sense in which that term is understood today. Cymbeline's court is not defined in a way that evokes a particular period, but is assimilated to the archetypal patterns of folk tale. His queen enacts the role of the wicked stepdame, analogous to that of her counterpart in *Snow White*, seeking to rid herself of her husband's daughter in order to augment her own position, while his sons correspond to the lost princes of fairy tale, stolen from him in infancy only to reappear in his hour of need bringing new

10. The contention that the play was influenced by Beaumont and Fletcher's *Philaster* (1608–10) is not explored here as the relationship between the two works remains a matter of debate. See J. M. Nosworthy (ed.) (1955) *Cymbeline*. Methuen, pp. xxxvii–xl (Arden edition).

hope to the suffering realm. Sexual disguise is thus placed in a very different context in this play from that in which it functions in the earlier stages of the dramatist's career. On the one hand it is divorced from the never-never-land of Italianate romance through its association with a historical actuality, while on the other it is assimilated to myth through its incorporation into the patterns of folk tale.

For all her non-dramatic origins, however, her Shakespearian ancestry clearly plays a part in Imogen's development. In the first place, the behaviour that she must adopt on assuming her new identity is defined in terms similar to those used by Portia (cf. *The Merchant of Venice*, III.iv.60–78, *Cymbeline*, III.iv.156–75), while Guiderius and Arviragus, like Orlando and Orsino, find themselves attracted to a seeming member of their own sex (cf. *Cymbeline*, III.vii.41–4). At the same time, the situation in which Imogen finds herself represents an extension of the negative aspects of role playing explored in *Twelfth Night*. Unlike her predecessors who (with the exception of Jessica) elect to assume their masculine roles, she is advised to shed her female identity by Pisanio, and is thus less in control than earlier heroines of her own situation. Similarly, the reasons for her change of gender constitute a heightening of the increasing urgency attendant upon the device in previous plays. Julia, in *The Two Gentlemen of Verona*, is motivated solely by her desire to be with her lover, and sets off for Milan of her own volition, while Portia chooses to go to Venice to be of service to her husband's friend. Rosalind and Celia, by contrast, don their disguises in order to escape from the tyranny of the court, while Viola, shipwrecked in Illyria, is obliged to construct a new identity for herself in an alien world. The assumption of a masculine persona thus becomes increasingly imperative in the course of these plays, but in every instance a change of identity affords the opportunity to enter the play world on a new footing. In *Cymbeline*, by contrast, the opposite is the case, in that the heroine adopts a disguise in order to leave her world rather than enter it. Her position at the start of the play is a highly prominent one. Not only is she the King's daughter and heir to the throne, but she has embarked upon a marriage that has attracted considerable public comment, and her metamorphosis into a youth is a means of discarding an identity that has become dangerous to her once her stepmother,

and her husband, seek her life. This progress out of her society
is carried a stage further, moreover, when she sets out for
Milford-Haven as Fidele. Having stumbled upon the cave that
serves as home to Belarius, Guiderius and Arviragus, she takes a
potion in the belief that it is medicinal and falls into a profound
sleep, which is mistaken by her hosts for death. Profoundly
moved by the loss of their guest, Guiderius and Arviragus carry
out a ritual funeral, strewing the body with flowers, and bequeathing it to the earth. The contrast here between disguise as a stage
in a progress towards dissolution, and the revitalization associated
with role playing in *The Merchant of Venice* and *As You Like It*,
could hardly be more striking. Where Imogen 'dies' to her husband
in her own person, and to Guiderius and Arviragus in her role
as Fidele, Portia enters Venice in order to dispel the shadow of
death, while Rosalind-as-Ganymede acts as a life-generating
agency in Arden, manipulating Phebe into marriage with Silvius,
and educating Orlando into a suitable husband for herself. Nevertheless, it would be a mistake to suppose that in *Cymbeline* sexual
transmutation is not associated with renewal – and it is here that
Shakespeare's additions to his source are of major importance. The
folk tale context in which Imogen's career is set serves to assimilate
her experience to a much larger process of loss and recovery
enacted in the course of the play. The negative actions of Cymbeline (who resists the marriage of his heir), the Queen (who seeks
the life of her stepdaughter) and Posthumus (who orders the
murder of his wife), disrupt the cycle of nature, plunging the court
(and, by extension, Britain as a whole) into a winter-like state, that
is symbolized by the disappearance and death of the next in line to
the throne. A state of sterility thus obtains in both public and
private spheres until a process of rebirth is set in motion with
Fidele's reawakening. Sexual disguise has thus been woven here
into that pattern of destruction and recovery, death and regeneration that underlies all those compositions associated with the final
phase of Shakespeare's career,[11] and the affinity with other plays of
this period is strengthened by the context in which Imogen's
'resurrection' takes place. Having travelled from courtly society

11. *Pericles* (1607–08), *Cymbeline* (1608–09), *The Winter's Tale* (1610–11), and *The
Tempest* (1611). *Henry VIII* (1613) and *Two Noble Kinsmen* (1613–16), written
in collaboration with Fletcher, also have some affinities with this group.

into the wilds, she is consigned to the earth and covered with flowers, and her return from death is consequently symbolic of the play world's reaccommodation to the rhythms of nature, and reassimilation to the cycle of the year.[12] The disguised heroine motif consequently carries very different connotations in this play than in either its dramatic or non-dramatic antecedents. Rather than serving as an instrument of discovery, or allowing access to unfamiliar areas of experience, it is emblematic of a universal process, representing the lapse into non-being that forms part of the rhythm of life.

It is not merely the fusion of the sexual disguise motif with the archetypes of folk tale, however, that distinguishes Shakespeare's use of gender exchange in *Cymbeline* from his handling of the device in earlier plays. The treatment of the attraction between individuals who are superficially of the same sex also shows a movement into areas rarely explored in the sources from which the epicene figures of Renaissance drama are ultimately derived. As noted above, Shakespeare does not invariably exploit the opportunities for sexual misalliance offered by the tales on which he draws. In *The Two Gentlemen of Verona*, for example, Proteus employs 'Sebastian' simply because he requires a more courtly servant than Launce, while in *The Merchant of Venice* Bassanio feels warmly towards 'Balthazar' not because he is attracted to 'him' as an individual, but because he has done him a valuable service. In *As You Like It* and *Twelfth Night*, by contrast, the sexual complications arising from gender exchange form a major element of the dramatic interest. Phebe and Olivia both fall in love with members of their own sex, while Orlando and Orsino are attracted to those who appear as masculine as themselves. In *Cymbeline* the sexual cross-currents are yet more unnatural. Guiderius and Arviragus find themselves powerfully drawn towards the 'boy' who unexpectedly presents himself in their home, and are consequently caught up in a situation that is unnatural in more than one respect. On one level they are emotionally engaged with a member of their own sex, while on another they are amorously involved with their own sister. The terms in which they address her are indicative of the sexual nature of the feelings her appearance elicits:

12. Compare the movement from Sicilia to Bohemia that takes place in *The Winter's Tale*, and the evocation of the rhythms of natural life in Act IV of the same play.

Gui.   Were you a woman, youth,
  I should woo hard, but be your groom in honesty:
  I bid for you as I do buy.
Arv.   I'll make't my comfort
  He is a man, I'll love him as my brother.

                                                  (III.vii.41–4)

The signals transmitted here to a theatre audience are curiously mixed. On the one hand, the attitudes of the princes affirm the potential value and beauty of human relationships, bearing witness to the bonds that bind together the family group, while on the other hand they generate an uncomfortable awareness that in the perverse world created by the Queen's influence the natural sympathy between brother and sister has led to a situation that is essentially unhealthy. It is only with the 'death' of Fidele, and his/her rebirth into a context that restores the play's familial relationships to a natural footing, that the darker elements involved in this situation are purged. The heroine's assumption of a masculine disguise in this instance thus allows the dramatist to explore the sexual impulse within the family group, without evoking the revulsion conventionally associated with incest.

Contemporary criticism of Shakespeare may be likened to a piece of photographic apparatus that permits an object to be viewed through a variety of filters. Each of the multiplicity of approaches currently reflected on the bookshop shelf (e.g. feminist, new historicist, structuralist) foregrounds (or negotiates with) one aspect of the dramatic composition, colouring the work of art (or highlighting one aspect of it) by the medium through which it is viewed. The epicene figures who stand at the centre of so many Shakespearian comedies lend themselves to this spectrum of interpretation, not least because the dramatist himself deploys them for different purposes at different stages in his career. Thus, for the reader concerned with the role of women in a society structured upon the assumption of male superiority *The Merchant of Venice*[13] may yield the most significant insights, while for the writer engaged in locating the artefact within the intellectual crosscurrents of a particular period, *As You Like It* and *Twelfth Night*

13. See M. French (1982) *Shakespeare's Division of Experience*. Jonathan Cape, p. 104.

are of particular interest.[14] For the student of intertextuality (i.e. the way in which literary compositions feed off or interact with one another), it is the development of Shakespeare's handling of his source materials, predicating this variety of interpretation, which is most illuminating. Julia, created at the start of the dramatist's career, remains, like her romance ancestors, within the parameters of female experience, while the later Portia and Rosalind transgress the barriers of their sex, entering more fully into their masculine roles. Similarly, where Julia is involved in a heterosexual courtship, Rosalind and Viola are drawn into both hetero- and homosexual relationships, while Imogen is implicated in a series of unnatural and destructive amatory drives. More broadly, where Julia is conceived as an element in a pattern of oppositions, Portia functions as a pole in a clash between value systems, while Imogen is assimilated into the cyclical processes of the natural world. In brief, a network of contrasts and analogies may be traced between the plays (and the above summary is by no means exhaustive), stretching back into the sources from which they originate. From the gritty Sebastian, via the magisterial Balthazar, through the quick-witted Ganymede, to the wistful Fidele, the epicene characters of Shakespearian comedy thus offer a textbook demonstration of the wealth of meanings that may be engineered, through adaptation, from a single motif. Bearing witness to man's lack of self-knowledge, his capacity for self-determination, his resilience, vulnerability and the cyclical nature of his experience, the metamorphosed maidens of Shakespearian drama testify, as they struggle with their doublets and wrestle with their codpieces, not to the paucity of their creator's imaginative resources, but to his capacity to cast a succession of highly original forms from his predecessors' well-worn moulds.

14. See S. Greenblatt (1988) *Shakespearean Negotiations*. Clarendon Press, Oxford, pp. 66–93.

Chapter 3

Scolding

The Comedy of Errors. The Taming of the Shrew. Much Ado
About Nothing. The Winter's Tale

To the late twentieth-century playgoer, accustomed to a concept
of sexual equality enshrined in law if not yet fully embraced in
practice, probably the least acceptable of the 'tales' on which
Shakespeare draws in the course of his comedies is that involving
the 'taming' of a domineering woman, or 'scold'. Distasteful as
this material may appear to the majority of modern readers, the
appetite for such stories stretches back to classical times, while the
battle between the sexes, often involving the physical correction of
a 'shrew', was a popular motif in both dramatic and non-dramatic
literature throughout the medieval and Tudor periods.[1] Since the
supremacy of the male constituted an integral part of the theological and social structure that the Renaissance inherited from the
Middle Ages, the assertive wife was regarded in the sixteenth and
seventeenth centuries not merely as disruptive of marital harmony,
but as a threat to the natural order, and her subjugation was
consequently posited as a highly desirable end. As both a grammar
school boy reared on Roman New Comedy, and an avid reader of
contemporary fiction, Shakespeare would have been familiar with
the 'scolds' of classical literature and the 'shrews' of folk tales from
his boyhood, and it is hardly surprising that the figure of the

1. For some typical examples of the genre, see below pages 76–7.

'termagant'[2] should have found her way (along with other traditional characters)[3] into his earliest plays. *The Comedy of Errors*, in which one of his first overbearing women appears, is heavily dependent (as noted in Chapter 1) on Plautus' *Menaechmi*, and the shrewish wife of the Roman comedy is carried over, together with her husband and his identical brother, into the Shakespearian version of the source. Nevertheless, the character has not simply been transposed into a new context. Adriana is much more sympathetically presented than her Plautine counterpart, and Shakespeare's treatment of her predicament (i.e. the way in which he 'altereth and changeth' his inherited material) constitutes a major step in the thought journey that was to lead him from the stereotypical image of the scold as a force for disruption, to a highly original respresentation of her as an agent of renewal.

The overbearing wife of the resident brother of Plautus' *Menaechmi* is introduced to the audience by her husband at the very start of the play, and his attitude towards her is overtly hostile. In a Tudor translation of the drama published not long after *The Comedy of Errors* was written (and therefore indicative of the way in which the characters of the classical play were regarded by Shakespeare's contemporaries), she is referred to as both a 'shrew' and a 'scold', and the way in which she seeks to dominate her husband is quickly established:

> [*Enter Menechmus talking backe to his wife within*]
>
> [MENECHMUS] If ye were not such a brabling foole and mad braine scold as yee are, yee would never thus crosse your husbande in all his actions. 'Tis no matter, let her serve me thus once more, Ile send her home to her dad with a vengeance. I can never go foorth a doores, but she asketh mee whither I go? what I do? what busines? what I fetch? what I carry? As though she were a Constable or a toll-gatherer . . . Well sith it is so, she shall have some cause, I mean to dine this day abroad with a sweet friend of mine . . . We that have Loves abroad, and wives at home, are miserably hampred, yet would every man could tame his shrewe as well as I doo mine. I have now filcht away a fine ryding cloake of my wives, which I meane to bestow upon one that I love better. Nay, if

---

2. The term came into popular use via medieval drama where it denoted a spurious Mohammedan deity of particularly violent disposition. In the course of the sixteenth century it came to signify an aggressive figure of either sex.
3. For example, the *servus* or witty slave (cf. the Dromios of *The Comedy of Errors*) and the *senex* or father figure (cf. Vincentio in *The Taming of the Shrew*).

she be so warie and watchfull over me, I count it an almes deed to
deceive her.

(I.ii.)[4]

Here, although the conduct of the wife is clearly reprehensible, the
behaviour of her husband is hardly worthy of respect, yet the
members of the audience are not encouraged to reflect upon
the woman's situation, or on the causes that have given rise to her
aggressive stance. Though the opening scene makes plain that she
has grounds of complaint against her husband, and the ensuing
errors occasion her considerable confusion and distress, her
responses to her situation are presented not as the product of a
unique set of circumstances, but as the typical behaviour patterns
of the class to which she belongs – cf. the comments of her father
whom she has summoned to her support:

> I will goe to my daughter, who I know hath some earnest businesse
> with me . . . I suppose it is some brabble between her husband and her.
> These yoong women that bring great dowries to their husbands, are so
> masterfull and obstinate, that they will have their own wils in everie
> thing, and make men servants to their weake affections.

(V.i.)

At the same time, the attitudes that she exhibits in the course of
the action are clearly not designed by the dramatist to elicit the
sympathies of the theatre audience. Her antagonism towards her
husband is motivated, not by frustrated affection or anxiety for his
well-being, but by a concern for possessions, and for her own
status. She takes exception to his 'trulls' because they are the
recipients of his gifts, rather than because they pose a threat to
their relationship, while she resents his conduct towards her not
because of the lack of affection that it implies but because it makes
her 'a stale and a laughing stocke to all the world' (cf. her exchange
with her father in V.1). At the close of the play no reconciliation is
effected between the couple, while Menaechmus' view of their
relationship is implicit in his willingness to sell her together with
the rest of his household goods:

> Mess[enio]. All men, women and children in Epidamnum, or elsewhere,
> that will repaire to Menechmus house this day sennight, shall there

4. All quotations from the Menaechmi are from the translation by William Warner
(1595) printed in the first volume of Bullough's Narrative and Dramatic Sources of
Shakespeare. No line numbers are given in this text.

finde all manner of things to sell: servaunts, household stuffe, house, ground and all: so they bring readie money. Will ye sell your wife too sir?

Men. Cit. Yea, but I thinke no bodie will bid money for her.

(V.i)

The basic grounds of contention between the Roman couple (most notably the husband's involvement with a courtesan) are transferred by Shakespeare from the *Menaechmi* to his own version of the 'errors' plot, but Adriana is not simply a reincarnation of her Plautine progenitor. Unlike her classical counterpart, she does not function in an exclusively masculine society, but is furnished with a confidante, in the person of her sister Luciana, through whom her own perspective on the situation is revealed. The exchanges between the sisters suggest that though she too is impatient and aggressive, her attitude to her husband is governed by a more intricate web of considerations than that determining the behaviour of her Roman antecedent. While Luciana speaks in terms of 'self-harming jealousy' (II.i.102), Adriana maintains that her conduct is the product of her husband's actions, and that her relationship with him is more important to her than his gifts:

> His company must do his minions grace,
> Whilst I at home starve for a merry look.
> Hath homely age th'alluring beauty took
> From my poor cheek? then he hath wasted it.
> Are my discourses dull? barren my wit?
> If voluble and sharp discourse be marr'd,
> Unkindness blunts it more than marble hard.
> Do their gay vestments his affections bait?
> That's not my fault, he's master of my state.
> . . . .
> Sister, you know he promis'd me a chain;
> Would that alone a toy he would detain,
> So he would keep fair quarter with his bed.
>
> (II.i.87–108)

Here, though the members of the audience concur with Luciana's view that her sister is contributing to her own unhappiness, they also recognize the pain and the admirable impulses underlying Adriana's position. Similarly, though her exchanges with Antipholus of Syracuse (whom she takes to be her husband) are ludicrous on one level because of the basic misconception on which they

depend, they command a measure of respect on another by virtue
of the emotion with which they are charged, and the vision of
marriage which they project. The passage is worth quoting at
length for the contrast that it affords with the attitudes of the
'shrew' of the Plautine model:

> The time was once when thou unurg'd wouldst vow
> That never words were music to thine ear,
> That never object pleasing in thine eye,
> That never touch well welcome to thy hand,
> That never meat sweet-savour'd in thy taste,
> Unless I spake, or look'd, or touch'd, or carv'd to thee.
> How comes it now, my husband, O, how comes it,
> That thou art then estranged from thyself? –
> Thyself I call it, being strange to me,
> That undividable, incorporate,
> Am better than thy dear self's better part.
> Ah, do not tear away thyself from me;
> For know, my love, as easy mayst thou fall
> A drop of water in the breaking gulf,
> And take unmingled thence that drop again
> Without addition or diminishing,
> As take from me thyself, and not me too.
> How dearly would it touch thee to the quick,
> Shouldst thou but hear I were licentious?
> And that this body, consecrate to thee,
> By ruffian lust should be contaminate?
> Wouldst thou not spit at me, and spurn at me,
> And hurl the name of husband in my face,
> And tear the stain'd skin off my harlot brow,
> And from my false hand cut the wedding-ring,
> And break it with a deep-divorcing vow?
> I know thou canst; and therefore, see thou do it!
> I am possess'd with an adulterate blot,
> My blood is mingled with the crime of lust;
> For if we two be one, and thou play false,
> I do digest the poison of thy flesh,
> Being strumpeted by thy contagion.
> Keep then fair league and truce with thy true bed,
> I live unstain'd, thou undishonoured.

(II. ii. 113–46)

Here, while the woman's whirling words and the man's implied
struggle to escape (cf. 'Ah, do not tear away thyself from me')

confirms the stereotypical view of the relationship between the sexes, the content of the speech runs counter to expectation, producing a much more complex species of comedy than that represented by the classical play. The line 'How comes it now, my husband, O, how comes it', with its repetitious phrasing, suggests the grief and bewilderment that the changed relationship has occasioned, while the endearments that the speaker employs (e.g. 'my love' at line 125), and her evocation of an earlier phase of the marriage (cf.lines 113–118) establish the emotional bond that once existed between husband and wife. The concept of marriage that she advances is a highly idealistic one, far removed from the mundane concerns of the conventional scold, while the anxiety that she exhibits is for her husband, and not solely for herself. In short, though those outside the play world undoubtedly laugh *at*, rather than *with*, Adriana in this scene, they do not wholly repudiate her position, respecting her ends, if not endorsing her means.

A similarly complex response to the domineering wife is achieved towards the close of the play. Antipholus of Syracuse having taken refuge in a priory, Adriana pursues him there in the belief that he is her husband, only to be taxed by the Abbess with having caused his disturbed state:

> *Abbess.* Hath he not lost much wealth by wrack of sea?
>   Buried some dear friend? Hath not else his eye
>   Stray'd his affection in unlawful love,
>   A sin prevailing much in youthful men,
>   Who give their eyes the liberty of gazing?
>   Which of these sorrows is he subject to?
> *Adr.* To none of these, except it be the last,
>   Namely, some love that drew him oft from home.
> *Abbess.* You should for that have reprehended him.
> *Adr.* Why, so I did.
> *Abbess.*   Ay, but not rough enough.
> *Adr.* As roughly as my modesty would let me.
> *Abbess.* Haply in private.
> *Adr.*   And in assemblies too.
> *Abbess.* Ay, but not enough.
> *Adr.* It was the copy of our conference;
>   In bed he slept not for my urging it,
>   At board he fed not for my urging it,
>   Alone, it was the subject of my theme;

In company I often glanc'd at it;
Still did I tell him it was vile and bad.
Abbess. And thereof came it that the man was mad.
The venom clamours of a jealous woman
Poisons more deadly than a mad dog's tooth.
It seems his sleeps were hinder'd by thy railing,
And thereof comes it that his head is light.
. . . .
In food, in sport and life-preserving rest
To be disturb'd, would mad or man or beast;
The consequence is then, thy jealous fits
Hath scar'd thy husband from the use of wits.
Luc. She never reprehended him but mildly,
When he demean'd himself rough, rude and wildly;
Why bear you these rebukes and answer not?
Adr. She did betray me to mine own reproof.

(V.i.49–90)

Here, the Abbess tricks Adriana into describing her conduct in
terms of that of the typical scold, encouraging her to convict
herself, as Adriana ruefully remarks. What is significant about this
scene, however, is the use that the dramatist makes, once again, of
the figure of Luciana. Though she too has warned Adriana in the
past against the attitude that she had adopted to her husband, she
fails in this instance to endorse the Abbess's position. Unlike the
old father in the *Menaechmi*, who is ready to see his daughter's
disagreement with her husband as a product of both her class and
disposition, Luciana comes to the defence of her sister, urging the
moderation of her response to her husband's behaviour, and the
provocation she has received. For all her religious vocation, the
Abbess does not, therefore, gain the unqualified approbation of
those outside the play world, and the distance between her
perceptions and those of the audience is heightened by the spectator's superior awareness of the situation. Though Antipholus of
Ephesus has undoubtedly been incensed by his wife's conduct, it is
not her jealousy that is responsible for the confusion at the priory
gates, nor is the man to whom the Abbess has afforded sanctuary
the wronged husband she believes him to be. Thus, though on one
level her castigation of Adriana is largely justified, on another it is
wholly misguided, allowing the members of the audience to retain
some sympathy for the overbearing wife even at the point in the
action at which she appears to come closest to the dramatic type.

The handling of the figure of the resident brother in the Shakespearian play also helps to modify the Plautine opposition between husband and wife. In Act III scene i, for example, Antipholus of Ephesus enters complaining that his wife is 'shrewish' (III.i.2) when he is unpunctual, but he himself flies into a violent rage on being denied access to his house, and determines to gain entrance to it by force. His behaviour draws a protest from his companion, a figure designed, like Luciana, to widen the spectator's view of the protagonists:

> *Eph. Ant.* Go, get thee gone; fetch me an iron crow.
> *Bal[thazar].* Have patience, sir, O, let it not be so;
>   Herein you war against your reputation,
>   And draw within the compass of suspect
>   Th'unviolated honour of your wife.
>   Once this, – your long experience of her wisdom,
>   Her sober virtue, years and modesty,
>   Plead on her part some cause to you unknown;
>   And doubt not, sir, but she will well excuse
>   Why at this time the doors are made against you.
> (III.i.84–93)

Balthazar's intervention here serves to afford the audience a fresh perspective on Adriana, who has largely been seen, prior to this point, in the context of her immediate family. The picture that he paints is a positive one, in stark (and amusing) contrast to the stereotype to which she seemingly conforms in locking her husband out of the house. He affirms the respect in which she is held by the community, and the 'wisdom', 'sober virtue' and 'modesty' (lines 89 and 90) with which she habitually conducts herself. The virtues assigned to her here by a wholly disinterested speaker allow the spectator to perceive her as a human being rather than a caricature, and thus to view her immediate behaviour, not as proceeding from a bias of nature, but as the product of a unique set of circumstances.

The concern with the marriage bond that runs through the scenes in which Adriana is involved also works to differentiate Shakespeare's treatment of the shrew theme from that of his Roman model. Where Plautus' wife is instrumental in promoting the errors of the classical play, contributing through her pursuit of status and goods to the image that the drama projects of a competitive, economically orientated society (see above, pages

13ff.), Adriana extends the disruption that the comedy enacts from the public to the private sphere, highlighting the emotional trauma that the play's errors involve. Rather than seeking to protect her possessions, Adriana is struggling to preserve her marriage, and though the means that she employs are prejudicial to her own ends, the ends themselves are far from unworthy.

In taking up the *Menaechmi* Shakespeare has thus considerably modified the conventional relationships that the Plautine comedy projects. He has divided the honours much more evenly between husband and wife, allowing those outside the play world, as well as those within it, a degree of respect for the latter's position. At the same time, he has complicated the straightforward caricature presented in the source by allowing the 'shrew' to reveal her motivation, affording the audience an insight into the psychology of scolding rather than focusing exclusively on its effects. Above all, he has used the figure of the assertive wife, not simply as a target for humour and a vehicle for the exposure of a type, but as an instrument for the exploration of the marriage relationship. It is this concern, far removed from the 'present purposes' of the classical drama, that he develops in the most notorious of his 'shrew' plays.

The Taming of the Shrew is one of Shakespeare's earliest comedies,[5] and it shares a number of themes (e.g. the nature of selfhood) with *The Comedy of Errors*. Nevertheless, though it too draws upon Roman New Comedy for specific incidents,[6] and includes a 'scold' among its dramatis personae, its principal interest does not derive from the work of Plautus or Terence. Although the immediate source of the play has yet to be established,[7] the Kate/Petruchio

5. Though the conventional chronology of the Shakespearian canon (in which *The Comedy of Errors* antedates *The Taming of the Shrew*) is assumed for the purposes of this discussion, it should be noted that some scholars have argued that *The Taming* was Shakespeare's first experiment in the comic mode. The precise order in which the early comedies were written does not materially affect, however, the argument of this chapter.

6. Act III scene i of *The Comedy of Errors* and Act V scene i of *The Taming of the Shrew*, for example, derive from the same scene in Plautus' *Amphitruo*.

7. The relationship between *The Taming of the Shrew* and *The Taming of A Shrew* (a very similar play of the same period) has been the subject of considerable debate (cf. B. Morris (ed.) (1981) *The Taming of the Shrew* (The Arden Shakespeare). Methuen, pp. 12ff.). Since the weight of evidence now points to *A Shrew* being a version of Shakespeare's comedy rather than its source no discussion of the relationship between the two structures is included here.

plot which gives the comedy its title clearly has its origins in the body of folk tales mentioned at the start of this chapter turning on the subjugation of an overbearing wife. Over four hundred versions of the story are extant, but two variations will suffice here to illustrate the tradition to which the play belongs. *A Merry Jest of a Shrewde and Curste Wyfe, Lapped in Morrelles Skin, for Her Good Behavyour* (*c.* 1550) is typical of the genre. A father (himself married to a shrewish wife), has two daughters, the elder overbearing like her mother, the younger pliant and good natured. The younger daughter, who has many admirers, marries and plays no further part in the tale, while the elder, who has only one suitor, becomes the focus of attention. The father attempts to dissuade her wooer from what he regards as an unwise match, but the young man persists with the courtship, and the marriage takes place. After a lapse of time, the wife's shrewish disposition begins to manifest itself, at which point the husband has his horse, Morrel, slaughtered, and orders its carcass to be flayed. Having forced his wife into a cellar, he beats her to the point of collapse, and then encloses her, naked, in the horse's hide. When she regains consciousness, her body stinging with the salt with which the animal's skin had previously been sprinkled, her husband threatens to keep her enclosed in the hide for the remainder of her life – thus effecting an immediate change in her attitude towards him. The husband then invites his parents-in-law to visit them, and exhibits the submissiveness of his wife, outraging his mother-in-law, who is promptly informed by her daughter that she too would have learnt obedience had she been wrapped in Morrel's skin.

The Handsome Lazy Lass[8] constitutes a variation on this kind of story in that a rather less brutal form of taming is employed. Here the wife's character is flawed by laziness, and the husband brings about the requisite improvement in her conduct by having his own food served to his hard-working servants, and reserving inferior fare for his own table. Recognizing that industry brings tangible rewards, the wife quickly abandons her antisocial conduct, volunteering for the most arduous tasks. Satisified of her reformation, her husband then reverses his former instructions, allowing her the food appropriate to her rank.

8. A traditional Scottish story included in J. G. McKay (1940) *More West Highland Tales*, Oliver and Boyd, Edinburgh, vol. 1, pp. 149–51.

It will be obvious to anyone familiar with the plot of *The Taming of the Shrew* that the play is heavily dependent on the tradition to which these tales belong, and that it draws upon both their physical and psychological methods of taming. The Shakespearian version of the story opens with the father's announcement that he will not consent to the marriage of his younger daughter, Bianca, until a husband has been found for her shrewish sister, Katherina. The arrival of the bold and wayward Petruchio in search of a rich wife provides a potential solution to this difficulty, and encouraged by Bianca's suitors he proceeds to woo, and eventually marry, Katherina. Determined to reduce her from a vixen to a dutiful wife, he decides to overgo her intemperance by the violence and irrationality of his own behaviour. He thus arrives for the wedding in clothes grotesquely inappropriate to the occasion, swears during the ceremony, strikes the priest, and throws wine over the sexton. He then insists on leaving the assembled company before the wedding breakfast, forcing his newly married wife to endure considerable physical hardship on her way to her new home. Once arrived there, he refuses her food on the grounds that the meal served to them is burned, denies her rest by finding fault with the making of the bed, and rejects the new clothes that have been made for her on the grounds that they are unfit to wear. Reduced to a condition of misery and exhaustion, Kate is forced to recognize the discord that will result from the crossing of his will, and consequently resolves to defer to his wishes. From the last scene of Act IV it is thus his will that governs her actions. She declares the sun to be the moon at his instigation, salutes an old man as a young virgin, tramples on her own cap in front of her father's household, and finally delivers a lecture to her fellow wives, at his command, on the duty that married women owe to their husbands.

Popular as such exemplary stories were in the sixteenth century, the kind of plot outlined above is patently not one likely to recommend itself to a contemporary audience. Not only is the assumed ideal on which it depends at variance with twentieth-century attitudes towards the relationship between the sexes, but the conduct of the husband in asserting his authority repels by its brutality rather than engaging admiration or respect.[9] The play as

---

9. The social acceptability of the husband's stance at an earlier period is indicated not only by the wide currency of shrew tales, but by the hostility of rural

outlined above lends itself to feminist readings, and is frequently discussed in terms of the oppressive nature of patriarchal institutions.[10] In fact, however, though the treatment that Kate receives from Petruchio smacks of the systematic cruelty of the 'Morrel' tale, Shakespeare does not present an unmodified version of the taming process. By adding to his inherited material he places the figure of the scold within a highly complex framework, simultaneously qualifying the audience's response to the central figures, while deepening the significance of the fabliaux[11] material on which he draws.

Though contemporary criticism of the play has tended to centre on the persons of the 'shrew' plot, in fact, it is not Kate and Petruchio with whom the members of the audience are first presented on taking their seats in the theatre. The play opens with an altercation between the 'hostess' of a tavern and a tinker named Sly, and it is upon the second of these characters that attention is focused in the opening scenes. The hostess having left in search of a constable, Sly falls into a drunken sleep, and is thus unaware of the arrival of a Lord and his followers, who decide to dress him up as a nobleman, and to enjoy his confusion at his translated state. This plan having been effected, a company of players present themselves at the Lord's house, and are requested to perform a play for his 'noble' guest. At the same time, the Lord instructs his page to disguise himself as a woman and to present himself to the tinker as his wife, while he himself waits on Sly in the guise of a servant. The play which is then begun (of which the shrew plot forms one strand) is consequently not, at this stage, the primary focus of audience attention. It is Sly who has been the central interest from the outset, and his responses with which the spectator

---

communities towards those who failed to fulfil their conventional roles. Domineering (or unfaithful) wives and subservient husbands were parodied by their neighbours in the 'skimmington', a burlesque enactment of their relations (cf. K. Newman (1986) 'Renaissance family politics and Shakespeare's *The Taming of the Shrew*' in *English Literary Renaissance* vol. 16, pp. 86–100 (reprinted in G. Waller (ed.) (1991) *Shakespeare's Comedies*, Longman, pp. 41–2)). The longevity of the tradition is attested by its role in Thomas Hardy's *The Mayor of Casterbridge* (1886).

10. See M. French (1982) *Shakespeare's Division of Experience*, Jonathan Cape, pp. 82ff.

11. The term (deriving from medieval French literature) denotes a type of humorous and often bawdy story satirizing human vices and failings in a boisterous and realistic vein.

is engaged when the characters played by the travelling actors are introduced. Shakespeare's Kate is thus first perceived by the theatre audience not as a 'real' person, but as a character in a play within a play, and is distanced from the spectator by the intervention of an internal audience between those outside the play world and the inset drama.

The scenes involving Sly do not simply serve, however, to impose a degree of distance between the spectators and the 'shrew' play, reducing the 'reality' of the action that they frame. They also introduce the themes of the central interest, and engineer a stance towards the events that are enacted. The Induction is concerned throughout with social inversion. It begins with a confrontation between the sexes, in which a blustering male is worsted by a woman. Having lapsed into a drunken sleep, Sly undergoes a further decline from man to beast (cf.Induction,i.32), only to be elevated through the intervention of the Lord from his true position in the social order to an inappropriately high one. At the same time, the Lord becomes a servant, and his page a woman, with the result that the 'shrew' play is performed, not before a conventional court, but in a topsyturvy world. This confused environment has, moreover, a dreamlike quality. Sly himself is unsure whether he is awake or asleep, cf:

> Am I a lord, and have I such a lady?
> Or do I dream? Or have I dream'd till now?
>   (Induction, ii. 69–70)

while the Lord suggests that Sly's brief period of ennoblement (during which the inset drama takes place) will later seem to him like a 'flatt'ring dream' (Induction, i.42). At the same time, this inverted, unreal world is the product of 'game'. The Lord has instigated Sly's metamorphosis into an aristocrat for 'pastime' (Induction, i.65), and his followers enter into the device with enthusiasm, deriving considerable amusement from the prospect of playing their parts (cf.Induction, i.129–36). The comedy performed by the travelling players is thus set in the context of courtly fun, adding a further dimension at its inception to the licensed misrule instituted in an aristocratic household as a means of passing a winter's day.

It will be apparent from the above that the scenes involving Sly are designed to soften the hard outlines of the principal action in a number of ways. The play within a play structure establishes the inset drama as art rather than life, while the social relationships that the shrew play projects function both as an aspect of Sly's dream, and as an extension of the species of Bacchanalia that is in progress in the Lord's household. It is not merely the intervention of the frame plot between the theatre audience and the play proper, however, that points to a more sophisticated treatment of the shrew theme than a summary of the story line suggests. The courtship of Kate and Petruchio is paralleled by the attempts of a number of suitors to gain the hand of Baptista's younger daughter, Bianca, and this plot is thematically related to both the Induction and the wooing of Kate. In the first place, the concern with role playing, initiated in the frame plot, invades every aspect of the drama. Just as Sly becomes a lord, while the Lord becomes a servant, so in the Bianca plot Tranio, Lucentio's servant, plays the part of his master, rich suitors disguise themselves as tutors, and a pedant assumes the role of a wealthy man. The overbearing conduct and aggressive masculinity of Katherina is thus placed in the context of an entire community in which roles have been exchanged or subverted. Far from being the single aberrant source of discord within a patriarchal society restored to order by her taming, Kate emerges as symptomatic both of the universe in which she exists, and the upside down world in which the comedy is played.

The closing scene of the drama also serves to underline the typicality, as opposed to the idiosyncratic nature, of Kate's conduct. The characters of both strands of the action come together for a banquet (traditionally representative of the restoration of harmony), but it soon becomes apparent that the relations between the members of the social group are far from ideal. The sexes jar both with one another and between themselves (cf.V.ii.14–47), while it quickly emerges that two of the three marriages made in the course of the play contain the seeds of future dissension. Hortensio, who has married a rich widow, is clearly afraid of his wife's anger (cf.V.ii.16ff.), while Lucentio, who has won the hand of Bianca, is disappointed in his expectation that she will automatically comply with his will (cf.V.ii.63ff.). Kate's defective relations with those around her are thus not the sole target of criticism. Rather than being exclusive to her own situation, her shrewishness is an instance of a universal phenomenon, the tendency of human beings – male and female – to undermine, through their 'froward-ness', the orderly functioning of the social group.

While the treatment of Bianca and her suitors suggests the typicality of Kate's conduct, the handling of the shrew herself is much more sympathetic than in the sources from which the play's action derives. Unlike the conventional scold, who is arrogant and self-assertive by nature, Kate is supplied with an explanation for her conduct – and one that reflects adversely on those around her. She first appears with her father and her sister's suitors, and the treatment that she receives invites her resentment of both:

> Bap[tista]. Gentlemen, importune me no farther,
>   For how I firmly am resolv'd you know;
>   That is, not to bestow my youngest daughter
>   Before I have a husband for the elder.
>   If either of you both love Katherina,
>   Because I know you well and love you well,
>   Leave shall you have to court her at your pleasure.
> Gre[mio]. To cart her rather. She's too rough for me.
>   There, there, Hortensio, will you any wife?
> Kath. I pray you, sir, is it your will
>   To make a stale of me amongst these mates?
> Hor[tensio]. Mates, maid, how mean you that? no mates for you
>   Unless you were of gentler, milder mould.
>
>   (I.i.48–60)

Here the rebuke that she delivers to her father is justified by his failure to protect her from abuse, while the contempt that she exhibits for her suitors is warranted by the rudeness of their behaviour. Similarly, though it appears at first sight that her hostility towards Bianca is motivated solely by the universal preference for the younger woman (cf.II.i.8–36), there are a number of indications that her resentment also derives from the knowledge that the assumptions made about her sister are ill-founded (cf.I.i.78–9). The action of the play, moreover, bears out the implication that Bianca's disposition is not what it appears to be. Though Lucentio, on first seeing the sisters, assumes that appearance and reality coincide – i.e. that one is a termagant, and the other the embodiment of 'mild behaviour and sobriety'(I.i.71) – as the comedy unfolds both the members of the audience and Lucentio himself are obliged to revise this assessment. Bianca shows herself capable of being as peremptory as her sister in her

conduct towards her 'tutors' (cf.III.i.16–20), while at the close of
the play she declines to come at her husband's command, rejecting
the dutifulness displayed by Kate towards Petruchio in terms that
bode ill for her own marriage:

> *Bian.* Fie, what a foolish duty call you this?
> *Luc.* I would your duty were as foolish too.
>   The wisdom of your duty, fair Bianca,
>   Hath cost me a hundred crowns since supper-time.
> *Bian.* The more fool you for laying on my duty.
>
>   (V.ii.126–30)

It is the ultimate status achieved by the central figure, however,
that constitutes Shakespeare's most significant adaptation of his
inherited material. At the outset of the action it is clearly established
that Kate's behaviour, warranted though it may be, is prejudicial
not only to the community at large but to her own happiness. She
is disrespectful towards her father (I.i.102–4), cruel to her sister
(II.i.1–22), and hostile both to Bianca's suitors and to the single
aspirant to her own hand (I.i.57–65 and II.i.182ff.). Her adverse
effect upon the social group is reflected in the extreme responses
that she elicits from those around her. Her father refers to her as a
'hilding of a devilish spirit' (II.i.26), while her sister's suitors
variously regard her as 'rough' (I.i.55), 'intolerable curst' (I.ii.88),
and 'shrewd, and froward . . . beyond all measure' (I.ii.89). She is
thus presented as an isolated figure existing in a society governed
by assumptions which she rejects, and it might appear at first sight
that the action of the play merely brings her from violent opposition to her world to an enforced conformity with its mercantile
values and hierarchical structures. In fact, Kate's progress may be
more adequately described as a process of education that leaves her
essential spirit unchanged, but transforms her relationship with
those around her. It is clear from the outset that although Petruchio's motivation in pursuing the match is initially financial, he is
also intrigued and impressed by the spirit that his prospective bride
exhibits. On being told, for example, that she has broken a lute
over the head of one of her tutors, he exclaims:

> Now, by the world, it is a lusty wench.
> I love her ten times more than e'er I did.
>
>   (II.i.160–1)

This appreciation of a strength of character equal to his own carries with it the promise of a more valuable relationship developing between the couple than Petruchio's pecuniary aspirations initially suggest, and it is the growth of this understanding, for all the physicality of the action through which it evolves, that the play traces. The course of conduct that Petruchio pursues – violating the decorum of the marriage ceremony, refusing to attend the wedding breakfast, subjecting his newly married wife to a long and arduous journey, depriving her of food, rest and new clothes on the pretence that nothing is too good for her – not only affords Kate a mirror image of her own behaviour, but brings her to recognize her own dependence on the orderly conduct of day-to-day life, and on the conventions she had previously scorned.[12] While Bianca learns nothing from her succession of tutors, Kate is thus educated into a fuller awareness of her own priorities (cf.IV.iii.2–29), while becoming more considerate of others through sharing the miseries to which intemperance and the abuse of authority lead (cf.IV.i.126–56). At the same time, she evolves a relationship with her husband that is more than a *modus vivendi*. The turning point in this process occurs during the return journey to Baptista's house, when she contradicts Petruchio for the last time over the seemingly incontrovertible question of the time of day:

> *Pet.* Good Lord, how bright and goodly shines the moon!
> *Kath.* The moon? The sun! It is not moonlight now.
> *Pet.* I say it is the moon that shines so bright.
> *Kath.* I know it is the sun that shines so bright.
> *Pet.* Now by my mother's son, and that's myself,
>   It shall be moon, or star, or what I list,
>   Or e'er I journey to your father's house.
> [*To Servants.*] Go on, and fetch our horses back again. –
>   Evermore cross'd and cross'd, nothing but cross'd.
>   (IV.v.2–10)

Recognizing that the journey will be abandoned unless he has his way, Kate elects to defer to him, not only on this point, but on any other position he cares to assume:

12. For a fuller discussion of this aspect of the play see A. Leggatt (1974) *Shakespeare's Comedy of Love*, Methuen, pp. 51–4.

> *Kath.* Forward, I pray, since we have come so far,
> And be it moon, or sun, or what you please.
> And if you please to call it a rush-candle,
> Henceforth I vow it shall be so for me.
>
> (IV.v.12–15)

Given the privations she has endured prior to this scene, and her anxiety to return to her father's house, this response might well be interpreted as representing the conventional cowing of the shrew to her husband's will. The encounter with Vincentio that follows, however, immediately qualifies this impression. Petruchio salutes the old man as a woman, inviting Kate to do the same, and is met, not with sullen acquiescence, but with a spirited entry into the game he has determined to play:

> *Pet.* [*To Vincentio.*] Good morrow, gentle mistress, where away?
> Tell me, sweet Kate, and tell me truly too,
> Hast thou beheld a fresher gentlewoman?
> Such war of white and red within her cheeks!
> What stars do spangle heaven with such beauty
> As those two eyes become that heavenly face?
> Fair lovely maid, once more good day to thee.
> Sweet Kate, embrace her for her beauty's sake.
> . . . .
> *Kath.* Young budding virgin, fair and fresh, and sweet,
> Whither away, or where is thy abode?
> Happy the parents of so fair a child,
> Happier the man whom favourable stars
> Allots thee for his lovely bedfellow!
> *Pet.* Why, how now, Kate, I hope thou art not mad.
> This is a man, old, wrinkled, faded, wither'd,
> And not a maiden, as thou say'st he is.
> *Kath.* Pardon, old father, my mistaking eyes,
> That have been so bedazzled with the sun
> That everything I look on seemeth green.
> Now I perceive thou art a reverend father.
> Pardon, I pray thee, for my mad mistaking.
>
> (IV.v.27–48)

Clearly, the Kate who speaks these lines is not a broken woman, but one who has learnt to accommodate her spirit and strength of will to the situation in which she is placed. The tone in which she speaks is suggested by Vincentio's subsequent reference to her as a 'merry mistress' (IV.v.52) and this sense of shared merriment

between the central couple is confirmed at the end of the exchange (IV.v.75), and carried forward into the final act. In the closing scene while divisions are exposed between the parallel couples (Lucentio and Bianca / Hortensio and the Widow), Petruchio and Kate operate in partnership, and it is they who finally emerge as the upholders of the social order. Faced with the recalcitrant attitudes of Bianca and the Widow, Petruchio charges Kate to bring the offending wives before their husbands, and it is she who instructs those who had formerly repudiated her on the attitudes that make for harmonious relationships within the social group (V.ii.131–80). In the topsyturvy world of the 'shrew' play it is thus the 'scold' who achieves marital happiness, while the initial object of male admiration falls short of the conventional ideal.

While *The Taming of the Shrew* transforms the misogynistic material of popular tradition into a vehicle for the exploration of a universal tendency, overturning audience expectations by its final alignment with the central figure, *Much Ado About Nothing* (1598) carries the rehabilitation of the literary type a stage further by suggesting the importance of the characteristics that the termagant embodies for the stability of the community at large. Though the play belongs to a later stage of Shakespeare's development, and was probably written between *The Merchant of Venice* and *As You Like It*, it nevertheless looks back to the earlier shrew play in a number of respects. Once again, a father-figure has charge of two marriageable young women, one gentle and accommodating (cf.II.i.46–9), the other wayward and self-assertive, and thus less likely to gain a husband (cf.II.i.16–18). While the pliant young woman has an eligible suitor, her cousin shows no inclination to marry, and exhibits little of the deference towards men convention-ally expected of women (cf.II.i.16–60). While her demure com-panion is modestly restrained in her speech, her cousin is quick to voice her opinions, and does not hesitate to engage in verbal combat with members of the opposite sex. Benedick's account of an exchange with Beatrice supplies a clear pointer to the latter's literary ancestry:

> O, she misused me past the endurance of a block! An oak but with one green leaf on it would have answered her: my very visor began to assume life and scold with her. . . . She speaks poniards, and every word stabs: if her breath were as terrible as her terminations, there were no living near her, she would infect to the North Star. I would not

marry her, though she were endowed with all that Adam had left him before he transgressed. She would have made Hercules have turned spit, yea, and have cleft his club to make the fire too. Come, talk not of her, you shall find her the infernal Ate in good apparel. I would to God some scholar would conjure her, for certainly, while she is here, a man may live as quiet in hell as in a sanctuary, and people sin upon purpose, because they would go thither; so indeed all disquiet, horror, and perturbation follows her.

                                        (II.i.223–45; Arden ed.)

Where *Much Ado* differs from *The Taming* is in the status of the marriageable women within the dramatic action, and their method of presentation. Whereas Kate is regarded as a threat to the social order, and as an obstacle to the happiness of her sister, there is no suggestion in *Much Ado* that Beatrice's attitudes are prejudicial to those around her, or that she is any the less popular than her cousin. At the same time, the elaborate distancing devices of the shrew play that served to locate its potentially distasteful material in the context of licensed misrule or dream have given place to a kind of structure that affords the audience a much greater degree of intimacy with the dramatis personae, and thus permits a fuller exploration of the psychology of scolding.

Much Ado About Nothing opens with the governor of Messina, Leonato, attended by his daughter and his niece, awaiting the return of their Prince, the victorious Don Pedro, from the wars. In the course of the scene the contrasting characters of the two young women are clearly established, with the vivacity of Beatrice set against the passive reserve of her cousin. In the exchange that precedes the Prince's entrance Hero speaks only one line, and that relates to her cousin, while Beatrice dominates the action, with nearly 50 per cent of the dialogue. Her language is witty and decisive, leading the messenger who has brought her uncle the news of Don Pedro's success to remark that he will be careful to 'hold friends' (I.i.83) with her, while her attitude to Benedick, the subject of conversation, is superficially scornful and evocative of the traditional conflict between the sexes:

Beat.   In our last conflict
      four of his five wits went halting off, and now is the whole man
      governed with one: so that if he have wit enough to keep himself
      warm, let him bear it for a difference between himself and his horse,

for it is all the wealth that he hath left, to be known a reasonable creature.

....

Mess. I see, lady, the gentleman is not in your books.
Beat. No; and he were, I would burn my study.

(I.i.59–72; Arden ed.)

What is notable about this scene, however, is Leonato's attitude towards his niece. He is careful to warn the messenger not to 'mistake' (I.i.55) her meaning, assuring him that her comments are merely part of a 'merry war' (I.i.56) in which she is engaged with Benedick, while he remarks wryly on her shrewdness (I.i.85). This last point is particularly significant in terms of the development that has taken place between this comedy and the earlier shrew plays. Whereas in *The Taming* Kate's heterodox attitudes were seen in negative terms as the product of insanity or contumaciousness (cf.'That wench is stark mad or wonderful froward': *Taming*, I.i.69), in *Much Ado* Beatrice's unconventional opinions are viewed in a positive light, as evidence of level-headedness or clarity of judgement (cf.'You will never run mad, niece': *Much Ado*, I.i.85).

The treatment of Benedick is also significant in relation to the presentation of the assertive woman in the later play. Whereas Petruchio is allied with the social order, and adopts his abrasiveness for a specific purpose, Benedick is Beatrice's masculine counter-part, and as aggressively independent as Beatrice herself. Beatrice thus emerges, not as a comic obstacle to the marriage of her gentler companion, the role in which Kate first appears in the earlier play, but as one element of a pattern of contrasts that is set up between two pairs of lovers. Just as Beatrice is vivacious and individualistic, so Benedick is high spirited and strong minded, while Hero and Claudio have a greater degree of respect for the social conventions, and are of a more pliant disposition. At the same time, the experience of the more accommodating couple provides an implicit justification for the stance adopted by the more combative pair. Claudio's readiness to defer to the judgement of others (cf.I.i.150ff.) makes him an easy target for the wiles of Don John, the Prince's malevolent brother, while Hero, defamed by her prospective husband on her wedding day, lacks the strength of character to defend herself, and is dependent upon the good offices of others both for her rehabilitation and eventual marriage. The elaborate defensiveness of Beatrice and Benedick functions as a contrast to this kind of vulnerability, and their resistance to any form of commitment consequently emerges as a means of protecting the personality from the kind of anguish that both Hero and Claudio suffer.

The development of 'scolding' from an instrument of unnatural dominance to a defensive mechanism is also implicit in the acute awareness of the harsh realities of human existence that both Beatrice and Benedick exhibit. Beatrice, for example, describes courtship and marriage to her cousin in terms that show a clear perception of the mutability of men's affections:

> Hear me, Hero: wooing, wedding, and repenting is as a Scotch jig, a measure, and a cinque-pace: the first suit is hot and hasty like a Scotch jig, and full as fantastical; the wedding mannerly-modest as a measure, full of state and ancientry; and then comes repentance and, with his bad legs, falls into the cinque-pace faster and faster, till he sink into his grave
>
> (II.i.66–73; Arden ed.)

while Benedick sees unfaithfulness as a concomitant of marriage:

> That a woman conceived me, I thank her: that she brought me up, I likewise give her most humble thanks: but that I will have a recheat winded in my forehead, or hang my bugle in an invisible baldrick, all women shall pardon me. Because I will not do them the wrong to mistrust any, I will do myself the right to trust none: and the fine is, for the which I may go the finer, I will live a bachelor.
>
> (I.i.221–8; Arden ed.)

It is also suggested that Beatrice's attitude towards Benedick has not always been as efficiently defensive as it is at the time at which the play opens. In Act II scene i, for example, after the battle of wits that takes place in the course of the masked dance, she answers Don Pedro's comment that she has 'lost the heart of Signior Benedick' (II.i.259–60) with

> Indeed, my lord, he lent it me awhile, and I gave him use for it, a double heart for his single one. Marry, once before he won it of me with false dice, therefore your Grace may well say I have lost it.
>
> (II.i.261–4; Arden ed.)

The comment implies that she has been hurt by Benedick in the past, and is determined not to place herself at a disadvantage for a second time. Her combativeness may thus arise (in part at least) from painful experience and is consequently more sympathetic than the unnatural assertiveness displayed by the conventional shrew.

It will be apparent from the differences outlined above that while in *The Taming of the Shrew* a psychological explanation for Kate's conduct is merely hinted at in her familial circumstances, in *Much Ado About Nothing* the members of the theatre audience are initiated much more fully into the mental processes of the central figures. At the same time, the characters of the later play are viewed from a variety of perspectives. Whereas Kate is a shrew to her entire circle, Beatrice is perceived by individuals in different ways. She is a 'pleasant-spirited lady' (II.i.320) to Don Pedro, 'too curst' (II.i.18) to her uncle Antonio, one who 'apprehend[s] passing shrewdly' (II.i.74) to Leonato, 'good coz' (III.iv.92) to Hero, and 'my dear Lady Disdain' (I.i.109) to Benedick. The figure of the scold has thus been modified from a caricature to a complex character, i.e. into one with a variety of facets to her personality. In addition, the members of the audience are invited, periodically, to view the action from her perspective. In Act IV scene i, for instance, she has the following exchange with Benedick following the defamation of Hero:

> *Beat.* You dare easier be friends with me than fight with mine enemy.
> *Bene.* Is Claudio thine enemy?
> *Beat.* Is a not approved in the height a villain, that hath slandered, scorned, dishonoured my kinswoman? O that I were a man! What, bear her in hand until they come to take hands, and then with public accusation, uncovered slander, unmitigated rancour – O God that I were a man! I would eat his heart in the market-place.
> *Bene.* Hear me, Beatrice –
> *Beat.* Talk with a man out at a window! A proper saying!
> *Bene.* Nay, but Beatrice –
> *Beat.* Sweet Hero! She is wronged, she is slandered, she is undone.
> *Bene.* Beat –
> *Beat.* Princes and counties! Surely a princely testimony, a goodly count, Count Comfect, a sweet gallant surely! O that I were a man for his sake, or that I had any friend would be a man for my sake!
>
> (IV.i.297–317; Arden ed.)

Here, though her language is intemperate, it is clearly not the reflex of an ungenerous or ungoverned spirit. It suggests her anger and indignation on Hero's behalf, the depth of her attachment to her cousin, and her sense of frustration at her own inability to right the wrong that has been offered to the more vulnerable woman.

The much more sympathetic treatment of 'scolding' in this play is also evident in the way in which the 'curst' woman is induced to discard her aggressive stance. In *The Taming of the Shrew*, though the assault that Petruchio mounts against Kate's overbearing disposition is essentially psychological, the means that he employs are largely physical, while the attitude that his wife ultimately adopts involves deferring to his will. In *Much Ado About Nothing*, by contrast, not only is Beatrice's jibing spirit curbed by wholly psychological means, but her final relationship with Benedick is one of equality. Tricked into overhearing a conversation staged by Hero and her ladies, she is led to believe that Benedick loves her, and that she is censured for her self-esteem:

> Urs[ula].   But are you sure
>   That Benedick loves Beatrice so entirely?
> Hero. So says the Prince and my new-trothed lord.
> Urs. And did they bid you tell her of it, madam?
> Hero. They did entreat me to acquaint her of it;
>   But I persuaded them, if they lov'd Benedick,
>   To wish him wrestle with affection,
>   And never to let Beatrice know of it.
> Urs. Why did you so? Doth not the gentleman
>   Deserve as full as fortunate a bed
>   As ever Beatrice shall couch upon?
> Hero. O god of love! I know he doth deserve
>   As much as may be yielded to a man:
>   But Nature never fram'd a woman's heart
>   Of prouder stuff than that of Beatrice.
>   Disdain and scorn ride sparkling in her eyes,
>   Misprising what they look on, and her wit
>   Values itself so highly that to her
>   All matter else seems weak. She cannot love,
>   Nor take no shape nor project of affection,
>   She is so self-endeared.
>
>   (III.i.36–56)

Beatrice's response to this exchange is indicative of the distance travelled by the termagant figure in the course of Shakespeare's work. Shocked by what she believes she has discovered about her public estimation, she resolves to lay aside her former abrasiveness, embracing the opportunity the conversation affords her of discarding the role she has assumed:

> What fire is in mine ears? Can this be true?
> Stand I condemn'd for pride and scorn so much?
>   Contempt, farewell, and maiden pride, adieu!
> No glory lives behind the back of such.
>   And, Benedick, love on, I will requite thee,
> Taming my wild heart to thy loving hand.
>   If thou dost love, my kindness shall incite thee
> To bind our loves up in a holy band;
>   For others say thou dost deserve, and I
> Believe it better than reportingly.
>
>   (III.i.107–16)

Here it is not the husband who subdues the wife but the prospective wife who grows in self-knowledge, consciously 'taming' her own heart to her future partner's 'hand'. Beatrice's conversion is not, moreover, an isolated instance. The Prince and his followers practise a similar device upon Benedick, and he too is brought to reflect upon the nature of his behaviour, and to renounce his former pride and contempt. At the close of the play, though both characters have grown in understanding, neither has assumed ascendancy over the other, while the verbal fencing in which they continue to engage serves as an index, not of either's desire for mastery, but of their intellectual equality.

The development of scolding through the Shakespearian corpus from a comprehensible, if misguided, response to a husband's neglect, to evidence of clear-sightedness and a means of self-defence is taken a stage further in *The Winter's Tale* (1610–11) in which the shrew evolves into a positive force. Paulina, fierce critic of the jealous Leontes, and assertive wife of the loyal Antigonus, is in some respects one of the most daring and original creations in the entire spectrum of Shakespearian comedy. She makes her first appearance in Act II scene ii after Leontes has condemned his virtuous queen (Hermione) to prison though she is on the point of bearing his child. The misguided nature of this action is evident to the entire court, but his conduct has met with little opposition, and it is in the context of deference towards a corrupt authority that Paulina's forthright behaviour is set. On hearing that the Queen has given birth in prison to a daughter, she resolves to confront Leontes with the truth about the folly of his delusions:

Paul. These dangerous, unsafe lunes i'th'king, beshrew them!
  He must be told on't, and he shall: the office
  Becomes a woman best. I'll take't upon me:
  If I prove honey-mouth'd, let my tongue blister,
  And never to my red-look'd anger be
  The trumpet any more.
....
  I'll use that tongue I have: if wit flow from't
  As boldness from my bosom, let't not be doubted
  I shall do good.

                                                (II.ii.30–54)

Here lunacy is associated with the object of the scold's invective, rather than with the scold herself, while scolding is viewed as a means of restoring the social order not as a cause of its disruption. The attitudes of the woman to whom she confides her decision to disabuse the King are also very different from those of the female characters with whom the shrews are contrasted in earlier plays. Emilia salutes Paulina as a 'worthy madam' (II.ii.42), speaks of her 'honour' and 'goodness' (II.ii.43), and describes her offer to intercede with Leontes as a 'noble' one (II.ii.48). In the following scene, Paulina succeeds in the face of masculine opposition in gaining access to the King, berating those about him as she does so for fostering his fantasies through their subservience, and describing her own mission as a curative one, designed to purge his misapprehensions:

Serv [ant]. Madam, he hath not slept to-night, commanded
  None should come at him.
Paul.   Not so hot, good sir;
  I come to bring him sleep. 'Tis such as you,
  That creep like shadows by him, and do sigh
  At each his needless heavings; such as you
  Nourish the cause of his awakening. I
  Do come with words as medicinal as true,
  Honest, as either, to purge him of that humour
  That presses him from sleep.

                                                (II.iii.31–9)

Leontes' attitude to her intervention is evocative of the responses of a succession of masculine figures to the overbearing women of earlier plays. He calls her an 'audacious lady' (II.iii.42), blames her husband for failing to 'rule' her (II.iii.46), and rejects her as a

'mankind witch' (II.iii.67). A catalogue of words and phrases
define her relationship with Antigonus as the stereotypical one
between hen-pecked husband and shrewish wife:

> Thou dotard! thou art woman-tir'd, unroosted
> By thy dame Partlet here.
>
> (II.iii.74–5)

>   A callat
> Of boundless tongue, who late hath beat her husband,
> And now baits me!
>
> (II.iii.90–2)

>   A gross hag!
> And, lozel, thou art worthy to be hang'd,
> That wilt not stay her tongue.
>
> (II.iii.107–9)

What is notable about this succession of insults, however, is that
they are largely directed towards Antigonus, rather than Paulina
herself, and they consequently emerge, not as a valid reflection on
the personality of the assertive woman, but as a means of evading
the substance of her attack. His frenzied insistence upon the
impropriety of her conduct is thus a measure of his failure to face
up to the aberrant nature of his own behaviour, while her attempts
to force him to recognize the true nature of his situation are a
yardstick not of her impertinence, but of her zeal as a subject.
Though she is undoubtedly outspoken, her aggressive stance
springs from love and duty rather than inherent contumaciousness,
while her torrent of words and belligerent attitude are directed
towards upholding the natural order rather than subverting it – cf.:

> Good my liege, I come, –
> And, I beseech you hear me, who professes
> Myself your loyal servant, your physician,
> Your most obedient counsellor, yet that dares
> Less appear so, in comforting your evils,
> Than such as most seem yours.
>
> (II.iii.52–7)

It is also important to note here that rather than seeking to
defend her personality or status through her assertiveness, Paulina
is consciously risking her life. On having her evicted from his

presence Leontes threatens her with death, only to have his words turned back on himself:

> *Leon.* I'll ha' thee burnt.
> *Paul.*   I care not:
>   It is an heretic that makes the fire,
>   Not she which burns in't.
>
>   (II.iii.113–15)

This exchange equates scolding not with self-protectiveness but heroic action and the reference to heretic and burning endow that heroism with spiritual dimensions.

Paulina does not appear again until the second scene of the following act, when she brings the news of Hermione's supposed death to the King. Stricken with grief, Leontes now accepts her admonitions as valid reflections upon his guilt, and it is as a stimulus to his conscience that Paulina functions during the sixteen-year gap that intervenes between the end of Act III and the start of Act IV. She herself does not appear again until Act V scene i, but her first words on her re-entrance serve to remind Leontes of his guilt. Her immediate return to the death of Hermione implies that she has continued to work upon his moral nature throughout the intervening years, 'scolding' him into repentance for the wrong he has committed. Her uncompromising speeches consequently emerge in the course of the action as a species of verbal scourging, with Paulina lashing the King with her tongue into active penitence, and thus paving the way for an ultimate reconciliation. It is notable, moreover, that in this play the restoration of social order is effected not by a husband or well-meaning friend as in previous shrew plays but by the ungovernable lady herself. Though Hermione's return to life and her reunion with Leontes form part of a pattern of renewal that has been ordained by a divine power (cf.III.ii.132–6), the means by which these ends are accomplished are engineered by Paulina. It is she who invites Leontes, Perdita and Florizel to view the 'statue' of Hermione, she who unveils the figure, and she who invites the 'sculpture' to descend into the world of flesh and blood (V.iii.1–103). At the close of the play, it is Leontes, not the woman who has berated him, who grows in understanding, while the scold is finally rewarded with a husband (cf.V.iii.130–46) not for her acquired docility, but unremitting outspokenness.

The figure of Paulina in *The Winter's Tale* clearly originates in the folk tales outlined at the start of this chapter. The very title of the play invites an awareness of this type of traditional material, and the antiquated nature of the action is enforced throughout (cf.II.i.21–5 and V.ii.1–29). In the eyes of Leontes, Paulina's assertiveness, volubility, and lack of deference towards her husband all mark her out as a shrew, while she displays none of the respect for male judgement expected of the female sex. Nevertheless, her progress through the play runs directly counter to the careers of the ungoverned wives of the conventions from which her attitudes derive. Where the stereotypical scold discovers the inappropriateness of a course of conduct at variance with the social norm, Paulina brings those about her to recognize the aberrant nature of their behaviour and is the upholder of the social order. The world created through Leontes' actions is a perverse one. He has imposed an unnatural winter on the summer time of his court, and it is therefore appropriate that in the inverted universe he has brought into being a figure traditionally presented in a negative light should function as an agent of renewal.

The battle between the sexes is a recurrent motif in the literature of every culture, and the taming of a shrewish wife ranks among the mouldiest of mouldy tales. Like his identical siblings and disguised heroines, Shakespeare's scolds bear witness to his fondness for familiar material, and his readiness to use the same character-type or situation on a number of occasions. At the same time, the figure of the termagant exemplifies one kind of originality that can arise through a succession of adaptations. Whereas in the previous chapter it was the range of meanings elicited from a single motif that was of particular interest, here it is the increasingly sympathetic way in which a literary stereotype is handled. Though Adriana in *The Comedy of Errors* at the start of Shakespeare's career, is supplied with an explanation for her conduct, the stance that she adopts is a misguided one, and her behaviour contributes to the disorder into which the society of the play is plunged. Similarly, Kate's behaviour in *The Taming* is initially antisocial, and though she emerges at the close as the upholder of the natural order her progress to self-discovery involves considerable privation. By *Much Ado About Nothing* the activity of scolding has become a means of self-defence, while verbal combativeness is a social asset, contributing to the intellectual pleasures of the play world. *The*

Winter's Tale completes the process of reversal implicit in this development. It is now the shrew who educates those around her, while her refusal to conform to the dictates of her society contributes to the welfare of the community as a whole. Where the overbearing woman of folk tale is forced to acknowledge her failings, and defer to the opposite sex, Paulina scolds the representative of the patriarchy into repentance, and induces his renunciation of a mistaken stance.

While the term 'shrew' has only one application in relation to human beings, the word 'scold' has a much wider range of implications. Both signify an assertive woman of unbridled tongue, but the latter also denotes the activity of rebuking or reproving, and is frequently employed in the context of the mother/child relationship. Given Shakespeare's notorious delight in word play, it is hardly conceivable that he was not alive to the different connotations of noun and verb, and it is possible that his awareness of the varying resonances, moral and social, of the term provided some of the impetus behind his treatment of the conventional figure. Though the development from Adriana to Paulina clearly derives in the main from a growth of interest in the psychology of scolds and scolding, it may also owe something to the interaction between a particularly receptive mind and a classroom training geared to exploiting the shifting nuances of the written word.

Chapter 4

Substitute Coupling

Love's Labour's Lost. Much Ado About Nothing. The Merry
Wives of Windsor. All's Well That Ends Well. Measure for
Measure

The activity of scolding, in both senses of the term, is one familiar
to theatre audiences of all generations. Though the passage of time
has modified the degree of acceptance that the conventional shrew
plot commands, it has heightened rather than diminished the
tension between the sexes, and thus given a new modernity to the
gender conflict upon which the story depends. Though the tale
itself is a mouldy one, in that it has a long literary history, it places
relatively little strain on the credulity of the spectator in that it
relates to everyday experience. The substitute coupling motif, by
contrast, is wholly different in kind. The situation belongs to the
world of romance (cf. Painter's *Palace of Pleasure* or Boccaccio's
Decameron)[1] rather than the arena of daily life, and many readers,
exploring the Shakespearian corpus in the library rather than the
theatre, find the concept of mistaking the identity of a sexual
partner too extravagant for serious consideration.[2] At the same

1. For a full account of the history of the motif see W. W. Lawrence (1931)
   Shakespeare's Problem Comedies, Penguin Shakespeare Library edition, Harmondsworth 1969, pp. 48ff.
2. It is worth noting that the device would not have appeared quite as improbable
   in Renaissance England as it does today. Though hardly commonplace during
   the period, some instances of sexual substitution were widely held to have
   occurred. The wife of the Earl of Oxford, for example, was believed to have
   taken his mistress's place in his bed in 1574, subsequently giving birth to the
   future Countess of Pembroke (cf. E. I. Fripp (1938) *Shakespeare Man and Artist*.

time, the resistance aroused by Shakespeare's use of the device is compounded by its repetition in related plays. Whereas the conflict between the sexes emerges as a source of plot complication at different stages of the dramatist's career, the 'bed trick' occurs in two of the three problem plays – *All's Well That Ends Well* and *Measure for Measure* – both of which were written *circa* 1603–4. The amorous adventures of Bertram (*All's Well*) and Angelo (*Measure*) thus attract hostile notice in two respects. On the one hand they flout probability, while on the other they suggest an overly economic use by the dramatist of his own plot material.

In fact, though *All's Well That Ends Well* and *Measure for Measure* are alone in the Shakespearian canon in extending this species of 'mistaking' to the intimacies of the bedchamber, they are not the only items in the corpus in which a false assumption is made about the identity of a sexual partner. Like a number of his fellow dramatists,[3] Shakespeare was interested in the device throughout his dramatic career, and explores a number of its popular variations. In the relatively early *Love's Labour's Lost* (1593–4), for example, a group of ladies assume masks and exchange favours when courted by the King and his lords, thus manipulating their suitors into misdirecting their attentions. The encounter serves to demonstrate the wit of the women on the one hand and the inadequacies of the men on the other, and it places no significant strain on audience acceptance as the two parties' knowledge of one another is minimal. A very similar scene (II.i.79–141) occurs in *Much Ado About Nothing*[4] but in this instance it anticipates a sequence of much more serious 'mistakings'. Claudio, one of the

---

Oxford University Press, vol. II, p. 601). The physical circumstances of life in sixteenth-century England also lent credence to the deception. Whereas absolute darkness is virtually unknown in the twentieth-century urban environment, in the narrow bedrooms of Tudor England, with their small windows and overhanging eaves, total darkness was an actuality. It is in this almost palpable blackness that the substitute couplings of fact and fiction were imagined to have taken place, and the 'blindness' of those involved in such encounters was one with which a contemporary audience could relate.

3. R. S. Forsythe has noted twenty-one plays of the period in which some kind of 'bed-trick' occurs (cf. *The Relations of Shirley's Plays to the Elizabethan Drama*. New York, 1914). Other types of sexual misidentification (e.g. turning on disguise) were even more common.

4. This scene constitutes a variation on the pattern in that the lady pretends to be deceived over the identity of a disguised partner in order to amuse herself at his expense.

play's central characters, is twice deceived over the identity of a sexual partner. He is first encouraged to believe that a young woman whom he sees talking to a man from her chamber window is the lady he is about to marry, and he consequently repudiates her at the altar bringing about her seeming death. His mistake having been revealed to him, he seeks to make amends for his conduct by marrying the 'cousin' of his betrothed, only to discover that the veiled lady is his former love. Here, though the events of the drama are clearly at a distance from daily life, the process that is enacted is a credible one. Claudio's youth and impressionability are stressed from the outset, and the ease with which he is misled, for both positive and negative ends, is consistent with his character. At the same time, since the veiled figure he takes in marriage is in fact his former bride, the sexual coupling beyond the scope of the play is unproblematic in terms of audience acceptance.

The Merry Wives of Windsor (1597?) offers a rather closer parallel with *All's Well* and *Measure for Measure* in that its mistaken pairings take place in the dark.[5] Slender and Dr Caius both hope to run away with Anne Page, but are tricked into eloping with boys. Here the sexual misalliances serve to expose the foolishness of the suitors and the inappropriateness of their pretensions to Anne, while their deception is made convincing by the use of disguise (cf. *Love's Labour's Lost*), an exchange of passwords, and the darkness and confusion of the forest in which the flight of the 'lovers' takes place. At the same time, the blindness of the suitors is credible in that it is not an isolated phenomenon. The play's central character, Falstaff, is repeatedly deceived by the merry wives, while his proposed dupe, Master Ford, persistently mistakes appearance for reality in his dealings with his wife. The confused sexual pairings of the final act thus form part of a sequence of similar misunderstandings, while being symptomatic of the disorder invading amatory relationships throughout the play world.

The substitute couplings of *Love's Labour's Lost*, *Much Ado About Nothing* and *The Merry Wives of Windsor* clearly require some degree of 'willing suspension of disbelief' on the part of the theatre audience in that the gullibility of their dramatis personae exceeds

5. A nocturnal exchange also takes place in *Much Ado About Nothing* with Margaret pretending to be Hero on the orders of Borachio. In this case, however, the lover is an observer of a scene played out for his benefit rather than being implicated in the deception.

that displayed by the generality of human beings in the course of their daily lives. Nevertheless, *All's Well That Ends Well* and *Measure for Measure* represent a quantum leap in terms of the demands that they make of the spectator. Both plays involve impersonation, not simply as a stage in the process of courtship, but in the privacy of the bedroom itself, and turn upon sexual encounters in which one partner is ignorant of the other's identity. In both cases a central male character assails the chastity of a virtuous young woman, only to have his intentions thwarted by the substitution of another lady (his repudiated wife/betrothed) for the threatened virgin. The repetitiousness of the pattern, together with the inherent incredibility of the plot, challenge acceptance on both aesthetic and common sense grounds, jeopardizing the intellectual satisfaction deriving from either work. It is thus in the bedrooms of Florence and Vienna, rather than the parks of Windsor or Navarre, that Shakespeare faces his sternest trials in the novel deployment of mouldy tales.

It is important to note at the outset that for all their obvious affinities *All's Well That Ends Well* and *Measure for Measure* have their origins in different sources. The exact date of the two plays is uncertain, but it is widely accepted that *All's Well That Ends Well* preceded the related piece, and it is consequently assumed here to be the earlier work.[6] The main plot derives, probably via Painter's *Palace of Pleasure*, from one of the stories (III.ix) in Boccaccio's *Decameron*,[7] in which substitute coupling is one element of a structure rich in folk tale motifs. The story turns on the way in which a rich and virtuous lady falls in love with a man of higher rank, and resolves to win him for her husband by curing the King of a malady that has defeated the skill of his physicians. Having restored her patient to health, she is invited, as she hoped, to choose a husband as her reward, and asks to be united with the man she loves. Though the request is granted (with some reluctance) the husband repudiates the match, declaring that he will not

6. *All's Well* is usually dated 1603–04, while *Measure for Measure* was performed in December 1604 and may well have been written earlier the same year. For a full discussion of the problems surrounding the dating of the two plays see G. K. Hunter's Arden edition of *All's Well* (1959), pp. xviii–xxv.
7. For a full account of the sources of *All's Well* see G. Bullough (1957–75), vol. II, pp. 375ff.; W. W. Lawrence (1931) *Shakespeare's Problem Comedies*. Penguin Shakespeare Library edition, Harmondsworth 1969, pp.48ff.; and G. K. Hunter's Arden edition of the play, pp. xxv–xxix.

acknowledge her as his wife until she has borne him a son and gained possession of the ring on his finger. In the course of a journey to Florence, the heroine learns that her husband has conceived a passion for a young gentlewoman, and she prevails upon this lady to agree to an assignation in return for her suitor's ring, and to allow her to take her place in the bedchamber. After a number of meetings, the lady becomes pregnant with twins, and is thus able to claim her lord as her husband having fulfilled both of his seemingly impossible conditions.

A number of traditional elements are drawn together in this tale, all of which Shakespeare employs in his play. The means by which the lady wins the gratitude of the King belongs to the tradition of the miraculous cure,[8] while her patience in the face of her husband's neglect places her within the convention of the long-suffering wife.[9] Her husband's imposition of conditions that are seemingly incapable of fulfilment as a prerequisite to the acknowledgement of their marriage derives from the 'tale of impossibilities',[10] while the recognition through rings is a familiar mechanism of romance.[11] Boccaccio's tale is thus woven from a number of equally improbable strands, with the bed trick subsumed into a larger structure in which all the threads of the narrative operate at a considerable remove from reality.

In taking up Boccaccio's story Shakespeare retains its conventional motifs, but he adapts the design of his borrowed plot in a number of ways. In the first place he marries the material derived from his principal source with a secondary strand of action that has no counterpart in the amatory adventures of the *Decameron*. This area of interest concerns the relationship between the reluctant husband, Bertram, and his friend Parolles, and it too is 'unoriginal' in that the latter has his starting point in a familiar dramatic type. As his name suggests, Parolles (French, *paroles*: words) is a man who is all words and no deeds, a *poseur* whose deficiencies

---

8. For a discussion of the ancestry of this tale see W. W. Lawrence (1931), *op.cit.*, pp. 62–3.
9. Examples of Tudor plays on this theme include John Phillip's *Patient and Meek Grissil* (1558–61) and the collaborative *Patient Grissil* (Chettle, Dekker and Haughton: 1600) The motif is discussed by W. W. Lawrence (1931), *op. cit.*, pp. 57–8.
10. See G. Bullough (1957–75), vol. II, p. 376.
11. The device is used, for example, in Ser Giovanni Fiorentino's *Il Pecorone* whence it is transferred to *The Merchant of Venice*.

(particularly in the military sphere) are revealed in the course of the play. The figure looks back through numerous intermediaries to the *Miles Gloriosus* of Plautus (and ultimately the *alazon* or braggart of Greek comedy), and appeared in a variety of contexts on the Tudor and Stuart stage.[12] By adding this secondary plot motif to the material derived from the *Decameron* Shakespeare effects a considerable shift in the focus of interest. Whereas Boccaccio's story is concerned with the means by which a deserving young woman secures the husband of her choice, and ultimately wins his respect, *All's Well* places the husband between two contenders for his loyalty, his worthless but seemingly honourable friend, and his worthy but superficially ignoble (in the sense of base born) lady.

The addition of the Parolles plot to the Bertram/Helena situation sustains, rather than violates, the folk tale aura of the structure in that it too draws on conventional material, inviting comparison with other literary works. Shakespeare's second departure from his source, however, is of a far more radical kind. Where Boccaccio maintains the distance between the romance environment in which his story is set and the day-to-day lives of his readers, Shakespeare reduces that distance by a succession of 'alterations' that enhance the credibility of events. Rather than being type figures – the witty wench, the noble husband, the ailing king, etc. – the characters of the play are fully fledged individuals whose conduct within the inherited plot is psychologically motivated. Bertram's extreme youth, for example, is stressed from the outset of the action (cf.I.i.66–8) and his lack of knowledge of the world provides an explanation (if not a justification) for his successive acts of misconduct. His repudiation of the bride assigned to him by the King is symptomatic of an immature concern with status and rank; his decision to fly to the wars is a product of youthful impetuosity and desire for glory; while his infatuation with Diana and ready deception by the bed trick spring from his inexperience in the sexual sphere. Similarly, Helena is not simply a capable and determined young woman intent on achieving her marital goals, but a complex character whose actions and attitudes are shaped by

12. The figure of Fynlaw of the Fute Band in Sir David Lindsay's *Ane Satire of the Thrie Estaitis* (1540–54) and Ralph Roister Doister in Nicholas Udall's play of the same name (1545–52) are typical sixteenth-century examples of the type.

events. Having succeeded in her original objective, she is shocked
by the discovery that in becoming Bertram's wife she has effectively banished him from his home (cf.III.ii.44–129), and her
decision to 'steal away' (III.ii.129) rather than be the cause of his
exile is indicative of a desire to resolve her difficulties not through
self-assertion, as in the past, but by self-abnegation (cf.III.iv.4–17).
The King, too, departs from the stereotypical role enacted in the
source. Rather than grudgingly fulfilling the obligations into which
he has entered, he recognizes the inherent worth of the woman
who has saved his life, and displays an unexpected broadminded-
ness in the lecture he delivers to Bertram on the relationship
between honour and rank (cf.II.iii.117–44).

The social structure in which these creations are placed by the
dramatist also represents, in its scope and variety, a significant
departure from the source. The husband figure is supplied with a
mother, who far from repudiating in conventional fashion a
socially inappropriate match, displays a surprising warmth and
generosity, embracing her daughter-in-law for her virtue, and
repudiating her delinquent son. This lady's household includes a
clown, who broadens the social spectrum that the play presents,
while Bertram has a number of male friends whose activities
furnish a context for his martial and amatory exploits. At the same
time, the idiom assigned to the dramatis personae contributes to
the creation of a much more familiar world than that of the source.
The scenes in which the clown is involved, for example, are bawdy
and colloquial (cf.I.iii.1–93), while the unmasking of Parolles is
conducted in everyday speech, cf.:

> *First Sold[ier]*. [*Reads*] *First, demand of him, how many horse the duke is*
> *strong*. What say you to that?
> *Par[olles]*. Five or six thousand; but very weak and unserviceable: the
> troops are all scattered and the commanders very poor rogues, upon
> my reputation and credit – and as I hope to live.
> *First Sold*. Shall I set down your answer so?
> *Par*. Do. I'll take the sacrament on't, how and which way you will.
> *Ber*. All's one to him. What a past-saving slave is this!
>
> (IV.iii.126–35; Arden ed.)

The incidents related by Boccaccio are also modified in order to
bring them closer to actuality. Shakespeare increases, for example,
the social disparity between his two central figures, providing

Bertram with a stronger and more convincing motive for disobeying the King's command, while he adapts the circumstances surrounding the bed trick, ironing out its more improbable aspects. Whereas in the *Decameron* a number of encounters take place between the husband and the presumed mistress, in *All's Well That Ends Well* only one meeting is arranged, heightening the likelihood of the deception remaining undetected. The consequences of the union are also more naturalistic in the Shakespearian play. Where Boccaccio's lady goes beyond her husband's demands by presenting him not with the requisite son but with a pair of twins, Helena merely conceives in the course of the action, and has still to give birth at the close of the play.

It might well appear at first glance that by accommodating the improbabilities of fiction to the realities of everyday life Shakespeare has translated the fanciful material on which his drama is based into a credible work of art, but in fact his alterations are often argued to have the reverse effect. A spectator's readiness to credit the events of a drama does not solely depend on the proximity of the action to the world of his or her own experience. Every drama operates within a set of conventions, and one element of an audience's pleasure derives from the realization of expectations raised by the form. It is not when the fiction departs from actuality, but when it violates its own conventions, that alarm bells sound in the reader's head.[13] Here it is the tension that Shakespeare sets up between the events of folk tale and the dramatic universe he creates that gives rise to many of the problems surrounding the play. These problems cohere, furthermore, around the substitute coupling of Act IV. Whereas the members of the audience are able to acquiesce in Boccaccio's never-never-land version of events, they resist the Shakespearian deception because of the moral issues that it raises in the world of flesh and blood. It is thus not the inherent incredibility of the inherited tale that is the source of the

---

13. A useful comparison may be drawn here with a modern popular literary form. Few devotees of detective fiction have themselves encountered a corpse, but they happily accept that certain elderly ladies and peers of the realm stumble on bodies at every turn and will expose the causes of their ends with ruthless logic. Though it might be closer to the harsh realities of police work if Lord Peter Wimsey or Miss Marple summoned the press at the end of a case to announce the failure of his or her enquiries, the reader would find the plot of the novel a disappointment, and experience an uncomfortable tension in the fiction between an exercise in deduction, and a species of documentary.

difficulty in *All's Well* but the strain that the structure exhibits between the elements which the dramatist retains and that which he 'altereth and changeth'.

It is important to note at this point that though the moral concern experienced by the audience is most acute in Act IV, it is not exclusive to this phase of the play. Unlike Boccaccio's story, which is firmly focused on the means by which a resolute young woman achieves a husband, *All's Well* involves the spectator from the outset in the moral health of the social group. A clear opposition is set up at the start of the action between an old, nobler, order and a present, fallen, condition. Two father-figures are newly dead when the play opens – the Count of Rossillion, Bertram's father, who is described as the epitome of honour (cf.I.ii.30–48), and Gerard de Narbon, Helena's father, a physician of unrivalled probity and skill (cf.I.i.16–20). These figures are mourned by contemporaries who are themselves worn by age, and aware of the deficiencies of the younger generation. The King is dying of a fistula, and is conscious of the limitations of 'these younger times' (I.ii.46), while Bertram's mother is a widow, concerned for her 'unseason'd' son (I.i.67). The sense of decay surrounding the court of the dying King is paralleled in the Countess's household through the presence of the Clown, Lavatch, a 'shrewd' and 'unhappy' knave (IV.v.60), who was once a favourite with the former Count. Though the principal representatives of the younger generation set out with high ideals – Bertram to emulate his father, and Helena to win a husband by desert – they fail in their immediate objectives, further tarnishing the tarnished times. The choices that Bertram makes are invariably misguided, functioning as a parody of his father's conduct. Where the late Count was 'discipled of the bravest' (I.ii.28), Bertram makes a companion of Parolles, a boastful coward prepared to betray his comrades, while the older man's magnanimity towards inferiors (I.ii.41–5) is overturned in his son's contempt for the low-born Helena, and readiness to seduce Diana. Similarly, though Helena's motives are positive, her actions do not lead to the universal recognition of her worth, nor do they promote right conduct in others. Her decision to win Bertram by healing the King is morally questionable, not least because it involves using the gifts inherited from her father for personal gain rather than altruistic purposes, while the reward that she claims for her services is the immediate cause of her husband's flight to Florence, and his increased dependence upon Parolles.

The moral implications of the characters' actions are also discussed throughout the drama, inviting the audience to reflect on the issues that are raised. The Countess and the King, for example, both reflect on the relationship between status and worth (cf.I.i.35–42 and II.iii.117–44), while the young Lords, the King, Lafew, and the Countess all explore aspects of Bertram's guilt (cf.IV.iii.1–35 and V.iii.1–27). At the same time the language of the play is redolent with moral and theological implications. The Clown, for example, asks the Countess's permission to marry, not in conventional romantic terminology, but with reference to man's sinful nature, cf.:

> I have been, madam, a wicked creature, as you and all flesh and blood are, and indeed I do marry that I may repent:
>
> (I.iii.33–5; Arden ed.)

while Bertram's friends, rather than being amused by his conduct, see it as symptomatic of human frailty:

> *Second Lord.* I will tell you a thing, but you shall let it dwell darkly with you.
> *First Lord.* When you have spoken it 'tis dead, and I am the grave of it.
> *Second Lord.* He hath perverted a young gentlewoman here in Florence, of a most chaste renown, and this night he fleshes his will in the spoil of her honour; he hath given her his monumental ring, and thinks himself made in the unchaste composition.
> *First Lord.* Now, God delay our rebellion! As we are ourselves, what things are we!
> *Second Lord.* Merely our own traitors. And as in the common course of all treasons we still see them reveal themselves till they attain to their abhorr'd ends; so he that in this action contrives against his own nobility, in his proper stream o'erflows himself.
>
> (IV.iii.9–24; Arden ed.)

The moral emphasis of the drama and fallen condition of the play world are most apparent, furthermore, at those points of the action at which the folk tale elements of the plot lie closest to the surface. The first half of the play, for example, moves towards the accomplishment of the miraculous cure, and the virtuous maiden's repudiation by her chosen husband. The healing of a king is traditionally associated with the renewal of a sick society through the exemplary virtue of one of its members, and is evocative of a universe in which miracles are possible, and stainless conduct an actuality. Boccaccio's story, drawing on this tradition, demonstrates the heroine's worth in two respects. She first displays her resourcefulness in restoring the King to health and then her patience and good judgement, on being repudiated by her husband, in returning to his estates and managing them effectively in his absence. In Shakespeare's version of the story, though the cure is effected and the King, who recognizes Helena's virtue, has every expectation that the fairy tale outcome of the situation will be achieved, the moral health of the community is further impaired through the conduct of Bertram. Not only does he refuse the wife assigned for him like his Decameronian predecessor, but he also fails in obedience as both a subject and a ward, entering a species of moral no-man's-land in that his subsequent exploits on the battlefield are not sanctioned by the King. Shakespeare's additions to his source, moreover, are crucial at this point. By giving Rossillion an alternative mistress in the shape of Bertram's mother, he deprives Helena of a second arena in which to demonstrate her virtue, while by assigning Bertram a friend in the form of Parolles, he displays the former's want of judgement in preferring a worthless companion to a worthy wife.

The process of subversion at work here in the treatment of the inherited plot is also evident in the second half of the play in the incidents leading up to and consequent on the bed trick. In the *Decameron*, the events surrounding the substitution are presented entirely from the wife's point of view, shielding the husband from adverse judgement. His interest in another woman is seen merely as the means through which his conditions for acknowledging the marriage are fulfilled, while her deception is unequivocally successful, leading to the birth of twins and the recognition of her value. In *All's Well That Ends Well*, by contrast, Bertram's attempted seduction of Diana is much more fully developed. The propriety of his conduct is commented upon by a number of characters (the Widow, Diana, the Lords, Parolles, etc.) and is universally regarded as dishonourable. His prosecution of the courtship is witnessed by the audience (cf.IV.ii.*passim*) and demeans him in the spectator's eyes, while the obtaining of the ring from his finger is charged with moral significance. Whereas in the romance the token that the lady requires in exchange for her maidenhead is merely an ornament that the count prized, in the play it is a family heirloom, symbolic of the honour passed from father to son. The exchange of Helena for Diana in *All's Well* thus has very different connotations from the substitution of Giletta for the gentlewoman's daughter in the *Decameron*. Unlike Boccaccio's heroine, who resolves a species of conundrum, demonstrating her resourcefulness for a third time, Shakespeare's salvages her husband's virtue, preserving his marital chastity, and subverting his intention of debauching an innocent and vulnerable young woman.

The final phase of the action also involves a process that runs counter to the inherited tale. Whereas in the *Decameron* the lady presents herself humbly before her husband, recounts what has passed between them, and sues for recognition as his wife, in *All's Well* attention remains focused on the husband, with the revelation of his sexual adventures leading to a further exhibition of vice. Rather than acknowledging his courtship of Diana, Bertram initially rejects her outright, before seeking to discredit her testimony by claiming that she is a strumpet (cf. V.iii.164–218). His lies and evasions lose him the esteem of his elders (cf. V.iii.175–6), bearing witness, once again, to the gulf between older and younger generations. Though the revelation of the bed trick relieves him of some measure of culpability, it does not enhance his moral status, offering him an escape route from guilt, rather than an opportunity, as in the source, to match virtue with magnanimity.

It will be evident from this necessarily brief outline of the moral loading of the Shakespearian play, that though the dramatist has retained the folk tale motifs around which *Decameron* III ix is structured, he has employed them for markedly different ends. Boccaccio's story operates in a world in which right action leads to reward, and the virtuous, though they may be tried, live happily ever after. In *All's Well*, by contrast, though the King and Countess look back to this older order, the universe in which the action is set is not inevitably conducive to virtue. Since the folk tale elements of the action are evocative of traditional codes of behaviour, they generate expectations in the audience which the characters fail to fulfil. The gulf between the potentialities encoded within the plot and the actualities that the drama enacts thus becomes a measure for the spectator of the distance between an ideal world and the real one, or between the universe inhabited by the late Count Rossillion and that represented by his son. The unease surrounding the bed trick is thus not simply a product of its inherent shabbiness or incredibility. The spectator experiences a sense of disquiet, not because the device is improbable, or distasteful, but because it derives from a different perspective on, or interpretation of, experience from that afforded by the play world. At the same time, this interplay between modes has wider implications. Not only is Bertram's failure to conform to the expectations of folk talk a measure of his own degeneracy, but that degeneracy, in turn, sullies the procedures of romance. Helena's substitution of herself for Diana salvages her husband's honour in the technical sense, but it also involves the conscious manipulation of others, raising uncomfortable questions for the audience in relation to the relative worth of husband and wife. In weighing the rightness of the characters' behaviour against the value systems of an implied ideal, the members of the audience are plunged, like the dramatis personae, into attempting to formulate judgements in an imperfect world. They experience the seaminess into which Helena finds herself drawn by her pursuit of Bertram, and participate in a process of evaluation in which a deception for honourable ends must be preferred to a dishonourable design.

As noted above, there is considerable evidence to suggest that both *All's Well That Ends Well* and *Measure for Measure* were composed during the period 1603–04, and the two plays undoubtedly have much in common. Just as the events of the former betray their romance origins by their distance from daily life, so the plot of *Measure for Measure* makes little contact with the experience of the seventeenth- or twentieth-century spectator. A ruler, having neglected the responsibilities of his position, delegates his office to a man of seeming probity in order that the rule of law should be restored, disguising himself as a friar to observe the outcome of events. Though intellectually committed to right conduct, the deputy finds himself attracted to a young woman who has come to him to plead for her brother's life, and he proposes the exchange of her virginity for her brother's release. Through the Duke's agency, the deputy's betrothed takes the lady's place, but though he fully believes that the sexual ransom has been paid he persists with the execution, obliging the Duke to devise a second stratagem – the substitution of the head of a dead prisoner for that of the threatened man. At the close of the play the full course of the deputy's conduct is finally exposed, and he is obliged to marry the woman he has unwittingly embraced.

Although, like the events of *All's Well*, these are patently not the kind of happenings that take place in the real world, they are set, once again, in a universe that is not an immeasurable distance from that to which the members of the audience belong. As in the earlier play, the characters are drawn from a wide spectrum of society, with heads of state rubbing shoulders with pimps and prostitutes, degenerates and fools. At the same time, like its predecessor, the play places considerable emphasis upon the less savoury aspects of human existence. Just as the means by which Helena secures a husband in *All's Well* robs their relationship of romance, while Bertram is engaged in seduction and makes a boon companion of a cheat, so the characters of *Measure for Measure* are enmeshed by their sexual drives, and function against a backdrop of prostitution. The idiom of the later play, like that of the earlier one, is frequently close to natural speech (cf.II.i.41–134 and IV.iii.1–62), while the action is set in everyday locations such as the prison or the street. Both plays, in short, deploy folk tale motifs in a context that is anti-romantic and familiar, setting up a tension between the actions the characters perform and the environment in which they are required to perform them.

The similarities that the two comedies exhibit are not, further-more, restricted to the clash which they exhibit between the archetypal and the everyday. The action of both plays is set in a universe that is in some sense a fallen one. Just as *All's Well* begins in mourning and proceeds to the court of a dying king, exploring the experience of a generation who are a source of disappointment to their elders and seem incapable of revitalizing their world, so *Measure for Measure* is set in a city that has fallen into corruption, where sexual laxity is pervasive, and the most self-disciplined fall victim to the vices of the flesh, augmenting the evils of their world rather than purging them. Angelo, in whom the Duke's authority and the moral health of the state are vested (cf.Bertram's role as the repository of his family's honour) seeks to corrupt an innocent young woman; Isabella is obliged to engage, like Helena, in an unpleasant deception; while Mariana in her moated grange seems fated to remain (cf.Helena) a virgin wife. The theological reso-nances of the two plays are also inescapable. The healing of the King in *All's Well* is saluted as a miracle (cf.II.iii.1–38), while the reclamation of Bertram is achieved through self-surrender and by way of a pilgrimage (cf.III.iv.4–17). Similarly, the very title of *Measure for Measure* invites an association with Christian teaching (cf.*Matthew*, chapter VII verse ii), while the names assigned to the characters (e.g. Angelo, Lucio) enforce an awareness of the play's metaphysical dimensions. Both dramas, moreover, are overtly concerned with the exploration of abstract ideas ('honour' in *All's Well*, 'justice' in *Measure for Measure*), while both expose man's failure to live up to his pretensions. Bertram, setting out to win honour, returns home to be publicly shamed, while Angelo, seeking to enforce absolute justice, is convicted of a gross abuse of the law. Even the language of the two plays affirms the intimacy of their relationship. Both range from the cerebral (cf.*All's Well*, II.iii.117–44 and *Measure for Measure*, II.ii.91–100) to the highly colloquial (cf.*All's Well*, I.iii.40–53 and *Measure for Measure*, II.i.41–107), while images of disease and animality abound (cf.*All's Well*, IV.iii.244–55 and *Measure for Measure*, I.ii.116–22). The amorous adventures of Bertram and Angelo are not isolated points of contact, in short, between otherwise unrelated works. They constitute the most striking instances of a similarity that invades every aspect of the two structures.

Though the resemblances between the two plays are too extensive to admit the possibility that Shakespeare did not have the earlier work in mind when the later was composed, it is important to reiterate at this point that the two dramas draw on wholly different sources and folk tale traditions. *All's Well* derives, as noted above, from the *Decameron* and the tale of seeming impossibilities, in this case the task of becoming pregnant by an alienated husband and obtaining a ring that he wears on his finger. The bed trick functions in this context as the vehicle through which the apparently unobtainable goal is achieved, and its success acts as an indicator of the resilience and worth of the central figure. *Measure for Measure*, by contrast, looks back through Whetstone's *Promos and Cassandra* (1578) to Cinthio's *Hecatommithi* (1565)[14] and belongs to the tradition of the 'monstrous ransom' – in this instance the exchange of the heroine's virginity for her brother's life. The bed

14. For a full discussion of the sources of the play see M. Lascelles (1953) *Shakespeare's* Measure for Measure, The Athlone Press, pp. 6–42; K. Muir (1957) *Shakespeare's Sources*, Methuen, vol I., pp. 101–9; and G. Bullough (1957–75), vol II., pp. 399–417.

trick functions in this convention not as a triumphant exhibition of ingenuity but as a means of evasion, and is designed to foil the deceived lover rather than win his approbation. The substitute bed-mate motif is interwoven, moreover, in the Shakespearian play, with a second folk tale device that has no place in Cinthio's story – the return of a disguised ruler to succour his people. Whereas in *All's Well That Ends Well* it is the forsaken lady who instigates the exchange of partners, in *Measure for Measure* it is the Duke, in his guise as the friar, who instigates the stratagem, shifting the emphasis away from the resourcefulness of the 'witty wench' to the restoration of order through rightful authority. For all the similarities between the two dramas which enfold them, the bedchambers of Florence and Vienna are thus arrived at by different routes, and the encounters that take place in their obscurity carry very different meanings.

The action of *All's Well That Ends Well* centres upon the business of gaining a husband. Helena's love for Bertram is established at the outset, and her healing of the King and exchange of places with Diana are stages towards the accomplishment of her marriage. *Measure for Measure*, by contrast (unusually for Shakespeare) is not concerned with the process of pairing. The central action of the play turns upon the Duke's attempt to restore order in Vienna, and his related testing of his deputy, and the sexual relationships that are presented in the course of the drama are of interest only in relation to these concerns. The impulse behind the action is not the individual's desire for self-fulfilment, but the civic necessity to grapple with vice, and it is this imperative, rather than his eligibility as a husband, that places the morally upright Angelo at the centre of the play's events. Similarly the love between Claudio and Juliet emerges as a focus of attention not because of its inherent worth as a human value but because it initiates successive violations of the law, while the marriages that take place at the close of the play are sentences imposed by the Duke rather than goals pursued by the parties throughout. Moreover, where *All's Well That Ends Well* sets the task of securing a husband against the background of a fallen world, *Measure for Measure* reverses these priorities, exploring the social and moral dilemmas to which the sexual appetite gives rise. The parallel sexual offences of Claudio with Juliet, Angelo with Isabella, and Lucio with Kate Keepdown illustrate the inequity of a law against 'fornication', while the blackmail of

Isabella by Angelo exhibits the susceptibility of the most self-disciplined to vice. Thus, whereas at the close of *All's Well* it is the reclamation of the individual (Bertram) which is of primary interest, in *Measure for Measure* the judgement of Angelo is subsumed into the larger problem of administering justice in an imperfect world.

The characters involved in the substitute couplings are also less similar than might appear at first sight. Considered in the abstract the dramatis personae of the two plays have much in common. All four (Bertram and Helena, Angelo and Isabella) set off in pursuit of theoretically laudable objectives, only to fall victim to their own passions, and to discover the compromising nature of human action. Bertram, pursuing the honour appropriate to his rank, finds himself drawn into a sequence of highly ignoble acts (disobedience, fornication, perjury), while Angelo, seeking to administer absolute justice, descends to blackmail and projected rape. Similarly, Helena, attempting to win a husband by desert, becomes a cause of Bertram's downward progress, while Isabella, having elected a life of sanctity, finds herself pleading for incontinence, and conniving at deception. Nevertheless, for all their similarities, the characters of the two plays do not simply duplicate one another. Bertram is presented from the outset as a very young man deprived of parental guidance by the death of his father, and then of the King's guardianship by his flight from the court. Though the resentment that he exhibits at having a wife assigned to him betrays want of judgement, it is not entirely unsympathetic, while his repudiation of marriage with a social inferior (though motivated by snobbery) is not unnatural in one of his rank. His decision to go to the wars rather than acknowledge his marriage consequently emerges as a product of youthful misjudgement, and the courage that he exhibits on the battlefield contributes to the image of juvenile impetuosity. Though his subsequent attempt to seduce Diana is clearly culpable, it is seen by his fellow lords as typical of the failings of humanity, rather than as an idiosyncratic deviation from virtue (cf.IV.iii.18–26), while his conduct is made explicable by his enhanced dependence on Parolles following his divorce from the moral authority of the King. The play thus traces the comprehensible slide from virtue of a not ill-intentioned young man, and though his final shifts and evasions are contemptible, they largely serve to damage himself, rather than endangering the social group.

Helena, too, for all the 'miracle' that she performs in healing the King, is presented as an erring human being with very earthly objectives. Her aim is to win and then reclaim the husband of her choice, and the means by which she achieves that goal exhibit the difficulty of acting rightly in a fallen world. Her pursuit of Bertram regardless of his own wishes contributes, as noted above, to his moral decline, while both she and the Widow are conscious of the dubious morality of her plans in relation to Diana (cf.III.vii.1–7 and 44–7). Notwithstanding the religious imagery surrounding the cure performed in Act II, or the self-abnegating nature of the pilgrimage that brings her to Florence, her motives throughout are wholly mundane. It is towards marriage with Bertram that her energies are directed – and at the close she is expecting his child.

The central characters of *Measure for Measure*, by contrast, are presented in much more absolute terms. Angelo is not merely well intentioned, like Bertram, he is a man of achieved virtue, whose self-discipline (cf.I.iv.57–61) and abstinence from vice (cf.I.iii.12) qualify him to govern Vienna in the Duke's absence. Moreover, the objective to which he has dedicated himself is as absolute as his nature. Where Bertram pursues a private virtue, Angelo seeks to cleanse a corrupt society through the unflinching administration of the penal code. Presented with a plea for mercy, he rejects any species of clemency, convinced that the ultimate well-being of the individual and the moral health of the community depend upon a strict adherence to the letter of the law:

> Isab[ella].   Yet show some pity.
> Ang. I show it most of all when I show justice;
>   For then I pity those I do not know,
>   Which a dismiss'd offence would after gall,
>   And do him right that, answering one foul wrong,
>   Lives not to act another.
>
> (II.ii.100–5)

Similarly, Isabella is not simply a strong-minded, positively motivated young woman like Helena – she is much more zealous crusader for right action. Unlike her more wordly predecessor who seeks a physical union, Isabella has renounced the world for the service of God, and is to become the bride, not of an earthly husband, but of Christ. Indeed, the degree of her spiritual

aspiration is such that she regrets that the order she is entering is
not more rigorous in its restraints:

> *Isab.* And have you nuns no farther privileges?
> *Nun.* Are not these large enough?
> *Isab.* Yes, truly; I speak not as desiring more,
> But rather wishing a more strict restraint
> Upon the sisters stood, the votarists of Saint Clare.
> (I.iv. 1–5)

The broader social concerns of the later play and the more
absolute nature of its protagonists have a significant impact upon
the meaning of the events leading up to and flowing from the bed
trick. Bertram's solicitation of Diana in *All's Well* constitutes one
stage in a step-by-step progress from honour which is initiated in
Act II and completed in the final scene. Angelo's passion for
Isabella, by contrast, represents a total reversal of his former
attitudes, and his decision to blackmail her into his bed is a decisive
one that determines his conduct throughout the remainder of the
play. Confronted by an overwhelming temptation, he plummets
from exemplary virtue to absolute vice, and his subsequent actions
are uniformly base. Where Bertram's experience may be described
as a mingled yarn (his seduction of 'Diana', for example, is
complemented by a growth of understanding in relation to Parolles), Angelo see-saws between moral extremes, and his nocturnal
encounter with 'Isabella' is a pivotal point in this experience. The
extreme nature of this reversal is indicated, moreover, by the
responses that it elicits from those around him. Whereas Bertram's
solicitation of Diana is seen as symptomatic of human frailty, and
its everyday nature is implicit in Helena's quickness to grasp the
situation (cf.III.v.63–70), Angelo's advances to Isabella are highly
aberrant, and are met with incomprehension (cf.III.iv.40–75) and
incredulity (cf.II.iv.113–46).

The difference in gravity between the two seductions (and thus
in the significance of their circumvention) is also indicated by the
means by which the would-be seducers pursue their goals. Though
Bertram's suit is an adulterous one given his previous marriage to
Helena, his courtship of Diana is conventional in that he serenades
her outside her window (cf.III.vii.39–43), sends her love letters
and tokens (cf.III.vi.108–112), and seeks to persuade her of the
enduring nature of his love (cf.IV.ii.15–17). The following

exchange is typical of the terms in which the courtship is conducted:

> *Ber.*   I love thee
>   By love's own sweet constraint, and will ever
>   Do thee all rights of service.
> *Dia.*   Ay, so you serve us
>   Till we serve you; but when you have our roses,
>   You barely leave our thorns to prick ourselves,
>   And mock us for our bareness.
> ....
> *Ber.* Be not so holy-cruel; love is holy;
>   And my integrity ne'er knew the crafts
>   That you do charge men with. Stand no more off,
>   But give thyself unto my sick desires,
>   Who then recovers. Say thou art mine, and ever
>   My love as it begins shall so persever.
>
> (IV.ii.15–37)

The phraseology Bertram employs here is drawn from the language of Petrarchan love, and serves to locate his suit in an amatory context, albeit for the listeners a debased one. The terms in which Angelo addresses Isabella, by contrast, carry radically different associations. Where Bertram seeks to seduce, Angelo is engaged in blackmail, and he makes no attempt to disguise his lust with a colouring of romantic love. Where his predecessor sees himself engaged upon an amorous adventure, Angelo is keenly aware that he desires to ravish and exploit, and is racked by the perception that his conduct is sinful in the extreme. The violence and harshness of his language is in striking contrast to the kind of vocabulary employed by Bertram, and is indicative of the far greater degree of moral depravity involved in the sexual encounters of the later play:

> *Ang.* What's this? What's this? Is this her fault, or mine?
>   The tempter, or the tempted, who sins most, ha?
>   Not she; nor doth she tempt; but it is I
>   That, lying by the violet in the sun,
>   Do as the carrion does, not as the flower,
>   Corrupt with virtuous season. Can it be
>   That modesty may more betray our sense
>   Than woman's lightness? Having waste ground enough,

Shall we desire to raze the sanctuary
And pitch our evils there? O fie, fie, fie!

(II.ii.163–72)

The heightened gravity of the context in which the later
exchange of bed mates is set is also indicated by the differences in
the situations of the women involved. Though neither Diana nor
Isabella is naturally inclined to wantonness, the latter's rejection of
sexuality is of a far more extreme kind than the former's. Diana (as
her name implies) is a lady of chaste disposition, who recognizes
the spiritual significance of physical purity (cf.IV.ii.21–9), but she
has not wholly renounced sexual relationships. Helena promises to
augment her dowry in return for her part in outwitting Bertram
(cf.III.vii.34–6), while the King makes a similar offer at the close
of the play, inviting her to make choice of a husband
(cf.V.iii.321–2). Isabella, by contrast, is a postulant, engaged in
entering a cloistered order. In enforcing her sexual surrender,
Angelo is not merely violating her physical being, but despoiling
that which has been dedicated to God, and the terms in which he
reflects on his conduct reveal his awareness of the spiritual implications of his actions (cf.II.ii.170–5). The seriousness of his offence
is compounded, moreover, by the seeming isolation, and consequent vulnerability, of the woman whose virtue he assails. Diana
is wooed by a man from a different country, an outsider in her
society, who has no direct influence over her own life, or over the
lives of those she loves. She is supported by the good counsel of
Mariana (cf.III.v.10–28), and by the advice of her mother, whose
virtue is attested by the pilgrims who direct one another to her
house (cf.III.v.30–1). She herself is aware that Bertram is already
married, and she has neither motive nor imperative for consenting
to his lust. Her agreement to the bed trick is not constrained,
therefore, by her situation, but is promoted solely by her desire to
be of service to another woman. Isabella's position is very different.
Her virtue is attempted not by a man outside her society but by
the acting head of state, and her brother's safety is dependent upon
the decision that she makes. Claudio himself has been arrested for
fornication, and the friend who urges her to plead for him is noted
for his licentiousness rather than his virtue. Unlike Diana's mother
who is wholly committed to the maintenance of the family honour,
Claudio wavers from his initial rejection of Angelo's terms for his

release and ultimately pleads with his sister to accept them (cf.III.i.114–150). Since both civil and judicial authority are vested in her would-be seducer, Isabella has no access to any public support or means of redress, and is incapable of extricating herself from her situation until the disguised Duke intervenes. The danger represented by the unwanted solicitation is thus far greater in the later play, generating a much deeper level of anxiety among those both inside and outside the play world.

The repercussions of the attempted seduction are also more far-reaching in the later version of the inherited tale. Bertram is a private individual, and the consequences of his attempt on Diana are personal ones that the play defines in terms of 'honour'. In attempting to corrupt a virtuous young woman he is undermining the probity of his house, while threatening to deprive a marriageable lady of the virginal condition on which her role in society depends. Angelo, by contrast, is a public figure, responsible for civil order, and entrusted with the moral health of the social group. In seeking to blackmail Isabella he engages not merely in tarnishing his own and another's honour, but in abusing the office that he holds, substituting tyranny for lawful government, inequity for justice, and actively promoting vice rather than curbing it. Isabella's response to his proposal is highly significant in relation to this final point. For all her spiritual aspirations, once the deputy's conditions come home to her she abandons her own moral stance, turning Angelo's own weapons against him by responding to blackmail with blackmail:

> Ha? Little honour, to be much believ'd,
> And most pernicious purpose! Seeming, seeming!
> I will proclaim thee, Angelo, look for't.
> Sign me a present pardon for my brother,
> Or with an outstretch'd throat I'll tell the world aloud
> What man thou art.

> (II.iv.148–53)

Similarly, Claudio descends rapidly down the moral ladder when told of the price of his freedom, urging his sister to comply with Angelo's demands (cf.III.i.109–35). His conduct, in turn, drives Isabella still further from the Christian ideal, her shock and anger at his behaviour causing her to question her mother's honour and to repudiate her brother in highly uncharitable terms:

What should I think?
Heaven shield my mother play'd my father fair:
For such a warped slip of wilderness
Ne'er issued from his blood. Take my defiance,
Die, perish! Might but my bending down
Reprieve thee from thy fate, it should proceed.
I'll pray a thousand prayers for thy death;
No word to save thee.

(III.i.139–46)

Angelo's conduct when the ransom has supposedly been paid contributes, furthermore, to this escalation of vice. Rather than keeping his side of the bargain by ordering Claudio's release, he persists with the execution, adding perjury and judicial murder (in intention, if not effect) to blackmail and rape, and instigating the further deceptions of the later acts.

The sexual substitutions lying at the heart of *All's Well That Ends Well* and *Measure for Measure* are thus set in distinct dramatic contexts, and they consequently carry very different meanings in relation to the dramas that enfold them. Bertram's encounter with the woman whom he believes to be Diana constitutes a further step in his downward progress, but it also represents a movement towards the restoration of social harmony. Helena consciously directs his misplaced desires towards a legitimate end, while his lust supplies the means through which the 'impossibilities' that he propounded may be fulfilled. Diana herself is never seriously threatened, while Helena secures a husband, and Bertram is saved from an action that would have discredited himself and his name. The impulse behind the substitution is ultimately therefore a comic one. A wrong is set right, and the members of the audience while deploring Bertram's conduct may be amused, on one level, by his deception. At the same time, the numerous suggestions that a divine power is at work in the play world help to convince the spectator that the bed trick was 'meant'. Helena's healing of the King is hailed as a miracle, while the chance encounter with the Widow that leads to the frustration of Bertram's designs occurs at the end of a pilgrimage. In short, seedy though it may appear at first glance, substitute coupling in this play is an instrument of renewal, functioning as an appropriately tarnished agent of reclamation in a fallen world.

In *Measure for Measure*, by contrast, Angelo's assignation with

Isabella constitutes the turning point of what might be termed a hypothetical tragedy. Though the members of the audience are aware of the Duke's device to subvert the monstrosity of the bargain, for Angelo the ravishing of Isabella is an actuality not a fiction, and it has terrible repercussions for both the deputy himself and those whose lives he controls. Whereas Bertram believes that he has had a pleasurable adventure with a marriageable woman, and gives no further thought to the affair until confronted with the lady in the final scene, Angelo is convinced that he has violated a novice, and is driven by fear of the consequences to renege on his agreement, and persist with Claudio's execution. Unlike *All's Well*, in which a single substitution is sufficient to resolve Diana's dilemma and satisfy Bertram's conditions, in *Measure for Measure* a second is needed (Ragozine's head for Claudio's) suggesting the escalation of evil from the initial deed. For Isabella, too, the consequences flowing from her attempt to intercede on behalf of her brother are terrifyingly real. For her, ignorant of the Duke's presence, the destruction of justice consequent upon the deputy's lapse from virtue is a continuing condition for which the bed trick offers only a local remedy, while unlike Helena who is secure in the success of her stratagem, she is obliged to come to terms with the knowledge that the device through which she preserves her virginity is ineffectual in saving her brother's life (cf.IV.iii.110–20).

The addition of the disguised ruler motif to the tale of the monstrous bargain also contributes to the darker implications of the later play. In *All's Well That Ends Well* it is the heroine of the tale of impossibilities who proposes the nocturnal exchange, whereas in *Measure for Measure* the threatened lady has no means of extricating herself from her situation and believes herself to be faced with an insoluble dilemma. The remedy in this instance lies in the hands of another, and but for the Duke's intervention as the Friar the choices faced by brother and sister were equally unacceptable. The movement from hypothetical tragedy to comedy is thus much more arbitrary in the later play in that the means by which the resolution of the action is arrived at is dependent upon a set of circumstances (the Duke's decision to observe his deputy) independent of the sequence of events through which the difficulties faced by the dramatis personae arose. At the same time, substitute coupling does not in itself constitute the mechanism through which social reconciliation takes place. Though it supplies a solution for a specific problem it leads to a further eruption of vice, and it is only the Duke's reappearance that permits the restoration of order within the state. The reimposition of rightful authority through an external agency suggests the heightened degree of difficulty with which man's negative impulses are controlled in the later work, with the events that take place in Angelo's bedchamber functioning as a measure of the deputy's depravity rather than as an instrument of his reclamation.

It is not merely their relative gravity, however, that distinguishes the sexual exchanges of the two plays, they are also differentiated by the meanings that they carry in relation to the 'problems' that are posed. *All's Well That Ends Well*, as noted above, is structured around varieties of honour, and Bertram's supposed seduction of Diana supplies an index to his decline from the values of his house. The substitution of Helena for Diana rescues him from an action that is demeaning to himself and damaging to another, while allowing him to experience transgression without bearing the burden of an enduring guilt. *Measure for Measure*, by contrast, is concerned with a public, rather than a private issue – the problem of administering justice in a flawed world. Angelo's projected rape of Isabella signals his own susceptibility to the vices of the flesh, but it also identifies him with those he judges, widening the problem that the play addresses from the balance between justice and mercy in specific instances to the difficulty of assessing human failings when even the most upright are capable of sin. Here, though the exchange of Mariana for Isabella subverts one particular misuse of power, it adds to the complexities of the central issue, inviting the audience to reflect upon the precise nature of Angelo's offence, to weigh it against those of others, and to question the simple equation between crime and punishment offered by the deputy at the start of the play.

The relationship between *All's Well That Ends Well* and *Measure for Measure* is patently a close one. Both are overtly concerned with moral issues, project worlds that have fallen away from an implied ideal, and employ sexual substitution as a means of resolving their actions while complicating the ethical problems with which they deal. Nevertheless, for all their common characteristics, neither the plays as a whole nor the bed tricks on which they depend may be adduced as evidence of creative lethargy. The two works draw on different sources, and by weaving additional folk tale motifs into the fabric of an earlier composition Shakespeare has transformed the experience that it affords. Through the process of altering and changing he has turned comedy into potential tragedy, amusement into trepidation, amorous adventure into criminal activity, and a personal lapse into a social catastrophe. Though both Bertram and Angelo unwittingly embrace a wife in a physical obscurity that is emblematic of their mental states, the former's action is simultaneously a local failure and a larger success, while the latter's is a violation and a desperate expediency. The gnomic utterances with which the two incidents are heralded gives some indication of the numerous potentialities and moral complexities inhabiting for the dramatist this most unlikely of inherited tales:

> Craft against vice I must apply.
> With Angelo tonight shall lie
> His old betrothed, but despised:
> So disguise shall by th'disguised
> Pay with falsehood false exacting,
> And perform an old contracting.
> (*Measure for Measure*, III.ii.270–5)

> Let us assay our plot; which, if it speed,
> Is wicked meaning in a lawful deed,
> And lawful meaning in a lawful act,
> Where both not sin, and yet a sinful fact.
> (*All's Well That Ends Well*, III.vii.44–7)

Chapter 5

Exile

2 Henry VI. The Two Gentleman of Verona. Romeo and Juliet.
Richard II. As You Like It. King Lear. Coriolanus. Cymbeline.
The Tempest

The sentence of banishment is pronounced upon a variety of
characters in Shakespearian drama and is used as a source of plot
complication, like a number of the devices explored in previous
chapters, throughout the dramatist's career. Where scolds and
identical siblings are exclusive to the comedies, however, and
sexual disguise is gender specific, banishment spans the entire
spectrum of the corpus, and is suffered by both male and female,
young and old. Moreover, unlike some, at least, of the plot motifs
discussed elsewhere in this book, exile was not a condition remote
from the everyday lives of a Renaissance audience. Though banishment no longer forms part of the English judicial process, it was
an integral part of the legal system as late as 1829,[1] and was
invoked on a number of occasions during the political and religious
upheavals that marked the Plantagenet and Tudor eras. Richard II,
for example, banished both disaffected nobles (e.g. the Earls of
Nottingham and Derby) and ecclesiastics (e.g. the Archbishop of
Canterbury), while Henry VI's chief counsellor, the Duke of
Suffolk, was murdered on his way into exile in 1450.[2] A statute

1. See J. Burke (1959) *Jowitt's Dictionary of English Law*. Sweet and Maxwell, vol. I
   s.v. Banishment, and T. E. Tomlins (1835) *The Law Dictionary*, 4th edn (2 vols),
   vol. I *s.v. Exile*.
2. These events would have been known to Shakespeare from Holinshed's
   Chronicles.

was enacted during Shakespeare's own lifetime providing for the banishment of dissentious rogues (1597), while others in 1592 and 1605 obliged Popish recusants to abjure the realm. Given the considerable interest in historical drama during the closing decades of the sixteenth century, it was inevitable that instances of banishment should find their way on to the Tudor stage, and that once established as a plot mechanism exclusion from the body politic should become an instrument of the corrupt courts of Jacobean drama. The depraved world of Webster's *The White Devil* (1612), for example, is introduced with the exclamation 'Banished!', while the horrors of *The Duchess of Malfi* (Webster: 1612–14) include the exile of the central figure.

Contemporary example and historical precedent are not the sole causes, however, of the recurrence of banishment in the Shakespearian corpus. Tales turning upon exile have formed part of the literary stock since classical times, and the romances on which Elizabethan–Jacobean dramatists drew for their plots frequently involved some species of self-imposed or involuntary exclusion. Two perspectives upon the exiled state are perceptible within this tradition. On the one hand, as in the variants of the Romeo and Juliet story, banishment represents an enforced separation from the loved one and hence a condition of loss, while on the other, as in the pastoral literature exemplified by Lodge's *Rosalynde*,[3] it points to the further impoverishment of a corrupt society, and signals a shift towards an alternative value system at one with the rhythms of nature and the simplicities of a golden age world (cf. the related Robin Hood tales).

The complex ancestry of the banishment motif is evident in Shakespeare's earliest work. The device is employed on no less than seven occasions[4] during the first phase of the dramatist's career,[5] with two of the better known examples looking back to a single source. The dating of a number of these plays is uncertain but *2 Henry VI* is undoubtedly among the the earliest of the group. The play turns upon the power struggle, occasioned by the

---

3. See below pages 133ff. The romance, first published in 1590, is the principal source of *As You Like It*.
4. Banishment plays some part in the action of *1 Henry VI*, *2 Henry VI*, *Titus Andronicus*, *Richard III*, *The Two Gentlemen of Verona*, *Romeo and Juliet* and *Richard II*.
5. That is, up to 1595–96.

weakness of Henry VI, which culminates in the communal violence known as the Wars of the Roses. In the course of the action, the Duke of Suffolk (who was responsible for arranging the King's unpopular marriage) is accused of complicity in the death of the Duke of Gloucester and consequently banished. His response to his sentence is of interest here because it is not simply developed in terms of regret for the loss of a position of power. Shakespeare drew on the chronicles of Hall and Holinshed for the historical background to the play,[6] and both writers give some indication that Suffolk was in love with the Queen. Holinshed notes, for example, that Margaret 'entirely loved' the Duke, while Hall remarks that Suffolk was the 'Quenes dearlynge'.[7] Neither chronicler develops this implication in any depth, but Shakespeare builds on the suggestion to produce a parting that has more in common with the amatory experience of romance than the drives of *realpolitik*:

> Queen. I will repeal thee, or, be well assur'd,
>   Adventure to be banished myself;
>   And banished I am, if but from thee.
>   Go; speak not to me; even now be gone.
>   O! go not yet. Even thus two friends condemn'd
>   Embrace and kiss and take ten thousand leaves,
>   Loather a hundred times to part than die.
>   Yet now farewell; and farewell life with thee.
> Suf. Thus is poor Suffolk ten times banished,
>   Once by the King, and three times thrice by thee.
>   'Tis not the land I care for, wert thou thence;
>   A wilderness is populous enough,
>   So Suffolk had thy heavenly company:
>   For where thou art, there is the world itself,
>   With every several pleasure in the world,
>   And where thou art not, desolation.
>   I can no more. Live thou to joy thy life;
>   Myself can joy in nought but that thou liv'st.
>   (III.ii. 348–65)

Here, parting from the homeland is not seen as loss of influence, but as a state of deprivation analogous to death, and it is this

6. For a more detailed account of the sources of the play, see G. Bullough (1957–75), vol. III, pp. 89–100.
7. See R. Hosley (1968) *Shakespeare's Holinshed*, G. P. Putnam's Sons, New York, p. 178, and G. Bullough 1957–75, vol. III, p. 112.

concept of banishment that is recalled in later plays. *The Two Gentlemen of Verona* (1593) and *Romeo and Juliet* (1594–96), for example, both look back to *Romeus and Juliet* (1562), a narrative poem by Arthur Brooke, but they also represent a development of the ideas explored in *2 Henry VI*. In *The Two Gentlemen of Verona* an idealistic young man (one of the 'two gentlemen' of the title) falls in love with the daughter of a ruler (variously referred to as the Emperor and the Duke) and plans a nocturnal meeting with her, to be accomplished with the help of a rope ladder (cf. II.iv. 174–9 and III.i.1–152). The project is betrayed, however, by a supposed friend, and the lover is consequently banished. The similarities with *Romeo and Juliet* here are obvious. Romeo also falls in love with a young woman from whom he is divided by a social barrier, visits her by means of a rope ladder, and is banished by an outraged prince. Moreover, although the immediate causes of their punishment differ, the central figures respond to their sentences in similar ways. Brooke's Romeus falls into a passion of grief on learning of his enforced parting from Juliet, rails against his fate, and declares that he would prefer a 'spedy death' to a life removed from his beloved (cf. 1291ff.). This last assertion may well have reminded Shakespeare of his handling of Suffolk's banishment in *2 Henry VI* in that both Valentine (*The Two Gentlemen of Verona*) and Romeo develop the proposition that separation from a loved one is a species of death:

> *Val.* And why not death, rather than living torment?
>   To die is to be banish'd from myself,
>   And Silvia is myself: banish'd from her
>   Is self from self. A deadly banishment.
>   What light is light, if Silvia be not seen?
>   What joy is joy, if Silvia be not by?
>   Unless it be to think that she is by
>   And feed upon the shadow of perfection.
>   Except I be by Silvia in the night,
>   There is no music in the nightingale.
>   Unless I look on Silvia in the day,
>   There is no day for me to look upon.
>   She is my essence, and I leave to be,
>   If I be not by her fair influence
>   Foster'd, illumin'd, cherish'd, kept alive.
>   I fly not death, to fly his deadly doom:

Tarry I here, I but attend on death,
But fly I hence, I fly away from life.
(*The Two Gentlemen of Verona*, III.i.170–87)

Compare:

Romeo. Ha! Banishment! Be merciful, say 'death'.
For exile hath more terror in his look,
Much more than death. Do not say 'banishment'.
Friar L[aurence]. Hence from Verona art thou banished.
Be patient, for the world is broad and wide.
Romeo. There is no world without Verona walls
But purgatory, torture, hell itself;
Hence 'banished' is banish'd from the world,
And world's exile is death. Then 'banished'
Is death, misterm'd. Calling death 'banished'
Thou cut'st my head off with a golden axe
And smilest upon the stroke that murders me.
Friar L. O deadly sin, O rude unthankfulness.
. . . .
This is dear mercy and thou seest it not.
Romeo. 'Tis torture and not mercy. Heaven is here
Where Juliet lives, and every cat and dog
And little mouse, every unworthy thing,
Live here in heaven and may look on her,
But Romeo may not.
. . . .
Hadst thou no poison mix'd, no sharp-ground knife,
No sudden mean of death, though ne'er so mean,
But 'banished' to kill me?
(*Romeo and Juliet*, III.iii.12–46)

For all the similarity of the views and emotions projected in these speeches, the careers of Valentine and Romeo subsequent to their exile are very different. *Romeo and Juliet* remains close to Brooke's narrative throughout, tracing a literal progress towards the grave as Romeo leaves Verona for Mantua, buys poison from an apothecary on hearing of Juliet's 'death', and returns to kill himself in the Capulet tomb. In *The Two Gentlemen of Verona*, by contrast, Shakespeare weaves elements of Brooke's poem into a structure compounded of a number of other strands – including the 'greenwood' literature popular with all classes of society in the sixteenth century.[8] Banished from the court, Valentine encounters a band of outlaws while on his way to Verona, and on being called upon to give an account of his situation, supplies himself with a history that clearly confirms his relationship with Romeo:

> 2 Out[law]. Whither travel you?
> Val. To Verona.
> 1 Out. Whence come you?
> Val. From Milan.
> 3 Out. Have you long sojourned there?
> Val. Some sixteen months, and longer might have stay'd,
>   If crooked fortune had not thwarted me.
> 1 Out. What, were you banished thence?
> Val. I was.
> 2 Out. For what offence?
> Val. For that which now torments me to rehearse:
>   I kill'd a man, whose death I much repent,
>   But yet I slew him manfully, in fight,
>   Without false vantage, or base treachery.
>
>   (IV.i.16–29)

At this point, however, the Shakespearian versions of Brooke's central figure part company. Having established that the bandits 'do no outrages / On silly women or poor passengers' (IV.i.71–2), Valentine agrees to become their chief, making 'a virtue of necessity' (IV.i.62) as the outlaws have done themselves. The life he embraces in the greenwood is only briefly evoked, but it is clearly not represented as a condition of extreme hardship. The bandits are associated through their field of reference with the world of Robin Hood (cf. 'By the bare scalp of Robin Hood's fat friar': IV.i.36), while their occupation is referred to as 'an honourable kind of thievery' (IV.i.39–40) that has yielded them 'treasure' (IV.i.75). Though Valentine continues to regret his distance from his beloved, he comes to regard his isolated existence as preferable to human society, in that it affords him an opportunity to reflect on his emotional state:

> How use doth breed a habit in a man!
> This shadowy desert, unfrequented woods,

---

8. Prose examples include Sir Philip Sidney's *Arcadia* (published 1590), while the dramatic tradition is represented by Anthony Munday's *The Downfall and Death of Robert Earl of Huntingdon* (1598).

I better brook than flourishing peopled towns:
Here I can sit alone, unseen by any,
And to the nightingale's complaining notes
Tune my distresses and record my woes.

                    (V.iv.1–6)

His association with the outlaws also allows him to control his situation in a way that was not available to him in Milan. Whereas at the Emperor's court he was dependent upon the advice of others (cf.II.iv.180–1), and blind to the deceptions taking place around him (cf.II.i.82–159 and III.i.51–169), in the greenwood he controls his forest companions, for all their lawless inclinations (cf.V.iv.13–17), and discovers the truth about his supposed friend (cf.V.iv.19–72). His former diffidence in love gives way to a new strength, and he asserts his claim to Silvia in the presence of her father, and against the man of the Duke's choice (cf.V.iv.124–9). Where for Romeo the progress into exile is a movement towards death, for Valentine the sojourn in the greenwood is a period of emotional growth, and the recuperative nature of the experience is reinforced through the careers of the outlaws who return to Milan with him, 'reformed, civil, full of good,/And fit for great employment' (V.iv.154–5).

The positive and negative potentialities of exile explored through 'altering and changing' Brooke's narrative are drawn together in *Richard II* (1595?). Bolingbroke and Mowbray, having accused one another of treachery, are on the point of settling their quarrel by single combat, when both are banished by the King, to the anguish of Bolingbroke's father, John of Gaunt. The background to the incident is supplied by the chronicles of Hall and Holinshed (cf.*2 Henry VI*), but the dramatist makes some significant additions to the historical accounts. Although neither chronicler gives any indication of Mowbray's immediate response to his sentence,[9] Shakespeare assigns him a very substantial speech in which he develops a view of the outcast state that has analogies with the equation between exile and death advanced by Romeo and Suffolk, but which shifts the emphasis away from the emptiness of a life

9. Hall merely indicates that he was 'sore repentant of his enterprise, and departed sorrowfully out of the realme', while Holinshed records that he received his sentence 'humblie' although 'it greeved him not a little' that the King had not supported him (see G. Bullough (1957–75), vol. III, pp. 387 and 394).

removed from the beloved, to the meaninglessness of an existence robbed of human intercourse:

> A dearer merit, not so deep a maim
> As to be cast forth in the common air,
> Have I deserved at your Highness' hands.
> The language I have learnt these forty years,
> My native English, now I must forgo,
> And now my tongue's use is to me no more
> Than an unstringed viol or a harp,
> Or like a cunning instrument cas'd up –
> Or being open, put into his hands
> That knows no touch to tune the harmony.
> Within my mouth you have engaol'd my tongue,
> Doubly portcullis'd with my teeth and lips,
> And dull unfeeling barren ignorance
> Is made my gaoler to attend on me.
> I am too old to fawn upon a nurse,
> Too far in years to be a pupil now:
> What is thy sentence then but speechless death,
> Which robs my tongue from breathing native breath?
>
> (I.iii.156–73)

Bolingbroke's banishment is even more fully developed than that of Mowbray, again by substantial additions to the source. Where Holinshed merely indicates that 'the duke of Hereford [i.e. Bolingbroke] tooke his leave of the king at Eltham, who there released foure yeares of his banishment',[10] Shakespeare explores the responses of both father and son to the abrupt change in their situations that the sentence entails. While Bolingbroke stresses the 'grief' (I.iii.274) of the exiled state, and the pain of separation from those he loves (I.iii.268–70), Gaunt declares that his own death will be hastened by the loss of his son, implying the further impoverishment of the social group through the act of expulsion. The imagery that the principal speakers employ in this scene is also significant in this respect. Richard's initial judgement upon Boling-broke is couched in seasonal terms. He banishes his cousin, not for 'ten years', but 'Till twice five summers have enrich'd our fields' (I.iii.141), while he later remits the term to 'Six frozen winters' (I.iii.211). Bolingbroke and Gaunt, in their turn, draw on the same field of reference. The former reflects on the way in which 'Four

10. See G. Bullough (1957–75), vol. III, p. 394.

lagging winters and four wanton springs' (I.iii.214) may be struck from his sentence by a word from the King, while his father attempts to cheer him by maintaining that 'six winters . . . are quickly gone' (I.iii.260). The cumulative effect of this strand of imagery is to establish an equation between banishment and sterility, and this equation does not solely relate to those excluded from the realm. Though Richard thinks of his kingdom enjoying 'twice five summers' (I.iii.141) in his cousin's absence, Gaunt associates his son's departure with barrenness (cf. 'But little vantage shall I reap thereby': I.iii.218), and sees the conduct of the King as contributing to the negative aspects of natural processes (cf. 'Thou canst help time to furrow me with age': I.iii.229). The emphasis upon the attitudes of father and son in the closing phase of the scene (lines 253–309) ensures that it is their view of the situation that impresses itself on the spectator's imagination. Banishment is thus established as a winter-like state, not merely for the exiled individual, but for the society from which that individual is excluded – and this concept has clear implications for Richard himself. In Act II scene iv, for example, a captain ominously reports:

'Tis thought the king is dead . . .
The bay-trees in our country are all wither'd,
And meteors fright the fixed stars of heaven,
The pale-fac'd moon looks bloody on the earth,
And lean-look'd prophets whisper fearful change.
                                                            (II.iv.7–11)

For all its negative aspects, however, the parting between Gaunt and Bolingbroke does contain suggestions of the more positive potentialities of the exiled condition. In a speech echoing words and phrases from *The Two Gentlemen of Verona* the older man attempts to reconcile the younger to his situation by suggesting that his hardships may be alleviated by embracing them as a product of choice, rather than compulsion:

All places that the eye of heaven visits
Are to a wise man ports and happy havens.
Teach thy necessity to reason thus –
There is no virtue like necessity.
Think not the king did banish thee,
But thou the king. Woe doth the heavier sit

Where it perceives it is but faintly borne.
Go, say I sent thee forth to purchase honour,
And not the king exil'd thee; or suppose
Devouring pestilence hangs in our air,
And thou art flying to a fresher clime.
Look what thy soul holds dear, imagine it
To lie that way thou goest, not whence thou com'st.
Suppose the singing birds musicians,
The grass whereon thou tread'st the presence strew'd,
The flowers fair ladies, and thy steps no more
Than a delightful measure or a dance;
For gnarling sorrow hath less power to bite
The man that mocks at it and sets it light.

(I.iii.275–93)

While there is no suggestion in these lines that the experience of a
less courtly society is inherently life enhancing, they do advance
the position that 'the mind is its own place' and thus look forward
to the much more positive view of exile propounded in *As You
Like It*.

Though the sentence of banishment (as will be clear from the
above) is a frequent motif in Shakespeare's early work, it functions
in the majority of instances as a mechanism of the plot rather than
constituting a principal focus of dramatic interest. Suffolk's exile
in *2 Henry VI* reflects his decline in political influence, and is
quickly followed by his death, while his parting exchange with
Margaret allows the audience a fresh perspective on the lives of
those caught up in the historical process, rather than initiating an
exploration into the outcast condition. Similarly, though the
banishment of Bolingbroke is more fully developed in personal
terms, the sentence itself is significant, not for the insight that it
allows into the woes of exclusion from the social group, but for
the political machinations to which it gives rise. Even in *Romeo and
Juliet* in which the parting between the lovers is fully delineated
and the play follows the hero into exile, the sojourn in Mantua is
quickly passed over, with the attention of the audience focused
upon the tragic consequences of Romeo's absence, not on his
experiences in a new location. It is only in *The Two Gentlemen of
Verona* that the exile state itself plays a part in the evolution of
events, and even in this instance Valentine's life among the outlaws
is only briefly sketched. In a number of the plays of Shakespeare's

middle period, by contrast, not only are the positive and negative aspects of exile explored more fully than in previous plays, but the outcast condition becomes the backcloth against which much of the action is set.

As You Like It (1598–1600) is directly indebted to Lodge's *Rosalynde*, a prose romance first published in 1590 and reprinted in 1592, 1596 and 1598. Lodge's romance (as noted in Chapter 2 of this book) traces the history of a pair of lovers – Rosader, a younger son, abused by Saladyne, his elder brother, and Rosalynde, the daughter of a King, driven into exile by a usurper (Torismond). Fearing that she will make an advantageous match that will prove dangerous to his position, Torismond banishes Rosalynde from the court, and she journeys to the forest of Arden disguised as a youth, accompanied by Torismond's daughter Alinda, disguised as Aliena. Once in the forest Aliena and 'Ganimede' purchase a farm, and become involved in the amatory experience of the shepherd Montanus, who is in love with the arrogant Phoebe. Rosader, meanwhile, having been further abused by his brother, is also forced to flee to the forest, enabling Torismond to use Saladyne's unfraternal conduct as an excuse to banish him from the court and expropriate his estates. Rosader finds his brother sleeping and saves him from a lion, but the ensuing harmony is disrupted by a band of outlaws who attempt to capture Aliena. Rosader fails in an effort to save her, but Saladyne comes to his assistance, only to fall in love with the lady he rescues. Having made contact with the woodland court of the exiled King, the various couples (Rosader and Rosalynde, Aliena and Saladyne, Phoebe and Montanus) are united, and the courtiers return from the forest following Torismond's defeat in battle.

To anyone familiar with the plot of *As You Like It* it will immediately be evident that Shakespeare follows the story-line of his inherited tale with considerable fidelity. Nevertheless, in adapting Lodge's leisurely narrative for the two hours traffic of the stage, he has made a number of significant alterations to the source material. In the first place, he has set up an opposition between the world of the court and that of the forest which is far more systematic than the distinctions drawn in the romance. In the course of Lodge's narrative a number of characters – Rosalynde, Rosader, Saladyne, etc. – are excluded from the society that Torismond governs, and these figures have both positive and negative inclinations. In *As You Like It*, by contrast, the exiles – Duke Senior and his followers, Rosalind and Orlando (who is forced to seek shelter in the forest, though not formally expelled) – are uniformly virtuous,[11] and their ejection from the domain of Duke Frederick implies the repudiation of specific values by the society that he rules. Conversely, Lodge's Arden is home to both the virtuous and the vicious. While on the one hand the shepherds and shepherdesses who tend their flocks there are primarily concerned with love, the 'rascals' who prowl through its confines hope to advance themselves by preying on others.[12] Significantly, this second group of characters is not carried over into the Shakespearian play. Shakespeare's Arden is a place of physical hardship, where wild beasts are a source of danger (cf.IV.iii.104–32), and inclement weather occasions suffering (cf.II.i.5–10), but those who live within its limits are not given to the abuse of their fellow men.

The polarization between the two locations of Lodge's narrative is set in motion, by the dramatist, at the very outset of the play. The action opens in the world outside Arden, and is initiated by Oliver's abuse of his brother Orlando. This breach of familial bonds is then placed in a larger context through an account by the wrestler, Charles, of the true Duke's treatment at the hands of his brother, cf.:

> *Oli[ver]*. Good Monsieur Charles! What's the new news at the new court?
> *Cha[rles]*. There's no news at the court sir, but the old news. That is, the old Duke is banished by his younger brother the new Duke, and three or four loving lords have put themselves into voluntary exile with him, whose lands and revenues enrich the new Duke, therefore he gives them good leave to wander.
> ....
> *Oli*. Where will the old Duke live?
> *Cha*. They say he is already in the Forest of Arden, and a many merry men with him; and there they live like the old Robin Hood of

---

11. Shakespeare's treatment of the figure of Oliver is important in this respect. Whereas his counterpart in the source is banished by the usurper for his unfraternal conduct, Oliver is given twelve months in which to surrender Orlando to Duke Frederick, and is threatened with banishment if he fails (see *As You Like It*, III.i.1–14). The vicious brother thus becomes a tool of the corrupt court, rather than an outcast from the society that the usurper has created.

12. See the text of the romance printed in G. Bullough (1957–75), vol. II, p. 222.

England. They say many young gentlemen flock to him every day,
and fleet the time carelessly as they did in the golden world.

(I.i.96–119; Arden ed.)

A number of aspects of this exchange serve to establish the
antithetical relationship between Duke Senior's court in Arden and
the environment created by the usurper. The equation with Robin
Hood suggests that the greenwood court is a beneficent one,
hostile to tyranny, and this implication is supported by the fact
that the nobility 'flock' to join it. The reference to the golden age
is also important in this respect. Not only does it suggest that the
society gathered in the forest is a superior one, but it forges a link
with the pastoral tradition, drawing together native and classical
conventions to evoke a way of life in harmony with nature. At the
same time, the world beyond Arden is associated with unnatural-
ness and rapacity. Not content with driving out his brother, the
usurper Duke has expropriated the estates of the 'loving lords' who
followed him into exile, enriching himself at their expense.

The opposition between the two worlds initiated in this opening
scene is heightened by the banishment of Rosalind at the close of
the act. Convinced that her popularity represents a threat to his
own position, her uncle excludes her from his realm on pain of
death, further fracturing the bonds between the members of the
family group. The terms in which he pronounces the sentence
against her are indicative of the violence and authoritarianism of
the society he has brought into being:

Duke F[rederick]. Mistress, dispatch you with your safest haste
  And get you from our court.
Ros.   Me uncle?
Duke F.   You cousin.
  Within these ten days if that thou be'st found
  So near our public court as twenty miles,
  Thou diest for it.
Ros.   I do beseech your Grace,
  Let me the knowledge of my fault bear with me.
  If with myself I hold intelligence,
  Or have acquaintance with mine own desires,
  If that I do not dream, or be not frantic,
  As I do trust I am not, then dear uncle,
  Never so much as in a thought unborn
  Did I offend your Highness.

Duke F.   Thus do all traitors.
  If their purgation did consist in words,
  They are as innocent as grace itself.
  Let it suffice thee that I trust thee not.
Ros. Yet your mistrust cannot make me a traitor.
  Tell me whereon the likelihood depends.
Duke F. Thou art thy father's daughter, there's enough.
                                        (I.iii.37–54)

The tyranny represented in this scene is in direct opposition to
the relationship between ruler and ruled enacted in the opening
exchanges of the following act. The scene has shifted from the
court to Arden, where the true Duke salutes his followers as his
'co-mates and brothers in exile' (II.i.1) and celebrates a life divorced
from the trappings of power (II.i.2–17). The two physical locations
of Lodge's narrative have thus become metaphors for states of
mind, and the contrast between them is emphasized by a second
departure from the source, the positive stance adopted by the
dramatis personae to their exiled condition. Whereas in Lodge's
version of the story Rosalynde and Aliena regard their banishment
as a misfortune to be encountered with patience and alleviated
through companionship (cf. pp. 178–9), Celia and Rosalind are
much quicker to embrace their situation. In an inversion of the
conventional equation between banishment and death, Celia asserts
that to remain in the court without Rosalind would rob her of her
own life (cf. 'I cannot live out of her company': I.iii.82), and that
to leave her father's realm with her is not banishment but freedom
(cf. 'Now go we in content / To liberty, and not to banishment':
I.iii.133–4). The stance adopted by the cousins affirms their
relationship, moreover, with Duke Senior and his lords. Rather
than repining against his situation, the true Duke regards it as
beneficial, leading not to sterility and imprisonment within the
self, but to the enhancement of life through self-knowledge, cf.:

  Now my co-mates and brothers in exile,
  Hath not old custom made this life more sweet
  Than that of painted pomp? Are not these woods
  More free from peril than the envious court?
  Here feel we not the penalty of Adam,
  The seasons' difference, as the icy fang
  And churlish chiding of the winter's wind,
  Which when it bites and blows upon my body

Even till I shrink with cold, I smile, and say
'This is no flattery. These are counsellors
That feelingly persuade me what I am'.
Sweet are the uses of adversity,
Which like the toad, ugly and venomous,
Wears yet a precious jewel in his head;
And this our life, exempt from public haunt,
Finds tongues in trees, books in the running brooks,
Sermons in stones, and good in everything.
Ami[ens]. I would not change it. Happy is your Grace,
That can translate the stubbornness of fortune
Into so quiet and so sweet a style.

(II.1.1–20)

The attitudes expressed in this scene clearly constitute a development of the ideas advanced by Gaunt in *Richard II*, Act I scene iii,
as a means of reconciling Bolingbroke to his situation. In this
instance, however, the Duke is not simply seeking to convince
himself that his predicament is the product of choice, he is actively
welcoming his condition as educative, and thus finding sources of
'good' even in hardship.

The concept of banishment leading to self-knowledge, and
consequently as life enhancing, permits Shakespeare to invoke the
positive values conventionally associated with the pastoral or
greenwood location.[13] Once in Arden, the dramatis personae
embark on a period of personal growth that is much more firmly
charted than the progression that takes place in the corresponding
passages of the romance. This development is anticipated, once
again, in Shakespeare's own earlier work in Valentine's sojourn
among the bandits, but whereas in *The Two Gentlemen of Verona*
only three scenes are devoted to this phase of the action, in *As You
Like It* four acts of the play take place in the forest. The cousins are
assimilated to the pastoral life by their decision to buy a farm,
while the Duke and his followers live as foresters, subsisting on
the animals that they hunt. Both groups may be seen as undergoing
a development as a result of this return to a simpler life. The true
Duke, divorced from the court, is able to reflect upon its nature
(cf. II.i.1–17), while Rosalind not only learns more about herself
(specifically her feelings for Orlando), but becomes an agent in the

13. For an introduction to the pastoral tradition, see P. V. Marinelli (1971) *Pastoral*,
   Methuen (The Critical Idiom).

education of others (Orlando, Phebe, Silvius). At the same time, the regenerative nature of the greenwood location is evinced through the experience of those who enter Arden of their own volition. Oliver, pursuing Orlando in order to surrender him to Duke Frederick, is reduced in the forest to a condition of penury (cf.IV.iii.106), but he is elevated morally by the values and virtues he finds there (cf.IV.iii.75–137), and assimilated to the pastoral world by his decision to become a shepherd and marry Aliena (cf.V.ii.1–12). Similarly, in a further major departure from the source, the usurper Duke, having gathered an army in order to put down his brother, encounters an 'old religious man' on the fringes of the wood, and is promptly 'converted / Both from his enterprise and from the world' (cf.V.iv.153–64).

The interaction that has taken place in Shakespeare's imagination between Lodge's narrative, the pastoral tradition, and his own experiments with the banishment motif, has clearly given rise in *As You Like It* to a much more meaningful structure than that supplied by the romance itself. Lodge's court becomes a life-denying environment hostile to goodness, while those who remove themselves to the forest assert the value of commitment, and are capable of moral growth. The forest itself is not simply an idealized pastoral location, but a state of mind favourable to natural ties, while the return to the court at the close of the action represents not merely the restoration of the old order, but the enrichment of civilized society through the experience of a more natural state. Where *Rosalynde* alternates between amorous encounters and val-orous deeds, *As You Like It* shifts between value systems, one based upon love, and the other on self-interest, and it is those initially expelled from courtly life who now embody the former.

It is this opposition between mental landscapes – the attitudes of those in positions of power and the stances of those whom they expel – that Shakespeare develops to such terrifying effect in *King Lear*. Just as *The Two Gentlemen of Verona* and *Romeo and Juliet* may be seen as companion pieces in that they represent comic and tragic developments of Brooke's *Romeus and Juliet*, so *As You Like It* and *King Lear* may be regarded as related works in that they enact antithetical versions of exclusion from the state. Once again, the origins of the play may be traced to a specific source – in this instance the anonymous *King Leir* (1588–94), which itself draws on a complex of traditional stories – but the adaptations that

Shakespeare makes to his inherited plot are largely the product of a process of evolution taking place in his own work.

The old play of *King Leir* fuses two major mouldy motifs, the story of the love test, and the tale of the ungrateful child who abuses an aged parent.[14] At the start of the action the King, Leir, resolves to trick his youngest daughter, Cordella, into marriage with the man of his choice, by requiring each of his daughters to express her love for him, and then challenging the youngest to match words with deeds. Though the two older daughters are fulsome in their protestations of affection, Cordella refuses to flatter her father, and he consequently determines to divide his kingdom between his (seemingly) more dutiful offspring. The two older daughters abuse their father and make an attempt upon his life, but the King escapes to Gallia with a loyal follower, Perillus. Having been reconciled to Cordella whom he meets there, Leir is succoured by her husband, the Gallian King, who defeats the representatives of the wicked sisters in battle and restores his wife's father to the throne.

It might seem at first glance that, but for the rejection of the happy ending, Shakespeare has simply taken over the plot of his predecessor's play, but in fact a number of alterations have been effected in the design of the anonymous work in the process of 'converting' its 'substance' to a fresh use. In the first place, the Gloucester plot, which parallels the story of Shakespeare's Lear, is not derived from the play's dramatic antecedent but from the tale of the Paphlagonian King recounted in Sir Philip Sidney's *Arcadia* (pub. 1590). This story concerns an old father who is brought to suspect the virtue of his legitimate son through the machinations of his illegitimate offspring, and thus pursues the life of the former, while placing his trust in the latter. The corrupt son then displaces and blinds his father, who is comforted in his misery by the son he has abused. By bringing the two stories together, Shakespeare has considerably broadened their significance, transforming an idio-syncratic experience through repetition into a universal process. At the same time, he has turned the storm in which the story of the

14. For a fuller account of the sources of the Leir story, and the anonymous writer's treatment of his material, see G. Bullough (1957–75), vol. VII, pp. 271–83.

Paphlagonian King is recounted[15] into the setting for the central scenes of the play, relating the condition of hardship that it symbolizes to a further alteration to his models, the addition of a recurrent banishment motif. Whereas Cordella is cast off by her father as a bastard (lines 312ff.), Cordelia is 'stranger'd' by Lear with an 'oath' (I.i.204), while the loyal Perillus who follows his master's fortunes is transformed into the banished Kent.[16] Similarly, whereas the son of the Paphlagonian King suffers an attempt upon his life, Edgar hears himself 'proclaim'd' (II.iii.1) and is forced to renounce his own personality for that of 'poor Tom'. A pattern of exclusion is thus constructed in the Shakespearian play that has no counterpart in the sources from which its disparate elements are drawn.

King Lear opens with a conversation between Kent and Gloucester which serves as an introduction to the two strands of the plot – the division of the kingdom between Lear's heirs, and the apportioning of Gloucester's affection between his legitimate and illegitimate sons. The conversation is interrupted by the entrance of the King, and the remainder of the scene is taken up with the development of the first of these strands. Having declared his intention to divide his kingdom in proportion to the love his children bear him, Lear rewards his two elder daughters for their glib protestations of affection, and severs the ties that bind him to the third when she affirms that she loves him merely 'according to [her] bond' (I.i.93):

> *Lear.* But goes thy heart with this?
> *Cor.*   Ay, my good Lord.
> *Lear.* So young, and so untender?
> *Cor.* So young, my Lord, and true.
> *Lear.* Let it be so; thy truth then be thy dower:
>   For, by the sacred radiance of the sun,
>   The mysteries of Hecate and the night,
>   By all the operation of the orbs
>   From whom we do exist and cease to be,
>   Here I disclaim all my paternal care,

15. No storm occurs in the anonymous *Leir*, but one may have been suggested to the later dramatist by the thunder and lightning following Leir's words at lines 1632–3 (line numbers refer to the text in G. Bullough (1957–75), vol. VII).
16. The title assigned to this figure may have been suggested by Marlowe's *Edward II* in which the King's younger brother, also an Earl of Kent, is banished from the presence (cf. IV.i.5) for opposing the royal will over the exile of a favourite.

> Propinquity and property of blood,
> And as a stranger to my heart and me
> Hold thee from this for ever. The barbarous Scythian,
> Or he that makes his generation messes
> To gorge his appetite, shall to my bosom
> Be as well neighbour'd, pitied, and reliev'd,
> As thou my sometime daughter.

(I.i.105–20)

The cosmic forces Lear invokes here in metaphorically banishing his daughter from her natural place in the family group endows the process of expulsion that he enacts with a far greater significance than is involved in the sentencing of Shakespeare's earlier exiles. Where Valentine and Romeo, Bolingbroke and Rosalind are cast out by specific societies, Cordelia is expelled from the order of nature, and the terrible implications of this action are heightened when Kent attempts to intervene on her behalf. Interposing in the hope of persuading Lear to reconsider his decision, Kent himself becomes the target of the King's anger, and is literally banished from the realm:

> *Lear.*   Hear me, recreant!
>   On thine allegiance, hear me!
>   That thou hast sought to make us break our vows,
>   Which we durst never yet, and with strain'd pride
>   To become betwixt our sentence and our power,
>   Which nor our nature nor our place can bear,
>   Our potency made good, take thy reward.
>   Five days we do allot thee for provision
>   To shield thee from disasters of the world;
>   And on the sixth to turn thy hated back
>   Upon our kingdom: if on the tenth day following
>   Thy banish'd trunk be found in our dominions,
>   The moment is thy death. Away! By Jupiter,
>   This shall not be revok'd.

(I.i.166–79)

As in *As You Like It*, the repetition of the act of exclusion serves to transform an isolated incident into a universal phenomenon – the banishment of virtue from the state – and this process is continued in the following scene in which the Gloucester sub-plot is caught up. The bastard Edmund succeeds in convincing his legitimate brother, Edgar, that his father is incensed against him, tricking the other man into supplying him with sufficient 'evidence' to persuade Gloucester that his son is plotting against his life. Consequently, by Act II scene iii Edgar too has been 'proclaim'd' (II.iii.1) and no longer has a place, like his main-plot counterparts, in Lear's kingdom.

Though Kent, on hearing his sentence, asserts like Celia that 'Freedom lives hence, and banishment is here' (I.i.181), the play does not pursue the exiles into a new location outside the degenerate world brought into being by the misuse of power. Whereas *As You Like It* follows Rosalind and Celia into the forest, the domain of the true Duke, and explores the attitudes of mind capable of 'translating' exile to liberty, *King Lear* remains within the society created by the central figure, focusing upon the nature of the environment produced by his actions. Cordelia disappears from the play world until late in Act IV, while Kent and Edgar shed their former identities, serving Lear and Gloucester respectively as Caius and Poor Tom. The lack of any alternative setting creates the illusion that Lear's kingdom is not one specific location but the universe as a whole, and this impression is heightened by the cosmic imagery the characters employ (cf.III.ii.1–9 and 14–24). The exclusion of Cordelia, Kent and Edgar thus represents the banishment of piety (in the fullest sense of that term) from the entire arena in which the action takes place, while the events that follow their expulsion trace, not the re-establishment of natural ties as in *As You Like It*, but the cataclysmic results of their severance. Thus where the earlier drama, drawing on the greenwood motif, explores the regenerative potentialities of the outcast state, *King Lear* examines the negative aspects of proscription, exhibiting the self-destructive nature of an action that militates against the principles on which lawful authority itself depends.

The diminishing of the community implied in earlier plays through the expulsion of one or more members of the social group becomes in *King Lear* a descent into a horrific universe in which man is indistinguishable from beast. Once altruism has been expelled from the body politic, and the natural bonds that bind parent to child and monarch to subject have been severed, self-interest flourishes unchecked by moral obligations, and power is divorced from the contraints of justice. The resulting world is typified by competing egoism (cf.the conflict between Goneril and Regan for the hand of Edmund), unnatural cruelty (cf.the driving out of Lear and blinding of Gloucester), and disorder on both local and national scales (cf.the death of Cornwall at the hands of a servant and the invasion of the realm by a foreign power). The monstrous condition of humanity is signalled, moreover, through the imagery of the play in which an insistent equation is set up between human beings and predatory beasts, cf.:

> *Albany* [to Goneril].   What have you done?
>   Tigers, not daughters, what have you perform'd?
>   A father, and a gracious aged man,
>   Whose reverence even the head-lugg'd bear would lick,
>   Most barbarous, most degenerate! have you madded.
>   Could my good brother suffer you to do it?
>   A man, a prince, by him so benefited!
>   If that the heavens do not their visible spirits
>   Send quickly down to tame these vilde offences,
>   It will come,
>   Humanity must perforce prey on itself,
>   Like monsters of the deep.
>   . . . .
>   Thou changed and self-cover'd thing, for shame,
>   Be-monster not thy feature.
>
>   (IV.ii.39–63)

The chaos brought about by Lear's actions is not restricted, moreover, to the social sphere. As in *As You Like It*, the physical world may be seen on one level as a representation of a mental state, with the anarchy within the kingdom functioning as an externalization of the tumult within Lear's mind. The social monstrosity consequent upon the repudiation of primary bonds and obligations is thus a literalization of the intellectual equation that Lear sets up between man and beast (cf.III.iv.109–11), while the convulsions in the realm and the cosmos both image and trigger the disintegration of his mind. Banishment, or casting out, in this play is thus both an external and an internal process, resulting in abnormality in the human frame, and barbarism in the body politic.

It is this equation between banishment and monstrosity in both public and private spheres that Shakespeare takes up in *Coriolanus* (1608). The historical background to the play is largely supplied by North's translation of Plutarch's *Lives of the Noble Grecians and Romanes* (1579), but Shakespeare also drew on a number of other historical works, including Holland's *Romane Historie of T. Livy* (1600). These sources agree in describing the process whereby Coriolanus, a valiant soldier, having sued as was customary for the consulship, is repudiated and banished by the common people for the pride and hostility that he exhibits towards them, but they part company in their treatment of their subject's response to this reversal of fortune. Where Livy simply records that Coriolanus was 'condemned in his absence, for contumacie, [and] departed into banishment to the Volscians, menacing his own countrie as he went, and carying even then with him the revenging stomacke of an enemie',[17] Plutarch develops the situation more fully, describing the responses of both patricians and plebians, and relating his protagonist's demeanour to his state of mind:

> Neither in his countenaunce, nor in his gate, dyd [he] ever showe him selfe abashed, or once let fall his great corage: but he only of all other gentlemen that were angrie at his fortune, dyd outwardly shewe no manner of passion, nor care at all of him selfe. Not that he dyd paciently beare and temper his good happe, in respect of any reason he had, or by his quiet condition: but bicause he was so caried awaye with the vehemencie of anger, and desire of revenge, that he had no sence nor feeling of the hard state he was in.[18]

Though Shakespeare's Coriolanus clearly has his origins in these accounts, he is neither condemned in his absence like Livy's protagonist, nor silenced like Plutarch's by his own anger. Though his fellow patricians urge restraint in his dealings with the people (cf. III.iii.31 and 67), he rises instantly to provocation, responding furiously to his sentence by violently repudiating the society he had formerly striven to defend:

> You common cry of curs! whose breath I hate
> As reek o'th'rotten fens, whose loves I prize
> As the dead carcasses of unburied men
> That do corrupt my air: I banish you!
> And here remain with your uncertainty!
> Let every feeble rumour shake your hearts!
> Your enemies, with nodding of their plumes,
> Fan you into despair! Have the power still
> To banish your defenders, till at length

17. Quoted from G. Bullough (1957–75), vol. V, p. 501.
18. Quoted from G. Bullough (1957–75), vol. V, pp. 525–6.

Your ignorance – which finds not till it feels,
Making but reservation of yourselves,
Still your own foes – deliver you as most
Abated captives to some nation
That won you without blows! Despising
For you the city, thus I turn my back.
There is a world elsewhere!

(III.iii.120–35)

The stance that Coriolanus assumes at the close of this speech
appears at first glance to be very similar to that propounded by
John of Gaunt and adopted by Duke Senior and Rosalind, but in
fact there is a significant distinction between the two positions.
Although the statement 'There is a world elsewhere' apparently
echoes Celia's 'Now go we in content / To liberty, and not to
banishment' (As You Like It, I.iii.133–4) or Kent's 'Freedom lives
hence, and banishment is here' (King Lear, I.i.181), it carries a
different range of implications in that it functions as the climax of
a tirade that effectively reverses the roles of banisher and banished.
Coriolanus does not simply leave his native city in order to seek a
freedom it no longer offers, he rejects his society as degenerate,
departing not with regret but contempt. The sentence of exile is
thus transformed from a punishment imposed by others into a
voluntary act, and this process of reversal is extended in Coriolanus' description of the society he spurns. Whereas for the outcasts
of earlier plays it was the exiled condition that represented a species
of death, for Coriolanus it is the society that condemns him that
reeks with the stench of physical decay (cf. III.iii.120–3).

The act of repudiation initiated by the people of Rome has
damaging consequences in Shakespeare's sources for both parties.
Consumed with anger towards his countrymen, Coriolanus leads
a force of Volsces against them, only to be killed by his new allies
when he spares Rome at his mother's entreaty. While remaining
close to his authorities, Shakespeare develops the events they relate,
turning their account of one man's divided loyalties into a vision
of universal monstrosity. Having embraced the breach between
himself and his compatriots, Shakespeare's protagonist, rather than
simply surrendering himself to wrath, regards himself (and is
regarded by others) as divorced from the human condition. On
leaving Rome for example, he describes himself as

> a lonely dragon that his fen
> Makes fear'd and talk'd of more than seen,
>
> (IV.i.30–1)

while the Roman general, Cominius, views him as outside the
natural order, cf.:

> He leads them [the Volsces] like a thing
> Made by some other deity than nature.
>
> (IV.vi.91–2)

Unlike Kent and Cordelia who remain loyal to the King who
expels them and seek to succour him in distress, Coriolanus is
dedicated to destruction, solely bent on the overthrow of the city
he once served. The dislocation of the natural order that banishment now represents is associated, furthermore, with a loss of
identity. Urged by Cominius to spare his countrymen, Coriolanus
refuses to answer to his former titles, disclaiming all selfhood but
that afforded him through the sack of Rome:

> Com. I urg'd our old aquaintance, and the drops
> That we have bled together. 'Coriolanus'
> He would not answer to; forbad all names:
> He was a kind of nothing, titleless,
> Till he had forg'd himself a name o'th'fire
> Of burning Rome.
>
> (V.i.10–15)

While Coriolanus is severed from the natural world through his
repudiation of his native city, Rome is diminished through the
expulsion of her former champion and defender. Not only are her
citizens at the mercy of the Volsces (cf.IV.vi.75–80), they are
increasingly torn by internal divisions, turning inward upon themselves in an orgy of destruction, cf.:

> Vol[umnia]. Anger's my meat: I sup upon myself
> And so shall starve with feeding.
>
> (IV.ii.50–1)

> Com[inius]. You [the Tribunes] have holp to ravish your own daughters, and
> To melt the city leads upon your pates,
> To see your wives dishonour'd to your noses –
> ....
> Your temples burned in their cement, and

> Your franchises whereon you stood, confin'd
> Into an auger's bore.
>
> (IV.vi.82–8)

This state of degeneracy has obvious analogies with the condition of Lear's Britain after the banishment of Cordelia and Kent, but whereas in the earlier play the loyalty of the outcasts is productive of a return to the natural order, in *Coriolanus* the mutual repudiation of the bond between society and the individual leads to further impoverishment and disaster. Though Rome is finally saved through the intervention of Volumnia, who persuades her son to forgo his revenge, the state that he spares remains a degenerate one, its citizens vacillating and divided (cf.IV.vi.130–56 and V.iv.36–40). At the same time, Coriolanus himself is not reintegrated into the community that has expelled him through his decision to renounce his vengeance. As a commander of the Volsces, he returns to Antium rather than Rome, but in sparing the latter he has betrayed the former and is consequently killed by his adopted countrymen as a traitor. In the closing scene, it is not a rediscovered oneness with family or people that he asserts, but the isolated self-sufficiency that has become his sole means of self-definition:

> Cut me to pieces, Volsces, men and lads,
> Stain all your edges on me . . .
> If you have writ your annals true, 'tis there,
> That like an eagle in a dove-cote, I
> Flutter'd your Volscians in Corioles.
> Alone I did it.
>
> (V.vi.111–16)

The phrase 'alone I did it' stands in stark contrast to the assertions of kinship, however tentative and exclusive, that are formulated in earlier plays. Where in *As You Like It* or *King Lear* banishment constitutes a step towards some form of reintegration, in *Coriolanus* it represents a condition of alienation that is the inevitable consequence of the severing of natural ties. Exile here, in short, involves considerably more than a state of deprivation. It is symbolic of the isolation and meaninglessness that attends the disintegration of the social group.

If *Coriolanus* constitutes Shakespeare's bleakest exploration of the negative aspects of the banishment motif, the plays of the last period represent his most profound exploration of the forces of renewal set in motion through exclusion. *Cymbeline* (1608–09), the second of the plays of this final period, and the first in which the sentence of exile is imposed, is structured upon a number of sources, including an anonymous comedy, *The Rare Triumphs of Love and Fortune*, written during the 1580s. This play concerns the adventures of a princess and a fatherless young man who has been brought up by the King at court, but is banished following the discovery of his love for his patron's daughter. The lovers plan a secret meeting, but their intentions are revealed to the King's son, and the heroine is obliged to seek shelter in a cave inhabited by a former courtier, who has himself been sent into exile through the treachery of a friend. After a number of further tribulations the lovers are eventually united, and harmonious relationships re-established in both the state and family group.

The similarities between this sequence of events and the plot of *Cymbeline* leave little room for doubt of the later dramatist's knowledge of his predecessor's work. Once again an orphaned young man, brought up in the court of a king, is exiled for falling in love with his benefactor's daughter, while the princess whom he marries, having also fled the court, seeks shelter in the cave of a courtier wrongly exiled in the distant past. While the Shakespearian drama clearly looks back to *The Rare Triumphs of Love and Fortune*, however, the anonymous play itself draws on a wealth of folk tales turning on the love between a beautiful princess and a poor but worthy young man, and it is to this stock of traditional stories underlying his immediate source that Shakespeare turns in 'converting' the 'substance' of the earlier work. Thus in *Cymbeline* the Princess (Imogen) incurs the enmity not only of her stepbrother but of his mother – the stereotypical stepdame (as noted in Chapter 2 of this book) of such stories as *Snow White* – and is cast through her agency into a death-like sleep, while the banished courtier, Belarius, has not simply withdrawn from public life, he has stolen away the King's sons and reared them as 'mountaineers'.[19] The amorous adventures that illustrate the title of the source play are subsumed through these additions into a larger

19. See G. Bullough (1957–75), vol. VIII, pp. 23–4 and 20–1. A much fuller account of the play's sources than the scope of the present chapter permits may be found in J. M. Nosworthy (ed.) (1955) *Cymbeline*, Methuen, pp. xvii–xxviii (Arden edition).

structure – and that structure conforms to the patterns of a fertility myth. The King's offspring, upon whom the renewal of the state depends, are lost through successive acts of misjudgement, and both King and kingdom enter a winter-like state until evil dies in the person of the wicked stepmother and her son, and new life blooms with the rediscovery of the 'dead' princess and her brothers. Banishment is thus equated here with a species of blight upon the realm, initiating a period of sterility that can give way to a new life only with reconstitution of the social group.

The movement from court to country plays a crucial part in the pattern of loss and recovery enacted in the course of the play, and it is here that the immediate and ultimate sources of the drama come together in Shakespeare's imagination with elements of his own earlier work. Just as Valentine grows in stature during his sojourn among the outlaws, and the banished courtiers of *As You Like It* develop in understanding during their residence in the forest, so the protagonists of *Cymbeline* are nurtured and regenerated in the pastoral environment beyond the confines of the court. Guiderius and Arviragus, the young princes snatched by the banished Belarius and brought up in the wilds of Wales, display a natural nobility, untainted by the corruptions of civilized society (cf. III. iii. 10–95), while the slandered Imogen, having followed her husband to Milford Haven, fallen into a drugged sleep, and been ritually consigned to the earth, wakens into a new existence in which her relationship with her husband is restored and reaffirmed (cf. V. v. 261–4). The terms in which Belarius, echoing Duke Senior (cf. *As You Like It*, II. i. 1–17), celebrates the virtues of the natural life are indicative of the Shakespearian origins of the play's stance towards the pastoral world:

> Now for our mountain sport, up to yond hill!
> Your legs are young: I'll tread these flats. Consider,
> When you above perceive me like a crow,
> That it is place which lessens and sets off,
> And you may then revolve what tales I have told you
> Of courts, of princes; of the tricks in war.
> This service is not service, so being done,
> But being so allow'd. To apprehend thus,
> Draws us a profit from all things we see:
> And often, to our comfort, shall we find
> The sharded beetle in a safer hold

Than is the full-wing'd eagle. O, this life
Is nobler than attending for a check:
Richer than doing nothing for a robe,
Prouder than rustling in unpaid-for silk:
Such gain the cap of him that makes him fine,
Yet keeps his book uncross'd: no life to ours.

(III.iii. 10–26)

While allowing for the development of the regenerative aspects of social exclusion, Shakespeare's additions to his source material also serve to emphasize its negative facets. The King's repudiation of his son-in-law is not an isolated act of misjudgement – it is part of a cycle of misconduct that has robbed the kingdom of its natural heirs. The banishment of the loyal Belarius has deprived the King of his sons, foreshadowing the casting out of Posthumus which loses him his daughter. The association between banishment and deprivation, established in Shakespeare's early work, is thus strongly enforced here, and so too is the degeneracy that follows from expulsion. Just as the exile of Duke Senior in *As You Like It* gives rise to the corrupt court of the usurper Duke, and the rejection of Cordelia, Kent and Edgar produces the savage animality of *King Lear*, so the banishment of Posthumus and Belarius permits the vicious Queen to flourish, breeding a court that is home to intrigue (cf.I.vi.4–45), obsequiousness (cf.I.iii.1–29) and perversion (cf.III.v.124–47). In place of the noble Guiderius, whose worth is amply attested both in single combat and on the battle-field, the heir to the throne is the unlineal Cloten, whose physical, intellectual and moral deficiences establish him as a parodic version of the son-in-law whom Cymbeline has repudiated. Thus, while the recuperative aspects of expulsion are stressed in the pastoral scenes of the play, the malignancy arising from the King's conduct is also powerfully evoked, with the interaction between the two perspectives on the process of exclusion generating a sense of relieved wonder at the close (both inside and outside the play world) when the 'lopp'd branches' of the kingdom are once more 'jointed to the old stock' (V.v.439 and 441).

Where *Cymbeline* enacts a cyclical process of rejection and recovery, placing equal emphasis on the society from which the exiles are excluded and the physical and mental landscape that brings about its renewal, *The Tempest* (1611) is unique in Shakespearian drama in that it is set exclusively in the exiled state. The play differs, moreover, from those discussed earlier in this chapter in that the central figure is not banished by a judicial process, or by an arbitrary exercise of power, but is divested of his authority through intrigue, and left to drift at sea to his death (cf.I.ii.53ff.) Nevertheless, the inclusion of *The Tempest* in this chapter is warranted in two respects. In the first place, Prospero's situation has obvious analogies with Duke Senior's in *As You Like It*. Both characters, having been driven from their positions by a younger brother, establish an alternative existence in a world remote from the sophistication of the court, returning after a lapse of time to reclaim their dukedoms, their minds enriched by their experiences. More tellingly, perhaps, Shakespeare pointedly invites comparison between the conduct of Prospero and that of the 'foul witch Sycorax' (I.ii.258), banished from Argier before the start of the play. In many respects this female magus may be regarded as Prospero's antithesis, or *alter ego*. Whereas he was renowned for his knowledge of the 'liberal Arts' (I.ii.73), loved by his people (I.ii.141), and loving towards the brother who abused his trust (I.ii.66ff.), she was a 'damn'd witch' (I.ii.263), who for 'mischiefs manifold, and sorceries terrible' (I.ii.264) was justifiably banished. It is not merely the histories of the two characters before their arrival on the island, however, that points to their contrastive relationship. Just as Miranda, Prospero's daughter, saves her father's life by endowing him with the fortitude to bear misfortune (I.ii.151–8), so Caliban, Sycorax's son, preserves his mother from death, in that she is pregnant with him when the sentence against her is pronounced, and is consequently spared the full rigour of the law (I.ii.263–70). Once on the island, the responses of the two sorcerers to the spirit whom they find there are diametrically opposed. Sycorax pins Ariel in a 'cloven pine' (I.ii.277) for failing to carry out her 'earthy and abhorr'd commands' (I.ii.273), while Prospero liberates him from confinement (cf.I.ii.291–3), employing him to act on the consciences of those who have wronged him, before freeing him 'to the elements' (V.i.317). Two facets of the exiled state are thus embodied in these opposing figures. Whereas Sycorax represents the mental deformity of those divorced from the social group, Prospero personifies the enlarged understanding achieved through the contemplation of nature (in the fullest sense of the word), by which regeneration may be achieved.

While under the sway of Sycorax, the magical island in which the action of the play is set reflects the monstrosity of its mistress. Prospero's account of the condition that obtained prior to his arrival is crowded with references to violence, bestiality and deformity:

> [Thou, Ariel] was then her servant;
> And, for thou wast a spirit too delicate
> To act her earthy and abhorr'd commands,
> Refusing her grand hests, she did confine thee,
> By help of her more potent ministers,
> And in her most unmitigable rage,
> Into a cloven pine; within which rift
> Imprison'd thou didst painfully remain
> A dozen years; within which space she died,
> And left thee there; where thou didst vent thy groans
> As fast as mill-wheels strike. Then was this island –
> Save for the son that she did litter here,
> A freckled whelp hag-born – not honour'd with
> A human shape.
> *Ari[el]*.   Yes, Caliban her son.
> *Pros.* Dull thing, I say so; he, that Caliban,
> Whom now I keep in service. Thou best know'st
> What torment I did find thee in; thy groans
> Did make wolves howl, and penetrate the breasts
> Of ever-angry bears: it was a torment
> To lay upon the damn'd.
>
>   (I.ii.271–90)

This evocation of a place of animality and death is in direct contrast to the image of the island that the audience receives. Though the action opens with the tumult of the storm, the spectators are quickly assured that no one has been harmed (cf.I.ii.25–32 and 217–32), while the beauty of the play's location, mirroring the minds of its current rulers, is constantly enforced (cf.I.ii.377ff.). Nevertheless, though the vision communicated to the audience is a positive one, the fluid nature of the island is suggested by the divergent responses of the ship-wrecked courtiers to the strange environment in which they find themselves. To the worthy Gonzalo it is a place of wonder, offering the opportunity for the creation of a Utopian society (cf.II.i.56–62 and 139–64), while to the degenerate Antonio and Sebastian it is filled with the stench of physical decay (cf.II.i.45–7). The region in which the action is set, in brief, is not simply a natural location, remote from the day-today world of the dramatis personae. It functions as an external representation of the mind divorced from the restraints governing human conduct – and thus engaged in the creation of its own actuality.

The two potentialities that the island holds in relation to its occupants exist as what might be termed text and subtext, or alternative possibilities, throughout. While Prospero achieves a greater degree of understanding (exhibited by his control over the physical world),[20] and a higher level of moral awareness (evinced in his decision to forgive his unrepentant brother, cf. V.i.130–2), his designs in relation to those he manipulates have only a limited degree of success. Though he achieves his goals in bringing Alonso to recognize his errors, and reforges social and familial bonds through the marriage between Ferdinand and Miranda, he fails to awaken Antonio and Sebastian to the consciousness of sin, or to open their eyes to the value of commitment. The outcast state into which the courtiers follow Prospero through the power of their former victim's art is not, therefore, presented as a greenwood world that is inevitably conducive to virtue. Though Prospero, Alonso, Ferdinand and Miranda return to enrich their society through the insights achieved through the process of exclusion, they carry with them in the persons of Antonio and Sebastian the negative impulses through which the whole cycle may begin afresh.

While being unique in the Shakespearian corpus in bringing together the positive and negative aspects of expulsion as alternative stances, or states of mind, *The Tempest* also stands apart from other items in the canon in that its central figure functions as a conscious agent of renewal.[21] Where the Duke in *As You Like It* learns from his experience in the forest, and Cordelia's conduct brings Lear to a fuller understanding of her worth, Prospero engineers the arrival of his enemies on his island, and sets out to educate them into an awareness of the wrongs they have committed. Unlike the exiles of previous plays who establish a metaphorical relationship between banishment and death, Prospero is literally dead to his own people, while the group he wrecks on the

20. For an excellent summary of Prospero's relationship with nature, see F. Kermode (ed.) (1954) *The Tempest*, Methuen, pp. xl–xli (Arden edition).
21. Though Edgar eventually undertakes this role in relation to Gloucester in the later acts of *King Lear*, this is not his intention at the start of the play.

island are subjected by him to a process of drowning, and then translated to a new world. By removing Prospero from any known society, and endowing him with supernatural power, the dramatist is able to examine the proposition, first put forward in *Richard II*, that the mind can create its own version of actuality, and explore the extent to which the liberated consciousness is all-powerful and self-sufficient. In the event, though the outcome of the action confirms the capacity of the individual to rise superior to misfortune, it also exposes the limitations of the human will. Though Prospero himself discovers that 'the rarer action is / In virtue than in vengeance' (V.i.27–8), and brings Alonso to a recognition of guilt, he is unable to impose his own moral vision on the courtiers as a whole. Though he subjects all his enemies to the same experiences, his educative programme is confounded by the intransigence of Antonio and Sebastian, and the company that returns to Milan is at once more enlightened and irremediably flawed.

Stories involving outlaws, whether dwelling comfortably in the forest or suffering in foreign lands, must undoubtedly be classed among the mustiest of mouldy tales, and the number of examples touched on in this chapter (and the list is by no means exhaustive) gives some indication of the readiness with which Shakespeare fell back on the device. Nevertheless, the meanings that he derives from his seemingly repetitive situations are far from uniform. Through the fusion of material derived from history, folk tale and romance, he evolves in the course of his career an increasingly complex motif that admits the exploration of a range of emotions and functions as a vehicle for both comic and tragic resolutions. For the protagonists of the early plays, rooted in historical and amatory works, the enforced division between the individual and his society constitutes a severance that deprives life of meaning, but with the addition of elements from the pastoral and greenwood traditions the concept of exile as death develops into a view of the outcast state as a testing ground for the resilience of the human spirit. The individual excluded from the body politic emerges as a potential source of regeneration, while the lopping off of a social member becomes a species of deformity. The assimilation of these concepts to the archetypal patterns of folk tale produces a yet richer tissue of meanings. The casting forth of a prominent figure now produces a state of sterility or moral decline, that can give way to a springtime of renewal only through reintegration into the rhythms of nature, and the reconstitution of the fractured state. While functioning throughout as a source of plot complication, the sentence of exile thus evolves into an instrument for the exploration of the relationship between the individual, the social group, and the order of nature – and ultimately for an examination of the limitations and capabilities of the human mind. The development that takes place between Suffolk's parting from Margaret and Prospero's return to Milan thus constitutes a considerable thought journey, and the extent of the distance travelled gives some indication of the imaginative energy expended by the playwright on the age old story of the 'wolf's head'.

Chapter 6

Putative Death

Romeo and Juliet. Antony and Cleopatra. Much Ado About Nothing. All's Well That Ends Well. Measure for Measure. Pericles. Cymbeline. The Tempest. The Winter's Tale

---

Of the many tales that Shakespeare draws on in the construction of his plays – and some of the more incredible have been touched on in previous chapters – there can be few as remote from day-to-day actuality as those involving a supposed death. Though many of us, in the course of our everyday lives, may be startled by the seeming interchangeability of a pair of identical twins, or embarrassed by a wife's aggressiveness towards her husband, few will be obliged to come to terms with the discovery that funeral obsequies have been performed over a living relative, or that a supposedly dead neighbour has returned to the arms of a grieving husband. Nevertheless, for all the rareness of such occurrences in daily experience, over a quarter of the thirty-seven plays generally attributed to Shakespeare include an incident of this kind – and the motif is used with increasing frequency as the dramatist's career evolves. While none of the early comedies or histories makes significant use of the device, the plays of the middle and late periods are crowded with instances, more than one variation on some occasions (as in *Pericles*, for example) being woven on the theme. The statistics are even more striking when the pattern of distribution over the various dramatic genres is taken into account. Only two of the ten tragedies (*Romeo and Juliet* and *Antony and Cleopatra*) involve any kind of hypothetical death, whereas six of the seven plays which incorporate both comic and tragic impulses (the so-called problem plays and romances)[1] make some use of this kind of false appearance as a vehicle for plot complication. Where the sexual substitutions of *All's Well That Ends Well* and *Measure for Measure* generate a degree of consumer resistance by virtue of their incredibility and seeming repetitiveness, the mass pseudo-mortalities of the late plays must give rise to some measure of scepticism with regard to an established dramatist's readiness to expand the frontiers of his art.

The fondness for this peculiarly non-naturalistic device was not, however, exclusive to Shakespeare. For all its apparent irrelevance to the grim realities of life in Elizabethan–Jacobean England, the supposed death was one of the most popular contrivances employed on the Renaissance stage. In Marston's *Antonio and Mellida* (1599), for example, the 'dead' Antonio rises unexpectedly from his bier when the father of his beloved Mellida rashly declares his readiness to do anything to reverse his death, while in Middleton's *A Chaste Maid in Cheapside* (1613) a pair of young lovers who have encountered parental opposition to their match, emerge from their coffins to be united by those originally assembled to mourn them. In other instances the practice is much less short-lived, and is designed to allow the 'deceased' to observe the living rather than manipulate their responses. In Middleton's *Michaelmas Term* (1605), for example, the comic villain, Quomodo, stages his own death in order to enjoy the spectacle of his wife's grief and his son's handling of his wealth, only to see his 'widow' take another husband and to discover that he has signed away his money. Similarly, the eponymous hero of Jonson's *Volpone* (1605–06) looks forward to enjoying the discomfiture of his prospective heirs by feigning his death and 'bequeathing' his property to his servant, only to be betrayed by his fellow conspirator who precludes his return to his former life. In yet grimmer vein are those plays in which a supposed death reflects a pervasive concern with mortality. In Webster's *The White Devil* (1612), for example, a number of murders precede Flamineo's apparent shooting by his sister Vittoria, while the ensuing quarrel between 'murderess' and 'victim' is cut short by a group of conspirators who conclude the lives of both.

The fascination that the device exercised for the dramatists of

1. That is, *All's Well That Ends Well*, *Troilus and Cressida*, *Measure for Measure*, *Pericles*, *Cymbeline*, *The Winter's Tale* and *The Tempest*.

the period is not difficult to understand. On the most basic level, it allows for an elementary species of 'discovery', affording a visually exciting and emotionally satisfying means of achieving a happy outcome in the face of seemingly intractable difficulties. At the same time, it supplies the playwright with a range of options in terms of actor–audience relationships. On the one hand, those outside the play world might be initiated into the stratagem, functioning as fellow conspirators, and thus relishing the misguided responses of the dramatis personae while anticipating, either gleefully or with trepidation, the moment of their enlightenment. On the other hand, the spectators might be kept in ignorance of the ruse, thus sharing the surprise of those within the drama at the moment of revelation, and participating in the fear or wonder that the denoument evokes. For the hard-pressed dramatist, under constant pressure to provide material for an expanding market, the device clearly offered a ready instrument for the construction of a variety of plots, a means of serving the Beaujolais nouveau within an existing supply of bottles.

It is not merely the intrinsic dramatic value of the contrivance, however, that is responsible for its repeated use on the Renaissance stage. As in the case of other devices explored in the course of this book, the sources to which Elizabethan–Jacobean dramatists turned for their plots, and the interaction between playwrights and companies, also played a part in promoting its use. Marston's *The Dutch Courtesan* (1604–05) affords a typical example of this kind of cross-fertilization. The play, which involves the apparent demise of the hero through the agency of his friend, has its origins in one of the stories in Montreulx's pastoral romance *Les Bergeries de Juliette* (1585–98), but it is also influenced by Shakespeare's *Much Ado About Nothing*, which itself involves a feigned death, and by Marston's own earlier work (e.g. *Antonio and Mellida*) in which the same motif occurs. A similar situation obtains in a number of Shakespearian plays, and the genesis of each example becomes more complex with each fresh use of the device. Whereas it is possible to make a straightforward comparison between the identical siblings of *The Comedy of Errors* and their counterparts in the *Menaechmi*, or to distinguish the separate traditions from which Shakespeare's substitute bed mates derive, in the case of the feigned death the increasingly intricate entangling of influences makes the process of altering and changing a much more difficult one to pursue. It is for this reason that the discussion of the device has been reserved for this stage of the book.

Romeo and Juliet (1594–96) and *Antony and Cleopatra* (1606–07), the two plays in which a hypothetical death appears in a tragic context, offer the simplest approach to the exploration of the motif. At first glance, the two works have much in common. Both enact the tragic process arising from the passionate attachment between a pair of lovers in a divided world. Romeo and Juliet are separated by the feud between their families, Antony and Cleopatra by the irreconcilable oppositions between the societies to which they belong. The hero of both tragedies commits suicide as a result of a false report that his mistress is dead, while the heroine takes her own life as a result of her lover's death. Moreover, in both tragedies the feigned death of the heroine is productive of a sense of waste, in that the tragic outcome is not felt by the audience to be inevitable. Romeo kills himself at the very moment that Juliet begins to waken from her drugged sleep, while Antony receives his death wound only seconds before learning that Cleopatra is alive. In both cases, the superior awareness of the theatre audience imposes a distance between those outside the play world and the central figures. Rather than being wholly involved in the hero's anguish, the spectator is agonizingly aware of his mistake, and is engaged on one level in willing him to delay his action in the hope that the truth will be revealed.

Nevertheless, for all the superficial similarities between the two structures, the plays draw on different sources and constitute very different kinds of dramatic experience. As noted in the previous chapter, *Romeo and Juliet* looks back to Brooke's *The Tragicall Historye of Romeus and Juliet*, a tale designed, according to the author, to exhibit 'a coople of unfortunate lovers, thralling themselves to unhonest desire, neglecting the authoritie and advise of parents and frendes, conferring their principall counsels with dronken gossyppes, and superstitious friers . . . finallye, by all meanes of unhonest lyfe, hastyng to most unhappye deathe'.[2] Shakespeare remains faithful to Brooke's narrative throughout (cf. pages 126–8 above), but he does not embrace its moral judgements, transforming what purports to be an exemplary 'history' into a tragedy of doomed love. The closing scene of the play is generally regarded as among the most poignant in the dramatist's

2. Quoted from G. Bullough (1957–75), vol. I, pp. 284–5.

work. Prevented from acknowledging their attachment, the lovers have married in secret, but are obliged to part after a single night together when Romeo is banished for killing Tybalt. Threatened with a second marriage, Juliet swallows a potion that induces a death-like sleep, but the letter informing Romeo of her intention fails to reach him, and he mistakenly supposes her to be dead. Making his way to her family vault he takes poison as she is about to regain consciousness, while she, finding his body beside her when she wakens, kills herself with his dagger.

The painful nature of this last scene clearly depends in large measure upon the awareness of the theatre audience that Juliet is not dead as Romeo believes, and that a tragic outcome could be averted. The fate of the couple is not presented as the inescapable product of a depraved life, the interpretation Brooke's 'To the Reader' invites, but as a consequence of a series of accidents, in that had Romeo received the letter, or Juliet awakened a moment earlier, the stratagem would have been a success. The role of chance rather than character in determining the fate of the lovers is integral, moreover, to the pattern of action that the drama as a whole enacts. The relationship between events is fortuitous rather than inevitable, while the fates of the dramatis personae are governed not by intention, or by the moral order, but by chance. It is chance that the lovers belong to rival families, chance that Mercutio dies through Romeo's agency, and chance that Romeo himself becomes the instrument of Tybalt's death.

The circumstances surrounding Juliet's feigned death serve, therefore, on one level, to heighten the spectator's awareness of other potentialities, of the proximity between disaster and triumph, and the ease with which the catastrophe might have been prevented. Paradoxically, however, they also contribute to the strong sense of fatality with which the play is infused. The Prologue refers to the lovers as 'star-cross'd' (line 6) and 'death-mark'd' (line 9), while both Romeo and Juliet, for all their rapture in their relationship, are conscious of a sense of foreboding. Juliet, for example, feels that their love is

> too rash, too unadvis'd, too sudden,
> Too like the lightning, which doth cease to be
> Ere one can say 'It lightens'
>
> (II.ii.118–20)

while Romeo reveals his sense of impending doom in an exchange with the Friar before his marriage:

> Do thou but close our hands with holy words,
> Then love-devouring death do what he dare:
> It is enough I may but call her mine.
>
> (II.vi.6–8)

The comments of the Prologue and the presentiments of the characters combine to locate the adverse circumstance that brings about the deaths of the lovers in the context of some larger design. While on the one hand the fate of the protagonists appears to depend on a series of accidents, on the other it emerges as the product of some supernatural agency, engaged in hurrying the couple towards a premature death. This last implication is further enforced by a number of speeches suggesting that the relationship between the lovers has been engineered by some divine power as a means of bringing about an end to the feud between their families. The Prologue, for example, links the 'star-cross'd' nature of the relationship with the healing of the divisions within Verona (lines 1–8), while the Prince at the close of the play sees a providential force at work in the succession of deaths that have taken place:

> Capulet, Montague,
> See what a scourge is laid upon your hate,
> That heaven finds means to kill your joys with love;
> And I, for winking on your discords too,
> Have lost a brace of kinsmen.
>
> (V.iii.290–4)

Two very different responses are thus brought into play by the dramatist in relation to the feigned death through which the tragic outcome is precipitated. On one level those outside the play world are acutely aware that Juliet is alive, that the opportunity for happiness is still available to the lovers, and that it is only a chance succession of mishaps that is leading them to their graves, while on another they are gripped by the conviction that the relationship is a doomed one, and that Juliet's 'borrow'd likeness of shrunk death' (IV.i.104) foreshadows the terrible actuality. Nevertheless, for all their contradictory aspects, both these responses involve an awareness of the central figures as pawns or instruments of forces larger than themselves, and it is this sense of the ultimate powerlessness of the dramatis personae to shape their own destinies that distinguishes the nature of the process that the drama enacts (and the role of the feigned death within that process) from the kind of tragic experience the playwright presents in the seemingly similar *Antony and Cleaopatra.*

Though Shakespeare was evidently familiar with more than one version of the Antony and Cleopatra story,[3] the principal source around which the play is constructed is undoubtedly North's translation of Plutarch's *Lives of the Noble Grecians and Romanes* (1579). As in his handling of *Romeus and Juliet*, Shakespeare remains close in plot terms to his copy-text throughout, and it is from the material supplied by Plutarch that Cleopatra's feigned death is derived. Like Brooke's 'To the Reader', Plutarch's commentary on his story is overtly moralistic, and it is in the avoidance of a judgemental stance that the dramatist's most significant departure from his inherited tale lies. Where Plutarch's Antony 'slue him selfe, (to confesse a troth) cowardly, and miserably',[4] Shakespeare's central figure is both a 'strumpet's fool' (I.i.13) and the 'crown o' the earth' (IV.xv.63), and the feigned death that precipitates his suicide plays a major part in the ambivalent responses generated by the playwright to his fate.

Unlike *Romeo and Juliet* in which the youthfulness of the central figures is constantly stressed, and the constraints exercised by others (e.g. their parents, the Friar, etc.) play a significant part in the action, the title characters of *Antony and Cleopatra* are presented as mature, sexually experienced individuals, accustomed to dominating their world. Cleopatra is Queen of Egypt, and her lovers have been the mightiest men of their day, while Antony is one of the 'pillars' (I.i.12) by which the Roman state is sustained. The tragic action is consequently a product, not of forces external to the wills of the protagonists, but of their own personalities, and the lovers are largely masters of their own destinies on the human stage. Unlike Romeo, who is banished from Verona against his own volition by the authority of the Prince, Antony elects to leave Egypt in order to attend to his affairs in Rome, while Cleopatra can require news of her lover from a messenger (cf.*Antony and*

---

3. For some of the materials available to him see G. Bullough (1957–75), vol. V, pp. 218–48.
4. Quoted from G. Bullough (1957–75), vol. V, p. 321.

Cleopatra, II.v.24–106) where Juliet can only sue (cf.*Romeo and Juliet*, II.v.18–65). Similarly, where the potion device in *Romeo and Juliet* is suggested to Juliet by the Friar, and carries the weight of his moral authority, the false report of the Queen's death in *Antony and Cleopatra* is proposed by Charmian, one of the Queen's ladies, and her mistress catches at it, not because she respects the other's judgement, but because it is of a piece with the kind of play-acting to which she is naturally disposed to resort. Cleopatra's supposed death is thus a product of disposition rather than circumstance, and so too are the events by which it is instigated and which it occasions. Following the defection of his navy to Octavius Caesar, Antony (who has had ample evidence of the Queen's fickleness) accuses her of betraying him, and it is fear of his anger that causes her to promulgate the news of her 'death'. The motive behind the deception is thus to buy time and procure safety following a breakdown of trust, rather than to pave the way for a physical reunion, as in *Romeo and Juliet*, after a period of enforced separation. At the same time, in contrast to Juliet, who fully intends to alert Romeo to the course she has elected to follow but is defeated by the operations of chance, Cleopatra sets out to deceive her lover, and is therefore directly responsible for his death. Consequently, though Romeo and Antony respond in superficially similar ways to the death of a mistress, the implications of their actions are very different. Romeo's prompt decision to kill himself reflects his total commitment to Juliet, and the ill-starred nature of their love, while Antony's resolution to 'Lie down and stray no farther' (*Antony and Cleopatra*, IV.xiv.47) exhibits his failure to comprehend not only the woman he has loved but the world in which he has sought to function.

Where *Romeo and Juliet* takes place in and around Verona, *Antony and Cleopatra* is set in a much larger context. A contrast is set up from the outset between the Roman and Egyptian worlds, and this contrast is epitomized in the mental landscapes of their respective rulers – Octavius Caesar and Cleopatra. The former is cold, committed to the military virtues, and intensely concerned with political power, while the latter is sensuous, fickle and devious, partaking of the fecundity and fluidity of the Nile that dominates Egyptian life. Unlike Juliet's decision to take the potion which is a deeply private one, Cleopatra's announcement of her 'death' is thus consistent with the character of her race – it is hasty rather than considered, born of fear rather than motivated by honour, and instinctively devious rather than forthright. At the same time, Antony's response to her supposed action is symptomatic of his conduct. Torn between his love for Cleopatra and his duty as a member of the triumvirate, he oscillates between Rome and Egypt, and his attempted suicide functions as a final demonstration of his inability to act coherently in either location. The decision to take his own life is itself ambivalent. The action is a typically Roman one, but the motive by which it is prompted, love for Cleopatra not defeat in battle, is Egyptian. His conduct is ineffectual, moreover, from either standpoint. The potential grandeur of the renunciation of life for love is undermined by the deception on which the gesture is based, while the attempt to die in 'the high Roman fashion' (IV.xv.87) is frustrated by his followers' refusal to assist him (cf.IV.xiv.54–95 and 105–10), and by his own failure to kill himself outright (cf.IV.xiv.95–106).

The behaviour of the lovers after Antony's attempted suicide also points to the very different significance of the feigned death in the later play. Romeo and Juliet elect to die within moments of one another, with Romeo's instantaneous decision to lie with his wife in the Capulet tomb (cf.V.i.34), and Juliet's equally swift response to the sight of his body (cf.V.iii.150–69) emphasizing the absolute nature of the relationship between them. Antony and Cleopatra, by contrast, do not die together. While the false report of Cleopatra's death is directly responsible for Antony's attempt on his own life, his suicide does not lead directly to hers, but contributes to the development of her character as woman and queen that takes place in the final act. Rather than being focused on a single tableau generating a sense of pity and waste, the attention of the audience is thus divided between the bungling and confusion through which Antony's once-heroic existence draws to its undignified close, and the impact of his death on those who survive him, both in the personal sphere and in the larger arena of Roman–Egyptian relations.

It will be apparent from the above that though Shakespeare moves away in both *Romeo and Juliet* and *Antony and Cleopatra* from the moralistic positions adopted in his sources, he uses the feigned deaths that determine the fates of his lovers to project widely divergent visions of man's relationship with the world he inhabits. In *Romeo and Juliet* the individual is a prey to external forces, an instrument of the stars, while the human will in *Antony and Cleopatra* plays a much larger part in shaping the outcome of events. The use of the putative death in the two plays is productive, nevertheless, in spite of their differences, of a similar kind of tragic effect. Since in both instances the incident that leads to the hero's suicide is hypothetical rather than real, the audience is aware of alternative scenarios (that Juliet might stir, for example, or Cleopatra repent of her rashness), and this awareness gives rise to a range of emotions – uncertainty, anxiety, even frustration – that imposes a distance between those inside and outside the play world. At the same time, the fact that the hero's decision is based on a false assumption undercuts in its arbitrariness the inevitability of the tragic process, while qualifying the spectator's acceptance of the protagonists' reflections on their experience. The fictive nature of a crucial link in the chain of the play's events thus serves to shift the drama away from that species of action in which the audience participates in the inescapable suffering of a central figure, towards the kind of theatrical experience evocative of both the positive and negative potentialities of human life.

It is this sense of alternative possibilities that links *Romeo and Juliet* and *Antony and Cleopatra* with *Much Ado About Nothing*, the first play in which Shakespeare explores the regenerative aspects of the feigned death motif. Like *Romeo and Juliet*, the Hero–Claudio plot of *Much Ado About Nothing* is based on a story which enjoyed wide currency in the sixteenth century, and was probably known to Shakespeare in a variety of versions. The basic plot involves three characters – a pair of young lovers and a villain who engineers a division between the two. Through the machinations of the latter, the hero sees a woman, whom he mistakes for his mistress, receiving the addresses of another man at her chamber window, and he consequently repudiates her, believing her to be false. The lady disappears and is presumed to be dead, but returns to be reconciled to her lover (in most versions of the story) when the villain's treachery is revealed. The tale admitted a variety of moral interpretations that afforded a justification for its relation. For Belleforest in his *Histoires Tragiques* (1569), for example, it demonstrated the way in which one sin gives rise to another; for Whetstone in *The Rocke of Regard* (1576) it afforded an example of 'the wretched end of wanton and dissolute living', while for Spenser in *The Fairie Queene* (1590) it supplied a warning against wrath.[5] The tap roots of the story, however, extend far beneath the moral topsoil of man's consciousness. On the one hand, the pattern of the tale allies it with a web of legendary material turning on man's unwitting destruction through deception or error of the thing he values most (e.g. the loss of the Garden of Eden through the wiles of Satan and the picking of the forbidden fruit: Genesis Chapter 3), while on the other it traces a cycle of death and rebirth, and thus has elements of a fertility myth (cf.the story of Persephone).[6] It is these more potent 'potentialities' underlying his sources that Shakespeare draws on in the construction of his play.

There can be no doubt that the characters of *Much Ado* may be readily accommodated within the moral categories of the inherited plot. Don John is unequivocally a villain, at odds with the society in which he functions; Claudio (the youthful lover) is both inexperienced and easily led; while Hero (the defamed lady) is the epitome of unsullied virtue and demure womanhood. The interaction between these figures plainly demonstrates the way in which human beings may be seduced from the path of virtue, and the ease with which the seemingly noble may be brought to evil and destructive courses. This moral statement is set, however, within a much larger context through a number of significant alterations to the basic tale. In the first place, the villain who brings about the heroine's 'death' is not simply a virtuous man corrupted by passion as in Bandello's version of the story, or a courtier given to dissimulation as in Belleforest's. Shakespeare's miscreant is the bastard brother of the Prince of Aragon, a man whose opposition to the divine order is implicit in the circumstances of his birth. 'Half-damned' from the moment of conception,[7] the bastard represented to Renaissance playgoers the embodiment of a malign

---

5. See G. Bullough (1957–75), vol. II, pp. 63–6. The direct quotation is from p. 66.
6. For an account of this tale see R. Graves (1955) (revised 1960) *The Greek Myths*. Penguin Books, Harmondsworth, vol. 1, pp. 89ff.
7. See *The Revenger's Tragedy* (Tourneur? 1605–06):

> O what a grief 'tis, that a man should live
> But once i'th'world, and then to live a bastard,
> The curse o'the womb, the thief of nature,
> Begot against the seventh commandment,
> Half-damn'd in the conception, by the justice
> Of that unbribed everlasting law.

(I.ii.159–64)

will, and Don John's destructive impulses towards Claudio and larger antagonism to love and virtue are typical of the class of beings to which he belongs. Shakespeare's second adaptation of his source material is equally significant. Whereas in the romances the disappearance of the heroine is a product of her own choice or the actions of her lover, in *Much Ado* Shakespeare turns back to his own work, ascribing the stratagem to a friar (cf. *Romeo and Juliet*). The interest of the tale is thus widened from the moral development of the hero to a clash between spiritual forces, with the feigned death of the heroine playing a crucial part in the progress towards the purgation of evil.

Though the Friar does not appear in the play prior to the defamation of Hero, he intervenes between father and daughter, following the departure of Claudio, with an authority that engages immediate respect:

> Pause awhile,
> And let my counsel sway you in this case.
> Your daughter here the princes left for dead,
> Let her awhile be secretly kept in,
> And publish it that she is dead indeed;
> Maintain a mourning ostentation,
> And on your family's old monument,
> Hang mournful epitaphs, and do all rites
> That appertain unto a burial.
>
> (IV.i.200–8)

There can be little doubt, that Shakespeare's mind has reverted here to *Romeo and Juliet*. In both instances a friar who has been called upon to officiate at a marriage ceremony proposes 'A thing like death to chide away [the] shame' (*Romeo and Juliet*, IV.i.74) of the sexual dishonour of the bride. The role assigned to Hero's father in the deception parallels that played unwittingly by Juliet's, while the emphasis on the rites of mourning, and the placing of the dead in a family vault, confirms the link between the two plays. The remainder of the Friar's speech, however, posits a development wholly different from that anticipated by his predecessor:

> *Leon.* What shall become of this? What will this do?
> *Friar.* Marry, this well carried shall on her behalf
>   Change slander to remorse; that is some good:

But not for that dream I on this strange course,
But on this travail look for greater birth.
She dying, as it must be so maintain'd,
Upon the instant that she was accus'd,
Shall be lamented, pitied, and excus'd
Of every hearer; for it so falls out
That what we have we prize not to the worth
Whiles we enjoy it, but being lack'd and lost,
Why then we rack the value, then we find
The virtue that possession would not show us
Whiles it was ours: so will it fare with Claudio.
When we shall hear she died upon his words,
Th'idea of her life shall sweetly creep
Into his study of imagination,
And every lovely organ of her life
Shall come apparell'd in more precious habit,
More moving-delicate and full of life,
Into the eye and prospect of his soul
Than when she liv'd indeed: then shall he mourn –
If ever love had interest in his liver –
And wish he had not so accused her:
No, though he thought the accusation true.
Let this be so, and doubt not but success
Will fashion the event in better shape
Than I can lay it down in likelihood.
But if all aim but this be levell'd false,
The supposition of the lady's death
Will quench the wonder of her infamy.
. . . .
Come, lady, die to live; this wedding-day
Perhaps is but prolong'd; have patience and endure.
                                        (IV.i.209–54)

Unlike those of his tragic counterpart, the Friar's aims here are
psychological rather than logistical, designed to manipulate the
attitudes of those responsible for Hero's plight, rather than to effect
a physical reunion between the lovers. This immediate objective
(which may be seen as the conventional moral one) is merely a
step, however, towards a much more significant species of change.
While the lady's accusers will be moved to 'remorse' (IV.i.211) by
the news of her supposed death, Hero herself will be cleansed of
the taint of her defamation as her virtues are re-established in the
public mind (IV.i.214–30). This process in turn is set in a larger

context through its association with the concept of rebirth. The anguish of Hero and her departure from life are seen as 'travail' (i.e. birth pangs) through which her reputation will be reborn, while the injunction 'die to live' (line 253) locates this experience within a cyclical process. Given the status of the speaker, and the context in which the scene takes place, the exhortation clearly has spiritual overtones, and the wider resonances of the scene would not have been lost on the play's original spectators. Where Juliet's feigned death is designed to frustrate the operations of chance, Hero's is thus a response to the workings of the forces of evil, initiating a period of self-examination and contrition leading ultimately to renewal.

The final act of the play reiterates the cyclical and religious processes implicit in the terminology in which the Friar's device is propounded. Leonato instructs Claudio to retract his accusation against Hero (V.i.275–6), requiring him to 'hang . . . an epitaph' (V.i.278) on her tomb in 'penance' (V.i.267) for his part in her death, and promising him 'almost the copy of my child that's dead' (V.i.283) in place of the lady he traduced. Mourning obsequies representative of Claudio's repentance for his misconduct, are consequently performed before the monument where Hero's body reputedly lies, with the mourners turning away at the completion of the ritual to prepare for the wedding that can now ensue. As Claudio affirms his willingness to embrace the woman who is to take the place of his former bride, the veiled lady removes her mask, revealing both the old Hero and a new one:

> *Claud.* Give me your hand before this holy friar.
>   I am your husband if you like of me.
> *Hero.* [*Unmasking.*] And when I liv'd, I was your other wife;
>   And when you lov'd, you were my other husband.
> *Claud.* Another Hero!
> *Hero.*   Nothing certainer:
>   One Hero died defil'd, but I do live,
>   And surely as I live, I am a maid.
>
>   (V.iv.58–64)

This scene could be regarded as fulfilling one of the alternative potentialities of which the audience is conscious in Shakespeare's earlier handling of the feigned death motif. Where Juliet wakens in the family monument with the dead body of her husband beside her, surrounded by images of mortality, Hero returns from the tomb to be reunited with her lover in a world in which 'wonder' is 'familiar' (V.iv.70), and a new order is instigated in the chapel.

It is the concept of dying to live, in both physical and spiritual senses, that is taken up by the dramatist in *All's Well That Ends Well*. As noted in Chapter 4 of this book, the play looks back to one of the tales in Boccaccio's *Decameron*, but Shakespeare has 'altered and changed' his material at a number of points. One of the most significant of these involves the conduct of the heroine after her repudiation by her husband. Boccaccio's lady demonstrates her worth as a wife through her management of her husband's estates, whereas Shakespeare's circulates the news that 'the tenderness of her nature became as a prey to her grief' (IV.iii.49–50), and disappears from the public eye. The similarities with Hero's situation (repudiation followed by a supposed death) are obvious, but Shakespeare has not simply transferred the events of the Hero–Claudio plot into a different dramatic context. In the first place, the status of the rejected maiden is markedly different. In *Much Ado About Nothing* the attention of the audience is divided between two pairs of lovers (Beatrice and Benedick – Hero and Claudio) whereas in *All's Well That Ends Well* Bertram and Helena are the sole object of interest, and the hypothetical death of one of these figures consequently has a larger significance within the scheme of the action than the corresponding incident in the earlier play. At the same time, the position of the repudiated lady has undergone an important change. Unlike Hero, whose repudiation is the product of a slanderous accusation that blemishes her reputation in the play world, Helena is rejected by Bertram on the grounds of class rather than moral condition, and is highly esteemed for her virtue throughout. Moreover, while Hero is a worthy but relatively passive young woman who is acted on by others (e.g. the Friar, Don John) for good or ill, Helena is a highly motivated individual who is responsible to a far greater degree for the situations in which she finds herself. In *All's Well That Ends Well*, in short, the feigned death of the heroine is a product not of expediency (as in *Romeo and Juliet* and *Much Ado About Nothing*) but of choice, and is motivated by considerations other than the preservation of love and honour.

It is in Act III scene ii that Helena embarks upon the course that is to lead to her supposed death. Having secured a husband of

superior rank by curing the King of a fatal illness and been rejected
by the man of her choice (see above, Chapter 4), she returns alone
to the family seat, only to discover that her husband has no
intention of joining her there but has departed for the wars.
Convinced that she is responsible for the dangers he will face, she
decides to expose herself to similar perils by leaving Rossillion,
thus enabling him to return home:

> Poor lord, is't I,
> That chase thee from thy country, and expose
> Those tender limbs of thine to the event
> Of the none-sparing war? And is it I
> That drive thee from the sportive court, where thou
> Wast shot at with fair eyes, to be the mark
> Of smoky muskets?
> ....
> Whoever shoots at him, I set him there;
> Whoever charges on his forward breast,
> I am the caitiff that do hold him to't;
> And though I kill him not, I am the cause
> His death was so effected. Better 'twere
> I met the ravin lion when he roar'd
> With sharp constraint of hunger; better 'twere
> That all the miseries which nature owes
> Were mine at once.
>
> (III.ii.102–20)

What is being suggested here is a species of substitution (i.e. that
she will suffer in his place), and the same implication underlies the
terms in which she writes to the Countess of the course she has
elected to take:

> I am Saint Jacques' pilgrim, thither gone.
> Ambitious love hath so in me offended
> That barefoot plod I the cold ground upon,
> With sainted vow my faults to have amended.
> Write, write, that from the bloody course of war
> My dearest master, your dear son, may hie.
> Bless him at home in peace, whilst I from far
> His name with zealous fervour sanctify.
> ....
> He is too good and fair for death and me;
> Whom I myself embrace to set him free.
>
> (III.iv.4–17)

The process of expiation through substitution and death initiated here is carried forward in the following act, but the actuality proves more complex than Helena originally conceives. Having died to the world with her disappearance from Rossillion, she arrives in Florence in the guise of a pilgrim, where she discovers that Bertram is engaged in the seduction of Diana. In order to preserve his honour and fulfil his conditions for acknowledging her as his wife, she offers to take Diana's place in the bedchamber, and is thus unwittingly embraced by her husband (see above, Chapter 4). Significantly for the concerns of this chapter, a discussion takes place between two lords while this nocturnal encounter is in progress, during which it is revealed to the audience that Helena has promulgated the news of her own death:

> *First Lord.* Sir, his wife some two months since fled from his house. Her pretence is a pilgrimage to Saint Jacques le Grand; which holy undertaking with most austere sanctimony she accomplish'd; and there residing, the tenderness of her nature became as a prey to her grief; in fine, made a groan of her last breath, and now she sings in heaven.
>
> *Second Lord.* How is this justified?
>
> *First Lord.* The stronger part of it by her own letters, which makes her story true even to the point of her death. Her death itself, which could not be her office to say is come, was faithfully confirm'd by the rector of the place.
>
> (IV.iii.45–57; Arden ed.)

Here, the fusion of two traditionally distinct stories – the feigned death and the bed trick – serves to heighten the significance of the latter device. Whereas Boccaccio's heroine proves her wit and worth in accomplishing her husband's conditions (see pp. 100–1 above), Helena redeems Bertram from error through an act of self-surrender that is given spiritual sanction through the 'rector' who bears witness to her death (cf. the Friars of *Romeo and Juliet* and *Much Ado About Nothing*). The old Helena 'dies' in order to liberate her husband, offering her body, on more than one level, for his social and spiritual deliverance. The outcome of the encounter between Bertram and 'Diana' is important, moreover, in this context. On his return to Rossillion, the young count stands accused not only of seducing Diana but of disposing of his wife, and he loses the respect of those around him through his evasiveness in relation to both charges. It is at this nadir of his fortunes that Diana paves the way for Helena's 'resurrection' with a riddling statement through which Bertram's burden of guilt falls away:

> But for this lord
> Who hath abus'd me as he knows himself –
> Though yet he never harm'd me – here I quit him.
> He knows himself my bed he hath defil'd;
> And at that time he got his wife with child.
> Dead though she be she feels her young one kick.
> So there's my riddle: one that's dead is quick.
>
> (V.iii.291–7)

What is being enacted in this phase of the play is a movement through death to new life. Helena is 'quick' in the sense of 'living' and consequently the agent of Bertram's release, but she is also 'quick' in the sense of 'pregnant' and therefore an instrument of renewal. The putative death of the heroine in this play may thus be seen in symbolic terms, functioning as the gateway to a new and better existence, rather than a mechanism for the evasion of suffering.

A similar use of a supposed death in the regeneration of a corrupt society occurs in *Measure for Measure*, a play closely related to *All's Well* (cf. Chapter 4, above). The play is structured upon Whetstone's version of a story in Cinthio's *Hecatommithi*, and it is from Whetstone's drama that the feigned death of the erring lover (Claudio) is derived. Nevertheless, Shakespeare's handling of Claudio's 'execution' is clearly influenced by his previous work. Once again, the device is propounded by a Friar (in this instance the disguised Duke), while the hypothetical death of a major character permits the expiation of guilt. Some aspects of the plot of the play have been outlined in a previous chapter, but further details of the action may be helpful at this point. A pair of young lovers, Claudio and Juliet (both names being carried over from earlier plays), have been found guilty of the crime of fornication, and Claudio is condemned to death. His sister is informed by the acting head of state (Angelo) that he will remit the sentence only in exchange for her virginity, but though her blackmailer believes that the sexual ransom has been paid he persists with the execution. The true head of state then proposes that the head of another condemned man should be sent to Angelo in place of Claudio's, only to be frustrated by the spiritual condition of the prisoner who proves unfit to meet his maker. It is at this point that the Provost reveals that another criminal, who closely resembles Claudio, has died in custody, and suggests that the head of this man should be used as proof that the sentence has been carried out. Angelo accepts the evidence with which he is presented, while Claudio's sister believes that her stratagem has failed and that her brother has been beheaded.

It will be apparent from this brief outline that a considerable distance is set up in the course of the action between the perceptions of those inside and outside the play world. The members of the audience are aware throughout that Claudio's life has been saved, while for the dramatis personae his death is an actuality. As noted in Chapter 4, Angelo is accused (and believes himself to be guilty) of judicial murder, while Isabella has to wrestle with the negative impulses unleashed in her by the deputy's conduct. The use of the feigned death in this context thus allows the perpetration, in intention, of the gravest offences (cf. the substitute bed mate motif), enabling the individual to recognize his or her failings without finally shouldering the responsibility for the errors to which they lead. Where the hypothetical deaths of *Romeo and Juliet* and *Antony and Cleopatra* admit the recognition of the comic potentiality within the tragic framework, the supposed loss of Claudio may, therefore, be argued to permit the reverse – the exploration of tragic experience within a comic structure.

As in *All's Well That Ends Well* the shift that takes place in *Measure for Measure* from the internal 'tragic' perspective to the external 'comic' one, is associated with the concept of rebirth. The muffled figure who 'should have died when Claudio lost his head' (V.i.486) is presented to Isabella as a substitute brother, and the revelation of his identity leads to a fresh upsurge of life. Claudio himself is pardoned, and his marriage to Juliet confirmed, while his 'unmuffling' saves Angelo in both physical and spiritual senses, cf.:

> *Duke.* By this Lord Angelo perceives he's safe;
> Methrinks I see a quickening in his eye.
> (V.i.492–3)

Superficially the Duke's observation here merely indicates that Angelo recognizes that his situation has changed, but the use of the term 'quickening' gives the comment a deeper resonance, suggesting the beginning of a new life (cf. the play on the word 'quick' in

All's Well That Ends Well, V.iii.297). Claudio is thus not the only character who 'dies' in the course of the play. Other figures die metaphorically with him, and are reborn into a new existence through the shedding of their corrupted selves.

The substitutions of *All's Well* and *Measure for Measure* (Helena for Bertram, Helena for Diana, Mariana for Isabella, Ragozine for Claudio) clearly link the two plays with that class of traditional story in which one object is sacrificed in place of another.[8] Numerous variations exist on this motif which has its origins in religious practice, and its ritual character is frequently suggested in the two plays. As suggested in Chapter 4 of this book, both comedies invite an awareness of the spiritual dimensions of their events, while the familiar dialogue of both works gives way at crucial moments to a language remote from natural speech. *All's Well That Ends Well*, for example, moves towards riddle, a common element of religious rites (cf. V.iii.282–7), while *Measure for Measure* employs the rhymed tetrameter, suggestive in its emphatic rhythms of chant:

> *Duke.* He who the sword of heaven will bear
> Should be as holy as severe:
> Pattern in himself to know,
> Grace to stand, and virtue, go:
> More nor less to others paying
> Than by self-offences weighing.
> Shame to him whose cruel striking
> Kills for faults of his own liking!
> Twice treble shame on Angelo,
> To weed my vice, and let his grow!
>   (III.ii.254–63)

It is this ritual aspect of the passage through a hypothetical death to an enhanced life which is developed in the plays of Shakespeare's last period (*Pericles*, *Cymbeline*, *The Winter's Tale*, *The Tempest*). In *Pericles* (1607–08), for example, the first play of the group, the eponymous hero undergoes a series of losses and recoveries which are associated from the outset with death and rebirth. The play is based on a Greek romance that enjoyed considerable popularity throughout Europe during the Renaissance and Middle Ages, and which was probably known to Shakespeare through Gower's

8. For a Biblical example see the story of Abraham and Isaac (Genesis, chapter 2).

Confessio Amantis (1393) and Laurence Twine's *The Patterne of Painefull Adventures* (1576). Shakespeare follows his sources closely,[9] but he structures his work far more systematically than his 'authors' (*Pericles*, 1 Chorus, 20) around a pattern of recurring situations involving some form of annihilation. At the start of Act II, for example, having been shipwrecked on leaving Tharsus, and tossed ashore bereft of possessions, Pericles addresses the elements in the following terms:

> Yet cease your ire, you angry stars of heaven!
> Wind, rain and thunder, remember, earthly man
> Is but a substance that must yield to you;
> And I, as fits my nature, do obey you.
> Alas, the seas hath cast me on the rocks,
> Wash'd me from shore to shore, and left me breath
> Nothing to think on but ensuing death.
> Let it suffice the greatness of your powers
> To have bereft a prince of all his fortunes;
> And having thrown him from your wat'ry grave,
> Here to have death in peace is all he'll crave.
>
> (II.i.1–11)

This passage has no counterpart in the *Confessio Amantis* in which Pericles is simply cast ashore 'in a poure plite' (line 643).[10] On the surface, the Prince is simply engaged here in expressing his deference to the gods and readiness to die, but on a deeper level (particularly in the first three lines) the vocabulary that he employs suggests a process of dissolution. At the very moment at which he emerges from his 'wat'ry grave', however, a group of fishermen come to his assistance, and offer him their aid in winning the hand of the Princess Thaisa. Thus where Gower's prince, at the corresponding point of the narrative, simply looks forward to 'joye after his sorowe' (line 673), Shakespeare's leaves the stage hoping to 'rise' (II.i.165).

The metaphorical journey that takes place here through death to

---

9. Though the authorship of parts of this play is disputed, I refer to the drama as Shakespeare's in the assumption that the design as a whole, as well as much of the execution, is his.

10. All quotations from Gower are from G. Bullough (1957–75), vol. VI, pp. 375–423. Twine's hero rebukes the sea for its untrustworthiness, and attributes his escape to providence (cf. *The Patterne of Painefull Adventures*, G. Bullough (1957–75), vol. VI, p. 434).

a fresh existence becomes literal in the following act. Having successfully wooed Thaisa, Pericles sets sail once again with his wife, but his Queen falls in labour during a tempest and seemingly dies while giving birth to her child. Urged by the sailors who believe that her corpse will bring them misfortune, the Prince consigns his wife's body to the deep, but her coffin is washed ashore at Ephesus, and carried to the house of the Lord Cerimon. It is at this point in the drama that the seesaw experience of the central figures acquires an overtly spiritual meaning, and is assimilated to ritual. Whereas Gower's Cerimon is simply 'A worthie clerke and surgien, / And eke a great phisicien' (1171–2),[11] the character of Shakespeare's Cerimon is more fully delineated, prior to the discovery of Thaisa's coffin, and the terms in which he speaks of himself establish him as a species of 'magus':

> I hold it ever,
> Virtue and cunning were endowments greater
> Than nobleness and riches; careless heirs
> May the two latter darken and expend,
> But immortality attends the former,
> Making a man a god. 'Tis known I ever
> Have studied physic, through which secret art,
> By turning o'er authorities, I have,
> Together with my practice, made familiar
> To me and to my aid the blest infusions
> That dwells in vegetives, in metals, stones;
> And can speak of the disturbances that
> Nature works, and of her cures; which doth give me
> A more content in course of true delight
> Than to be thirsty after tottering honour,
> Or tie my treasure up in silken bags,
> To please the fool and death.
>
> (III.ii.26–42)

Cerimon's learning and knowledge of herbs clearly associates him with the Friars of earlier plays (cf. *Much Ado*, IV.i.164–7, *Romeo and Juliet*, II.iii.1–16), but his potency is far greater than that of his predecessors. Though Juliet's spiritual adviser is capable of

11. Cf. Twine's Cerimon who is described as a 'physition' (G. Bullough (1957–75), vol. VI, p. 447). In Twine's narrative, however, it is Machaon, Cerimon's 'scholler in Physicke' (G. Bullough (1957–75), vol. VI, p. 449) who restores the lady to life.

inducing a death-like sleep, his designs are ultimately defeated by a power superior to his own, while the priest who officiates at Hero's wedding merely uses the appearance of death as an expediency, revealing the truth when his purposes have been achieved. In *Pericles*, by contrast, Thaisa's death is not a device but a seeming actuality, and it is an art akin to magic but emphatically aligned with virtue that restores her to life:

> *Cer.*   Make a fire within;
> Fetch hither all my boxes in my closet.
> Death may usurp on nature many hours,
> And yet the fire of life kindle again
> The o'erpress'd spirits. I heard of an Egyptian
> That had nine hours lien dead,
> Who was by good appliance recovered.
>
> *Enter Servant, with [boxes,] napkins, and fire.*
>
> Well said, well said; the fire and cloths.
> The still and woeful music that we have,
> Cause it to sound, beseech you. [*Music*]
> The viol once more; how thou stirr'st, thou block!
> The music there! [*Music*] I pray you, give her air.
> Gentlemen, this queen will live.
> Nature awakes a warm breath out of her.
> She hath not been entranc'd above five hours;
> See, how she 'gins to blow into life's flower again!
> *1 Gent.* The heavens, through you, increase our wonder.
>   (III.ii.82–98)

The words spoken by the First Gentlemen serve to link the raising of Thaisa with the operation of supernatural forces – forces of which Cerimon himself is an instrument. The use of music to revive the Queen suggests the evocation of a divine harmony, while the enhanced spirituality of the new life into which Thaisa 'blows' is indicated by her decision to become a votaress of Diana.

While Act II sees Pericles' resurrection from shipwreck, and Act III the death and rebirth of his queen, Act IV is concerned with the loss of their daughter, Marina. Having been entrusted to the care of Dionyza, Marina grows into a virtuous and talented young woman, but she excites the enmity of her guardian, who resents her superiority to her own child (cf. 1 Chorus, IV.1–52). Dionyza consequently plans her murder, but her instrument fails to carry out her commission when attacked by pirates, and is obliged to 'swear she's dead / And thrown into the sea' (IV.i.98–9). Convinced that her wishes have been carried out, Dionyza informs her appalled husband that she has disposed of their unwelcome charge, and describes the deception she plans to practise on Pericles:

> Cle[on].   What canst thou say
>   When noble Pericles shall demand his child?
> Dion. That she is dead. Nurses are not the fates,
>   To foster it, not ever to preserve.
>   She died at night; I'll say so. Who can cross it?
> ....
>   And as for Pericles,
>   What shall he say? we wept after her hearse,
>   And yet we mourn. Her monument
>   Is almost finish'd, and her epitaphs
>   In glitt'ring golden characters express
>   A general praise to her, and care in us
>   At whose expense 'tis done.
>   (IV.iii.12–46)

At first sight this episode appears to look back to *Much Ado About Nothing* and the funeral obsequies conducted over the 'dead' Hero, but in fact the pretence enacted by Dionyza occurs in both of the principal sources from which the plot of the play derives. The significance of the deception is considerably heightened, though, in the Shakespearian version of the tale, by the recurring patterns into which it is woven. Dionyza and Cleon deceive Pericles into the belief that Marina is dead, but they themselves are deceived by Leonine. At the same time, Leonine is mistaken in his assumption that Marina cannot escape the hands of the pirates, and thus wrongly believes her to be dead, while feigning to have carried out his commission. Pericles himself is convinced, erroneously, that he has lost both wife and child, passing into a state of suspended animation from which he in turn can be recovered only by Marina. All three principal characters die, therefore, in some sense to their own world, while being susceptible for the members of the audience of recovery.

As in a number of Shakespeare's earlier plays, the supposed death of the heroine is associated in both *Pericles* itself and the sources on which it draws with the taint of sexual dishonour. Having been carried off by the pirates, Marina is sold to a brothel keeper, and is consequently in danger of physical defilement. In *Pericles*, however, the contamination that threatens the heroine is placed in a larger context than in previous compositions through the adaptations that Shakespeare makes to his inherited tale. Catching up Marina's frequent appeals to the gods in Twine's *Patterne of Painfull Adventures*, and opposing them with a sequence of references to the diabolic (cf.IV.vi.164 and 1 Chorus, V. 11) Shakespeare transforms the bawdy house into a species of hell, implying that the heroine's progress through 'death' into the brothel is a descent from this world into the pit. Significantly Marina's virtue proves to be too great to be contained by this environment, and she emerges from the 'unhallow'd' (IV.vi.99) world of the brothel keeper into an existence explicitly associated with the divine, cf.:

> She sings like one immortal, and she dances
> As goddess-like to her admired lays.
> Deep clerks she dumbs, and with her neele composes
> Nature's own shape, of bud, bird, branch or berry.
>
> (1 Chorus, V.3–6)

It is at this point in the drama that some of the most powerful effects are elicited from the variations that Shakespeare has woven on the putative death motif. As in the sources, the supposedly dead Marina encounters her father, awakening him from the death-like trance into which he has passed, but unlike the incidents on which it is structured the Shakespearian reunion fuses the recovery of the individual with the ebb and flow of the sea, a cycle of death and rebirth, and the beneficence of the gods, cf.:

> *Per.* Give me a gash, put me to present pain,
>   Lest this great sea of joys rushing upon me
>   O'erbear the shores of my mortality,
>   And drown me with their sweetness. O, come hither,
>   Thou that beget'st him that did thee beget;
>   Thou that wast born at sea, buried at Tharsus,
>   And found at sea again. O Helicanus,
>   Down on thy knees! thank the holy gods as loud
>   As thunder threatens us: this is Marina.
>
> (V.i.191–99)

The spiritual plane on which this scene functions is further enforced by the incident which brings the episode to a close. Having been lulled to sleep by the music of the spheres, Pericles is visited by the goddess Diana, who instructs him to go to her temple in Ephesus and recite his story before her altar. The final phase of the action thus moves, once again, towards the enactment of ritual. Pericles formally rehearses his successive gains and losses in the presence of Diana's vestals, causing Thaisa in turn to tell her story, and initiating her return to her husband and child. All three principal characters consequently pass, in the course of the drama, through death to a fuller existence, one irradiated by the divine approval bestowed on the active pursuit of virtue, and submission to the will of supernatural powers.

It will be evident from this very brief account of the complex intermeshing of supposed and metaphorical deaths that takes place as the action unfolds that the hypothetical demise of a principal character is not simply a ruse here deployed by the dramatis personae for positive or negative ends, but part of a pattern of action with symbolic dimensions. The fictive state functions as a gateway to a different order of experience, and represents a ritualized expression of a movement through an extremity of suffering to an apprehension of the divine. The constant references to the sea, furthermore, serve to equate this process with the rhythm of the seasons. The storm in which Thaisa 'dies', for example, is evocative of winter, while Pericles wakens to embrace his child (and to give her in marriage) during Neptune's summer feast in Mytilene (cf. V.i.17). These larger implications of the supposed loss of a major character are common to all four of Shakespeare's final plays. In *Cymbeline* (1608–09), for example, the substitution motif of earlier comedies is once again caught up, but the exchanges that the drama enacts have a wider meaning than in previous compositions. Two antithetical figures are set before the audience at the start of the action – Posthumus, who is the epitome of virtue (cf. I.i.28–54) and Cloten, who is 'Too bad for bad report' (I.i.17). As noted in Chapter 2, Posthumus sins against his newly married wife, Imogen, by ordering her death in the belief that she is adulterous, and he offers his life to the gods in recompense when he discovers the magnitude of his error. Imogen's death, however, is doubly fictitious. In the first place, Pisanio, Posthumus' instrument, fails to carry out his orders (cf. III.iv.1–181), and in the second, the inanimate state into which she lapses after fleeing for her life is merely the product of a sleeping potion. Posthumus' misconduct in relation to his wife is thus hypothetical rather than real, and he 'dies' for it by proxy. Cloten, dressed in Posthumus' garments, is killed by his virtuous stepbrother, Guiderius, and his body is laid beside that of the supposedly dead Imogen. The heroine consequently wakens to find the corpse of her 'husband' beside her (cf. *Romeo and Juliet*), and suffers an agony of grief at his loss. Both Posthumus and Imogen thus 'die' to those closest to them in the course of the play, and embark on a regenerated existence at the close purged of calumny (cf. *Much Ado About Nothing*) and guilt (cf. *All's Well That Ends Well*).

Cymbeline, then, like *Pericles*, traces a process of renewal through loss, but the role played by the gods in its development is far more emphatic than in the previous play. Although the deities are constantly evoked in the earlier drama, and clearly influence the course of events, they act through human and natural agencies until the reunion between Marina and Pericles has been accomplished, when Diana appears to Pericles in a dream. In *Cymbeline*, by contrast, Jupiter descends from the heavens on an eagle to confirm his authority in the play world. Accused by the ghosts of Posthumus' immediate family of neglecting 'great Sicilius' heir' (V.iv.51), he chides them for their attempted intervention in matters beyond their reach, assuring them that the 'mortal accidents' (V.iv.99) endured by the characters are the product of his will.

The part played by the supernatural is yet more prominent in *The Tempest* (1611), the final play of the last group, in that a large part of the action is dictated by a magus and his spirits. The play has been discussed in a previous chapter, but the feigned death that contributes to its development is worthy of mention in this context since the drama as a whole (unusually for Shakespeare) is not dependent on any known source but develops ideas explored in previous plays. As noted in Chapter 5, the action turns on the means by which the exiled Duke of Milan regains his dukedom, and thus is concerned, once again, with renewal. Having been wronged by Antonio and Alonso, Prospero contrives their shipwreck on his island, convincing the latter that his son Ferdinand has been drowned. Alonso consequently suffers for his misdeeds through the seeming death of his heir, and is rewarded with the return of his child through his repentance for his errors. This pattern of action is clearly related to the cycles of death and rebirth enacted in previous plays, and as in the other romances this purgatorial experience is associated with the rhythms of nature and the operation of divine powers. The loss of the youthful Ferdinand and the consequent grief of the King, plunges the court into a winter-like state (cf.II.i.137–8), that gives way to a 'second life' (V.i.195) with the Prince's rediscovery. Moreover, though Prospero is immediately and overtly responsible for the experiences to which the courtiers are subject, it becomes increasingly clear as the action evolves that his authority is not absolute. It is 'bountiful Fortune' (I.ii.178) which has brought his enemies within his reach, and the gods who are the ultimate agents of the reconciliation of which Ferdinand's 'death' is the instrument, cf.:

> Gon[zalo].   Look down, you gods,
> And on this couple drop a blessed crown!
> For it is you that have chalk'd forth the way
> Which brought us hither.
>
>   (V.i.201–4)

Nevertheless, for all the potency of the supernatural forces impinging here on the circumstances surrounding a supposed death, it is not *The Tempest* but *The Winter's Tale* (1610–11) that constitutes Shakespeare's most profound and dramatically powerful treatment of this final species of mouldy tale. The play is a tragi-comedy, based on *Pandosto, The Triumph of Time* (1588), a prose romance by Robert Greene. Greene's story traces the history of a misguided monarch, Pandosto, who becomes suspicious of the relationship between his wife and his friend, pursuing the life of the latter, and causing the death of the former (and indirectly that of his elder child) through his baseless accusations. His wife having given birth to a daughter immediately prior to her death, Pandosto causes the infant to be exposed in the belief she is a bastard, but the baby is succoured by herdsmen, and eventually marries the son of her father's former friend. The first phase of this narrative has obvious affinities with the Hero–Claudio plot of *Much Ado*, and it may have been this resemblance that prompted Shakespeare's most significant departure from his source. Whereas Pandosto's queen collapses and dies on her husband's repudiation of the oracle affirming her innocence, Hermione lives on in secret after her supposed death, and is eventually reunited with her husband and child. At the same time, Shakespeare also 'altereth and changeth' the career of the erring monarch subsequent to the occasioning of the Queen's death. Unlike Pandosto, who passes from remorse at his misconduct to further crimes against his daughter and state, ultimately taking his own life, Leontes pursues the path of contrition, and is finally rewarded for his penitence through the restoration of his wife and child.

The pattern of action that Shakespeare constructs from Greene's narrative has obvious affinities with the redemptive processes enacted in previous plays. Once again, as in *Much Ado About Nothing*, the 'death' of a defamed lady permits the discarding of a tainted life, while her apparent loss initiates a period of mourning (cf. *Much Ado About Nothing* and *Cymbeline*) that allows for the purgation of guilt. Furthermore, as in previous compositions, the seeming death of a major figure is not an isolated phenomenon. Just as in *Pericles* the supposed death of Thaisa is followed by the loss of Marina and the trance-like state of the King, so Hermione's disappearance is symptomatic of a process that embraces not only her two children as in the source, but the King's instrument, the unfortunate Antigonus, whose celebrated pursuit by a bear has no place in Greene's work. In *The Winter's Tale*, however, unlike earlier plays involving a similar mesh of hypothetical deaths, the loss of the members of the royal household occurs virtually simultaneously. Where *Pericles* enacts a seesaw movement between loss and recovery, and Imogen 'dies' once in her own person and then a second time as Fidele, *The Winter's Tale* plummets from happiness to disaster, with the succession of blows that Leontes suffers following his repudiation of his wife and child constituting the nadir of his experience. The change in his situation is linked in the most emphatic terms, moreover, with the cycle of the year. Unlike *Pericles* and *Cymbeline* in which an association is implied between human experience and the rhythms of nature, *The Winter's Tale* establishes an overt relationship between the two, enlarging the significance of the pastoral passages of Greene's narrative. The title of the play invites an awareness of a particular time of year, and seasonal references abound throughout (cf.II.i.23–5 and IV.iv.70–135). The play opens with an evocation of the springtime youth of the central figures (cf.I.ii.60–74), moves through the jealousies of middle age (cf.Leontes' suspicions in relation to Hermione and Polixenes), to a winter of sterility and death (with the loss of Hermione and the casting out of Perdita in the storm), before a process of rebirth is set in motion with the blossom-time love between Perdita and Florizel, and the summer of marriages made and remade in the final act. At the same time, while enriching the meaning of the pastoral settings of Greene's narrative, Shakespeare has also heightened its spiritual implications. Just as the reunion of Thaisa and Pericles (like that of Imogen and Posthumus) is overtly engineered by the gods, so Leontes' recovery of Hermione is directly related to Apollo, whose potency is powerfully evoked (cf. III. i. *passim*).

The Winter's Tale may thus be seen on one level as an accommodation between Greene's *Pandosto* on the one hand, and the dramatist's own earlier work on the other, but it also represents a major departure from (or adaptation of) the strands that have combined in its development. In the first place, as noted above, the death of the traduced lady in the romance is not a fiction but an actuality and hence there is none of the wonder at the close of Greene's narrative that accompanies the closing scene of the Shakespearian play. At the same time, the nature of this wonder is quite distinct from that arising from the resolutions of the dramatist's previous compositions in that those outside the world of the drama are not initiated into the stratagem by which the action is resolved. When Hermione faints during her trial and is carried from the court, the spectator's attention is focused upon Leontes, and there is no break in the action to admit the revelation of the Queen's recovery before Paulina returns to the presence with the news that her mistress has expired. Already attuned to a universe in which man's errors are productive of terrible consequences (cf. the division between Polixenes and Leontes, the death of Mamillius, the casting out of Perdita), the members of the audience have no cause to suspect the truth of this announcement, and they consequently participate in Leontes' anguish, rather than being distanced by their superior knowledge from his experience. The spectator's belief in the actuality of the Queen's death is confirmed, furthermore, in subsequent scenes. The words of the oracle (III. ii. 132–6), which clearly point to the survival of Perdita, make no apparent reference to Hermione, while Antigonus recounts a dream in which the Queen appeared to him like one of 'the spirits o'th'dead' (III. iii. 16). Antigonus concludes from his experience that 'Hermione hath suffer'd death' (III. iii. 42), while the terms in which he describes the apparition which appeared to him suggest a being

from another world (cf.III.iii.16–37). The protracted mourning of
Leontes also helps to confirm the reality of his wife's loss, as does
the emphatic reiteration by Paulina of the King's responsibility for
his widowed state (cf.V.i.13–16). Consequently, at the close of the
play, when Leontes, Perdita, Florizel and Polixenes visit Paulina's
house to view the 'statue' of Hermione supposedly carved by Julio
Romano, those outside the play world are as unprepared as those
within it for the revelation that the Queen is alive, and they thus
share in the responses of the dramatis personae, rather than
anticipating (as in *Much Ado About Nothing* or *All's Well That Ends
Well*) the moment of their enlightenment. As the statue of Hermione gradually comes to life, the members of the audience, like
Leontes and his household, are gripped with a sense of wonder,
crossing with them into a universe made radiant by an apprehension of the power and benevolence of the gods.

It is not only the withholding of information from the theatre
audience, however, that distinguishes Shakespeare's use of the
supposed death in *The Winter's Tale* from his handling of the
device in earlier plays. Where *Romeo and Juliet*, *Much Ado About
Nothing*, *Measure for Measure* and even *Cymbeline* focus on the
means by which the deception is to be accomplished, and the
benefits it is designed to produce, *The Winter's Tale* stresses the
business of feigning, exploring the relation between fiction and
actuality. Confronted by the 'statue' of Hermione, Leontes and
Polixenes reflect on the differences between the artefact and the
living woman, implying through the comparison the superiority
of life to art (cf.V.iii.23–36 and 77–9). Nevertheless, while testifying to the wonder of existence, Leontes also bears witness to the
profound effect that the sculpture has upon him. The stone, he
declares, rebukes him 'for being more stone than it' (V.iii.38),
while conjuring his 'evils . . . to remembrance' (V.iii.40). The
words suggest an interaction between the work of art and the
perceiver's moral nature, with the artefact stimulating the erring
individual to meditate upon his conduct and repent of his transgres-
sions. The process of feigning in this instance is thus not simply an
instrument of reclamation or renewal, as in previous plays, or a
vehicle for the apprehension of the divine, it is assimilated into an
exploration of the nature and function of art itself.

Though it is not until the final scene of the play that its
culminating fiction is revealed, the artifice of the entire drama is

stressed by the playwright throughout. The members of the audience are constantly reminded that they are engaging with a work of art, and that the happenings they are witnessing are feigned rather than real. The very title of play invites comparison with a fireside story, while the traditional content of winter tales is referred to in Act II scene i. Leontes himself equates his conduct with that of an actor (cf. I. ii. 187–90), while an unnamed gentleman in Act V comments on the non-naturalistic nature of the drama's events (cf. V. ii. 22–9). The implication of this series of references is that those watching the Shakespearian play stand in the same relation to the drama that Leontes occupies relative to the statue of Hermione, and this equation between the two levels of spectators admits a justification by the playwright of the moral basis of his own art. Just as Leontes is encouraged to look deeper into himself through the artifice engineered by Paulina, so it is suggested the members of Shakespeare's audience may have their understandings enlarged through imaginative engagement with the fictions the dramatist presents. The seeming death at the heart of the action is thus considerably more than a theatrically effective means of supplying a happy ending. While permitting the achievement of a more far-reaching reconciliation than that attained by the source, and contributing to a pattern of death and rebirth enacted on both physical and spiritual planes, it constitutes an implicit *apologia* for the craft of the dramatist himself.

While functioning as a justification of its creator's own profession, the final act of *The Winter's Tale* may also be seen, in the context of the present study, as an endorsement of Shakespeare's procedures. The meaning of the last scene emerges through a process of regression, in that those outside the play world function as an audience to the experience of Leontes, while Leontes himself assumes the role of spectator to a scene produced by Paulina. In both instances, the imagination of the perceiver responds to the work of art, converting the riches created by another mind to its own use. The succession of audiences and artefacts does not end, however, with the statue of Hermione. Behind *The Winter's Tale* itself lies the fictional world of Greene's *Pandosto*, a world with which Shakespeare's imagination was at some point engaged. The process of 'conversion' that brought *The Winter's Tale* into being is thus analogous to Leontes' response to the statue of Hermione, or the spectator's own reaction to *The Winter's Tale*. Though every visitor to Stratford will not literally return home from the playhouse, fired with an impulse to rewrite Shakespearian drama, each member of the audience will reshape the artefact in his or her imagination, turning its substance, if not into an *Otello*, like Verdi, or a *West Side Story*, like Bernstein, into a drama uniquely relevant to its creator's own specific consciousness.

Of the many tales that Shakespeare drew on in the course of his career it was ultimately the feigned death that afforded him the widest range of dramatic effects. It could suggest the primacy of fate over human volition, contribute to the evolution of character, define a stage in a cyclical process, imply a movement to a different plane of experience, or promote an understanding of the nature of art itself. It could be deployed for positive or malign purposes, permitted the dramatist a variety of actor–audience relationships, and allowed the simultaneous exploration of the comic and tragic potentialities of human life. By enabling the persons of the drama to confront the hypothetical as an actuality it enabled the destructive nature of human impulses to be fully delineated while affording scope for a resolution affirming the existence of forces of renewal, and the possibility of enlightenment through suffering. In short, just as 'the truest poetry' according to Touchstone, 'is the most feigning' (*As You Like It*, III.iii.16), so some of Shakespeare's most profound insights into the nature of reality are achieved through the medium of the putative death.

Conclusion: Shakespeare's Mouldy Tales

Though the main thrust of the comment from which the title of this book is derived clearly relates to the staleness of the material Shakespeare presents, there is also the implication that it is deficient in 'wit'. The entire passage from Jonson's 'Ode' in which the allusion to *Pericles* occurs, not only levels the accusation of using well-worn devices, but condemns the worthlessness of the kind of drama currently in vogue, cf.:

> Say that thou pourst them [playgoers] wheat,
>   And they will acorns eat:
> 'Twere simple fury still thyself to waste
>   On such as have no taste:
> To offer them a surfeit of pure bread
>   Whose appetites are dead.
>   No, give them grains their fill,
>   Husks, draff to drink, and swill;
> If they love lees, and leave the lusty wine,
> Envy them not, their palate's with the swine.
>
>   No doubt some mouldy tale
>   Like *Pericles*, and stale
> As the shrieve's crusts, and nasty as his fish –
>   Scraps out of every dish,
> Thrown forth, and raked into the common tub,
>   May keep up the play-club:
>   There sweepings do as well
>   As the best ordered meal.
> For who the relish of these guests will fit
> Needs set them but the alms-basket of wit.
>
>   And much good do't you then:
>   Brave plush and velvet men

Can feed on orts; and safe in your stage-clothes
   Dare quit, upon your oaths,
The stagers and the stage-wrights too (your peers)
   Of larding your large ears
    With their foul comic socks,
    Wrought upon twenty blocks:
Which, if they are torn and turned and patched enough,
The gamesters share your guilt, and you their stuff.
                 ('Ode to Himself', 11–40)

The images employed here clearly register Jonson's disgust at the tired nature of the offerings presented to contemporary audiences, but they also communicate his disapproval of the intellectual limitations of the work of his fellow dramatists. 'Draff' (i.e. dregs), 'swill', 'lees', 'crusts', 'scraps', all carry this double sense of staleness and nutritional deficiency or impoverishment, and it is this final aspect of 'mouldiness', the inherent value of the tales themselves, that remains to be addressed in justifying Shakespeare's fondness for inherited materials. Though the 'turned and patched' fabrics from which the plays are pieced together are demonstrably employed in a variety of ways, the 'stuff' itself from which those plays are composed often seem unworthy of serious attention.

Although Jonson, like Shakespeare, both advocated and practised the art of imitation, proudly proclaiming his indebtedness to the 'ancients',[1] the series of comedies on which his reputation as a dramatist principally rests are closely in touch with the daily life of Elizabethan–Jacobean England. The settings are frequently familiar, the dialogue is racy and colloquial, and the action, with its exposure of contemporary abuses, has an immediate and obvious relevance to the audience to which it is addressed. Some parts of Shakespeare's work exhibit a similar capacity for social realism,[2] but the preponderance of his plays do not concern themselves, in the main, with the superficies of contemporary life. Settings are frequently remote – the forest of Arden, ancient Britain – the persons divorced from everyday existence – cf. the gathering in Navarre's park (*Love's Labour's Lost*) or on Prospero's island (*The Tempest*) – while the events that are enacted in the course of the drama frequently strain the credulity of the audience rather than

1. Compare *Sejanus* ('To the Readers') and *Volpone* (dedication).
2. Compare the tavern scenes of the two parts of *Henry IV*.

being drawn from daily experience (cf. the 'death' and recovery of Thaisa in *Pericles*, or the protracted concealment of Hermione in *The Winter's Tale*). Where Jonson's work is openly concerned with serious moral issues (e.g. the corruption consequent on the pursuit of wealth in *Volpone*), Shakespeare is less overtly moralistic, ushering his spectators into a kind of universe in which a vicious Duke may be converted to virtue through an encounter with a holy man (*As You Like It*), or a husband reunited with the wife 'killed' by his tyranical conduct (*The Winter's Tale*). The contrast between the two dramatists thus appears, at first sight, to bear out the contention that while one is a serious writer whose work is of enduring interest, the other is a purveyor of 'husks' of little relevance to everyday life.

The first point to be noted about Shakespeare's choice of plot material is the very fact, constantly reiterated in the course of this book, that his tales have been frequently retold. The apparent want of judgement that led him to the kind of story that Jonson derides was seemingly shared by a succession of writers stretching back to classical times. As noted in previous chapters, confusion between siblings, sexual disguise, banishment and scolding occur in a wide range of literary contexts, and the repeated use of these motifs might be seen as an index not of their worthlessness but continuing interest. The opening lines of *Pericles* are indicative of this attitude to certain tales:

> To sing a song that old was sung,
> From ashes ancient Gower is come,
> Assuming man's infirmities,
> To glad your ear, and please your eyes.
> It hath been sung at festivals,
> On ember-eves and holy-ales;
> And lords and ladies in their lives
> Have read it for restoratives:
> The purchase is to make men glorious,
> *Et bonum quo antiquius eo melius.*

These lines, as noted in the introduction, testify to the proven value of the tale that the drama presents, and its continued bearing upon the lives of successive generations. The occasions on which the story has been related are also significant in relation to this assertion of worth. 'Festivals', 'ember-eves' (evenings preceding periods of fasting), and 'holy-ales' all have religious connotations, and the association between Gower's 'song' and the church calendar implies that it has a bearing on man's spiritual self. *Pericles* is the only one of Shakespeare's plays to offer this kind of justification of its plot material, but a number of the recurrent motifs that the dramatist employs have their origins in religious beliefs. A return from the dead, for example, is a common element in European mythology, while a number of legends involve metamorphosis, including some variety of sexual disguise (cf. the various transformations of the Greek gods).

It would be ludicrous to suggest that the crowds flocking into the Elizabethan–Jacobean playhouses regarded the plays of Shakespeare in the same light that their ancestors viewed the Mystery and Morality plays that directly inculcated the truths of their faith. The stories that Shakespearian drama enacts have detached themselves through successive redactions from their mythological origins, and are no longer evocative of the beliefs in which some, at least, of them originate. The tales themselves, however, spring from the impulse to account for the circumstances of human existence, and the aspects of experience that they confront are consequently common to every generation. Though the specific faith in which a story has its origins may have been supplanted by more complex ways of explaining our universe, the tale itself remains of interest in that it deals with recurring fears and aspirations.

It would obviously not be possible in the scope of this final chapter to attempt a detailed exploration of the origins of Shakespeare's material and the consequent sources of its perennial appeal. What follows is simply designed as an indication of the possible attraction of certain tales, and the intellectual nutrition that they supply. Two major threads are discernable in the stories explored in previous chapters. In the first place, a significant proportion of Shakespeare's inherited plots are concerned with identity or self-definition. An interest in twins, for example, is a recurring sociological phenomenon deriving from the challenge that identical siblings represent to man's sense of his own selfhood. Duplication of feature implies duplication of personality, a concept inimical to the assumption of human individuality, and mysterious in its application to familial relationships. The existence of interchangeable individuals is unsettling to the social group, and it is this element of dislocation, exposing the individual to the unknown, which links the identical twin motif to other tales. Exile, for example, another common strand in European folk lore, also involves an assault on the security of the individual through a disruption of relationships within the social group. Cut adrift from the familiar, the outcast is deprived of those props – personal relationships, religious observances, civic responsibilities – which shore up his sense of life's meaning, and is forced to enter an alien environment in which previous assumptions about the nature of existence are threatened or undermined. The entering of uncharted territory links this kind of story with those involving the transgression of gender distinctions. Just as the exile is forced to function in an unfamiliar physical and mental landscape through his expulsion from the state, so the woman who adopts the attire and attitudes of a member of the opposite sex enters a new arena in which inculcated codes of behaviour no longer hold good.

In each of these instances the interest of the tale originates in a disruption of the norm through which the unknown, with its accompanying sense of fear and dislocation, disturbs the superficial security of human life. It is this sense of fear, specifically fear of the alien or unexplored, that associates this complex of plot motifs with the second major strand discernable in the tales, a confrontation with, and avoidance of, death. Resurrection, or translation to a different sphere of existence, are recurrent elements of the religious systems through which human beings have sought to come to terms with mortality, and, as old orthodoxies give way to new sets of belief, myths expressive of man's desire to evade the limitations of his own being enter the literary stock in the form of tales. A large number of Shakespeare's plays, as noted in Chapter 6, involve some kind of return from the grave, and the plot motifs that they employ – the purging of guilt through self-sacrifice (*All's Well That Ends Well*), substitution (*Cymbeline*), the raising of the dead through exemplary worth (*Pericles*) – all derive from archetypes designed to locate man's life within a larger, metaphysical, context. It is not only those plots concerned with a feigned or supposed death, however, that testify to humanity's abiding concern with mortality. Stories involving exile carry a set of related connotations (e.g. departure from the known, entry into a void, loss of selfhood) which serves to align them with tales more directly concerned with exploring the boundaries of human existence. Similarly, the assumption of disguise, for all its comic potentialities, has comparable implications, in that it involves the extinction of the self. When Viola in *Twelfth Night*, for example, recounts her supposed sister's fate, she is reflecting, as Cesario, on the attenuation of her own feminine being (II.iv.108–22).

The plot motifs on which Shakespeare draws in the construction of his plays are thus not concerned with fanciful, never-never-land predicaments but with perennial fears and aspirations. Rather than presenting his audience with 'husks' devoid of intellectual value, the dramatist offers the spectator new insights into the concerns that are common to every generation through his imaginative engagement with paradigmatic situations. The process of breathing new life into mouldy tales does not end, however, with Shakespeare himself. Drama is essentially a cooperative art, depending upon a creative interaction between director, actor and text. Just as Shakespeare altered and changed the stories handed down to him by previous writers, so successive companies of players have added to and deleted from their inherited scripts in accordance with theatrical exigencies, the capabilities of specific performers, and the tastes and preoccupations of their own age. Shakespearian drama, in short, is not a stable entity. The 'tale' enacted by David Garrick (1717–79) was not the 'tale' enacted by Macready (1793–1873), and the film of *Henry V* released during the Second World War carried a different meaning from that conveyed by the grim drama produced in Stratford during the 1980s. The Richard of Gloucester who lives in the memory of the present generation is not the figure who emerged for our predecessors from their reading of *Richard III*. He is the product of a creative interaction between *3 Henry VI*, *Richard III* and a twentieth-century theatrical imagination. It's not Shakespeare's mouldy tale that haunts the corridors of the modern mind – but Laurence Olivier's.

Further Reading

The starting point for any investigation of Shakespeare's use of inherited material must be G. Bullough (1957–75) *Narrative and Dramatic Sources of Shakespeare* (8 vols), Routledge and Kegan Paul. Bullough not only prints the major sources and analogues of the entire corpus, together with substantial bibliographies, he also discusses Shakespeare's handling of the material on which he draws, while his concluding chapter traces the history of source scholarship prior to the publication of his own study, and the nature of the insights to be achieved from this kind of approach to the dramatist's work. The primary materials supplied by Bullough, though extensive, may be supplemented by reference to the work of a number of editors who have concerned themselves with specific areas of Shakespeare's reading, notably W. H. D. Rouse (1961) *Shakespeare's Ovid*, Centaur Press; T. J. B. Spencer (1964) *Shakespeare's Plutarch*, Penguin, Harmondsworth; R. Hosley (1968) *Shakespeare's Holinshed*, G. P. Putnam's Sons, New York; T. J. B. Spencer (1968) *Elizabethan Love Stories*, Penguin, Harmondsworth.

While Bullough is primarily concerned with assembling the texts the dramatist employs, a second major study by K. Muir (1978), *The Sources of Shakespeare's Plays*, Yale University Press, New Haven, focuses on the use Shakespeare makes of his source materials, and the ways in which his reading informs the fabric of his drama. Muir's work, in turn, may be supplemented by reference to the introductions to modern editions of specific plays, the more scholarly of which (e.g. Arden, Signet, New Cambridge) offer a detailed analysis of the sources drawn on in the course of composition and the process of adaptation they undergo. A large number of books and articles have also addressed themselves to individual plays or particular areas of indebtedness. M. M.

Lascelles (1953) *Shakespeare's* Measure for Measure, The Athlone Press, for example, explores the complex of sources and analogues underlying one of the problem plays; C. T. Prouty (1950), *The Sources of Much Ado About Nothing*, Yale University Press, New Haven, focuses on one of the major comedies; while B. Spivack (1958), *Shakespeare and the Allegory of Evil*, Columbia University Press, New York, traces the history of the medieval vice, and the impact of the figure on Shakespearian tragedy. Other studies consider the influence of specific works, authors, or literary movements on the Shakespearian corpus as a whole, e.g. G. C. Taylor (1925) *Shakespeare's Debt to Montaigne*, Harvard University Press, Cambridge, Mass.; R. Noble (1935) *Shakespeare's Biblical Knowledge and Use of the Book of Common Prayer*, SPCK; C. Gesner (1970) *Shakespeare and the Greek Romance*, Kentucky University Press, Lexington; A. Thompson (1978) *Shakespeare's Chaucer: A Study in Literary Origins*, Liverpool University Press, Liverpool. The wide sweep of Shakespeare's reading has also been the subject of a number of important articles, including F. P. Wilson (1950) 'Shakespeare's Reading', in A. Nicholl (ed.) *Shakespeare Survey*, vol. 3 pp. 14–22, and G. K. Hunter (1971) 'Shakespeare's Reading', in K. Muir and S. Schoenbaum (eds.) *A New Companion to Shakespeare Studies*, Cambridge University Press, Cambridge pp. 55–66.

The educational background which helped to define Shakespeare's reading habits and to determine his method of composition may also be approached through both primary texts and scholarly accounts. Among the most accessible of the former are L. V. Ryan (ed.) (1967) *The Schoolmaster (1570) by Roger Ascham*, Folger Shakespeare Library, Cornell University Press, Ithaca, New York; and R. D. Pepper (ed.) (1966) *Four Tudor Books on Education*, Scholars Facsimile Reprints, Gainesville, Fla. Notable among the scholarly accounts are K. Charlton (1965) *Education in Tudor England*, Routledge and Kegan Paul, and the opening chapter of G. K. Hunter (1962) *John Lyly: The Humanist as Courtier*, Routledge and Kegan Paul. Sir Philip Sidney's *An Apology for Poetry*, ed. G. Shepherd (1975), Manchester University Press, and George Puttenham's *The Arte of English Poesy*, ed. B. Hathaway (1970), Kent State University Press, provide a useful introduction to Renaissance critical theory, while Renaissance attitudes to plagiarism are discussed in H. O. White (1935) *Plagiarism and Imitation during the English Renaissance*, Harvard University Press, Cambridge, Mass.

Relatively few studies have focused on Shakespeare's repeated use of a single source, though a number of scholars have been concerned with the repetitious use of plot motifs. Among the former is L. Scragg (1982) *The Metamorphosis of 'Gallathea': A Study in Creative Adaptation*, University Press of America, Washington DC. Among the more important of the latter are P. V. Kreider (1941) *Repetition in Shakespeare's Plays*, Princeton University Press for the University of Cincinnati, and M. W. Black (1962) 'Repeated Situations in Shakespeare's Plays' in R. Hosley (ed.) *Essays on Shakespeare and Elizabethan Drama in Honor of Hardin Craig*, University of Missouri Press, Columbia, pp.247–59.

Index